Voices from the Ming-Qing Cataclysm

VOICES FROM THE MING-QING CATACLYSM

CHINA IN TIGERS' JAWS

EDITED AND TRANSLATED BY
LYNN A. STRUVE

Yale University Press
New Haven and London

Excerpts from Martino Martini, *Bellum Tartaricum, or the Conquest of the Great and Most Renowned Empire of China* (London: John Crook, 1654), the translation quoted in Chapter 3, are published with permission of the Princeton University Library.

Designed by Jill Breitbarth and set in Janson type by Rainsford Type, Danbury, Connecticut. Printed in the United States of America by Vail-Ballou Press, Binghamton, New York.

Library of Congress Cataloging-in-Publication Data

Voices from the Ming-Qing cataclysm : China in tigers' jaws / edited and translated by Lynn A. Struve.

   p. cm.

   Includes bibliographical references and index.

   ISBN 0-300-05679-6 (cloth: alk. paper)

      0-300-07553-7 (pbk.: alk. paper)

   1. China—History—1644–1795. I. Struve, Lynn A., 1944– .

DS754.2.V65 1993

951'.032—dc20   92–43916

                                         CIP

A catalogue record for this book is available from the British Library.

The paper in this book meets the guidelines for permanence and durability of the Committee on Production Guidelines for Book Longevity of the Council on Library Resources.

10 9 8 7 6 5 4 3 2

For *Panthera tigris*—the real loser, after all

Contents

ACKNOWLEDGMENTS

THE PURSUIT OF ONE DETAIL or another in these varied translations has led me to plead at the doors, literally and figuratively speaking, of many fine colleagues in my departments, my university, the United States, China, Japan, and England. Contemplating my heartfelt obligation to acknowledge their help, I realized that it would appear as if I had set a secretary to work typing out in alphabetical order every third name from my lists and files of professional associates. To avoid demeaning anyone by inclusion in a long scroll, let me just express sincere thanks to all those who have responded patiently and conscientiously from their deep resources of scholarly knowledge to my out-of-the-blue queries. You have been wonderfully kind.

There are a few persons in Bloomington, Indiana, however, without whose skillful and unflagging services this volume would not have reached publication in its present form. First is my able research assistant, Shoucheng Yan, who helped me with many difficult phrases and checked each of my draft translations, thereby saving me from the public commission of innumerable errors and infelicities. Second is the stalwart head of the East Asian Collection of the Indiana University Library, Thomas H. Lee, who never fails to evince genuine enthusiasm for my textual escapades and who—through his excellent relationships with East Asian librarians around the world—usually manages to bring in the elusive items with dispatch. John Hollingsworth of Cartographic Services, the Department of Geography at Indiana University, patiently turned my awkward pencil sketches into immaculately professional historical maps. And Mark Simons of Photographic Services, Indiana University, performed near miracles in resolving problems with the photographs of illustrations, which often were from unclear, yellowed, or damaged old texts.

Some of the texts translated herein were obtained through the cordial cooperation of staff in the National Library of Beijing; the National Central Library in Taipei; the Library of Congress; the Lilly Library, Indiana University at Bloomington; and the Firestone Library, Princeton University. Over the years my sojourns to collect materials on the Ming-Qing transition have been subsidized by the Committee for Scholarly Communication with the People's Republic of China (with funds provided by the National Endowment for the Humanities), the American Philosophical Society, and the Institute for Advanced Study at Indiana University. Research supplements have been provided by the Indiana University College of Arts and Sciences through the Office of Research and the University Graduate School. Publication was partly subsidized by the Center for East Asian Studies at the university.

Last and surely least is my little yellow tabby, Xiao Huang, whose regular inspections and monitor-top supervisions neither hastened nor improved my work on this anthology but whose concern for the historical portrayal of her distant feline relations warrants praise from any true Confucian.

Voices from the Ming-Qing Cataclysm

INTRODUCTION

THE TIGER IS ALL but extinct in China today, but in earlier centuries the animal was greatly feared by people who lived in or traveled through sparsely populated areas. By the seventeenth century, human population growth had made bona fide sightings of tigers rare; it was often reported, nonetheless, that tigers would venture into cities to feed on human carrion after some disaster—pestilence, famine, or a massacre. Although tigers may have been present more in people's imaginations than in actual tooth, claw, or stripe, associations of the tiger with acute peril, calamity, ferocity, and intimidating aggressiveness—or, more positively, with dashing, thrilling savagery and martial courage—were frequent in Chinese expressions in the seventeenth century and remain so today. Contending with a perilous situation, for instance, is called being in a "tiger's mouth" (*hukou*), and surviving such a situation is called "life beyond the tiger's mouth" (*hukou yusheng*).

Because the tiger is native to neither North America nor Europe, the aura of exotic beauty that it carries in the Western mind has not been manifest in China. But the Chinese have associated the tiger with things from the outside in another way: their word for tiger, *hu*, is homophonous (except for tone) with their general, pejorative term for northern "barbarians"—who were viewed inimically by denizens of the "Central Florescence" from at least as early as the third century B.C.[1] In the eyes of Chinese south of the Ming-period civilizational demarcation line, the Great Wall,[2] such aliens became the most salient among several factors that made the middle seventeenth century one of the most trying periods in Chinese history.

The term *general crisis*, derived from scholarship on seventeenth-century European history, is often applied to comparable conditions in China during that century: climatic cooling, reduced agricultural yields, revenue shortfalls, political strife, social disruptions, economic dislocations, monetary instability, epidemic diseases, and so forth.[3] The one calamity that stands out most in Chinese cultural memory, however, and which exacerbated all the others, was the conquest of China by a coalition of "barbarian" peoples from the far northeast, led by the Manchus. From their base east of the Liao River the consummately martial leaders of the Qing dynasty (1636–1911) seized control of the Chinese government, both violently and by default, from the indigenous Ming dynasty (1368–1644), with its markedly antimartial bias.[4] But among the armed conflicts that ensued in China from the 1620s through the 1670s, those perpetrated or necessitated by Manchus, or even by those northeastern peoples allied with the Manchus,[5] constituted only a part. There also abounded huge roving armies of marauders, smaller local bands of outlaws or hired thugs, pirates of the lakes, rivers, and seas, and aborigine insurrectionists, not to mention Ming government troops, who—whether renegade or not—often pillaged to survive. It probably is safe to say that no locale in China escaped some sort of "soldier calamity" (*binghuo*) during the middle decades of the seventeenth century.

That terribly agonizing time—when people in all sorts of life situations had their social and political values, moral courage, and physical stamina put to severe tests—has been treated on the macro level for the most part. In trying to extract some general sense from the tumult of events, scholars of all ideologies have tended to use abstractions such as *scholar-bureaucrats*, *peasant rebels*, *local elites*, *urbanites*, *banner nobility*, and *landlord-capitalists* to speak about the responses of people to conditions of the day. Twentieth-century ideas about nationalism have tended to oversimplify both Ming and Qing loyalism, which in the seventeenth century involved complexes of factors not found in present-day Chinese patriotism.[6] Most textbooks characterize the Ming-Qing transition as a relatively short and smooth one, institutionally and culturally—a minor blip in the very long electrocardiogram of Chinese history.

Certain overlapping countertrends in scholarship have also promoted a sort of sanitization of the conquest period. Scholars in both East and West have tried to get away from the jingoistic anti-Manchuism that characterized Chinese studies of the conquest period from the time of the Republican revolution (which overthrew the Qing dynasty in 1911) until the 1950s. This sanitization, along with the official Chinese policy to treat the minority peoples of China more fairly by reducing "Great Han-Chinese chauvinism," has engendered reluctance to bring forth unflattering aspects of Manchu activities. In addition, the desire of scholars to move beyond the stereotypical moral condemnation of "bandits" in traditional Chinese writings on socially disruptive groups has coalesced with the glorification of such groups as "revolutionaries" in Communist Chinese historiography. Thus, the brutalities of both the Manchus and the rebels tend to be either glossed over or attributed with "historical functionality"—that is, with having been necessarily destructive aspects of certain teleologically conceived, positive or progressive developments in Chinese history.

Also distorting our view of that time has been the more voluminous production of historical source materials in the economically advanced and heavily populous lower Yangzi region than in other regions. The number and wide circulation of writings about what happened to places and personages in the area now encompassed by Jiangsu and Anhui provinces and the northern parts of Jiangxi and Zhejiang provinces have encouraged the mistaken notion that the violence and destructiveness of the Qing conquest occurred mainly there. As will be evident in several of the selections in this anthology, that was hardly the case. The rich lower Yangzi and Hangzhou Bay regions had much that was vulnerable to destruction, but they also had the greatest resources for recovery. Other parts of the country, once devastated, remained longer in that condition (map 1). The western provinces, in fact, suffered the worst and the longest. The slaughter of hundreds of thousands of people in Sichuan Province under the tyrannical regime of the rebel leader Zhang Xianzhong between 1644 and 1646 was but the beginning of armed strife in the Sichuan Basin[7]—which persisted until resistance to Qing control was eliminated in 1663. Perhaps worse, from the early 1640s through the late 1670s southern Huguang (present-day Hunan Province) was ravaged repeatedly—first by rebel armies, then by clashing Ming and Qing armies, then by forces loyal to the Qing and those supporting the breakaway southwestern feudatory, Wu Sangui—with the result that only 27 percent of the land registered in 1581 was being cultivated in 1679.[8]

In sum, although excellent studies of major literary and political figures of the conquest period are now available to Western readers, we have

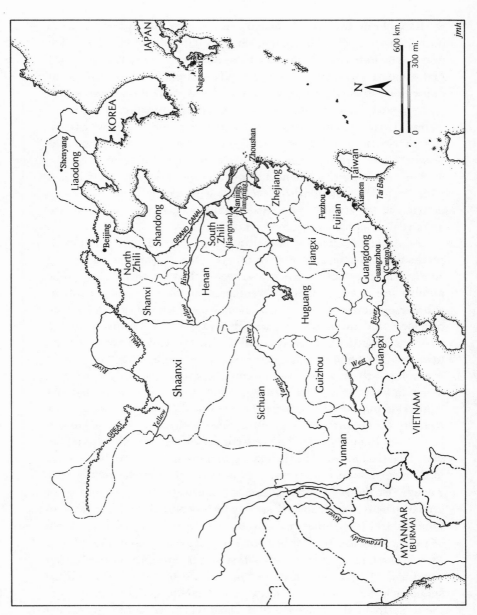

Map 1. China in the Mid-Seventeenth Century

yet to lend an open ear to the voices of a wider variety of people (including Europeans) in different parts of the country whose lives were deeply affected—and often terminated—by the dynastic cataclysm.[9] This is unnecessarily the case, for those voices have been waiting to be heard, as it were, for a long time. One feature of the general restlessness of late Ming thought that was not obliterated by early Qing conservatism was a marked willingness to abandon the reticence traditional in prose narratives and to describe personal experiences, including dilemmas.[10] Doubtless the traumas of the Ming-Qing transition reinforced this cultural development, and the bibliophilic, textually preservative ethos of Qing learning aided the survival of such narratives, even those by very obscure writers. It has remained only for someone to make them more accessible to present-day readers through selection, translation, annotation, and introduction. Any fictional elements in this anthology are those generated by the authors themselves, who give form to their observations, feelings, and memories—as we all do—with motifs supplied or conditioned by their cultural milieus.

In delving into this sort of literature, one soon realizes that the overwhelming motivation for writing down personal experiences in those trying times—whether the pen was used right there in the tiger's mouth or later on—was self-justification or self-vindication. This includes the guilt-tinged need of human beings in any culture to explain how it was that they lived when so many others died. Decisions made and courses of action taken under extreme duress seem to be suspect and to require painful articulation or reexamination. Though this may be generally true in any culture, the particular dilemmas that arise, the models that are looked to for guidance, the values that motivate people in different, stressful situations, the manner in which spiritual release is sought—these are culture specific. Indeed, the stories presented here could be regarded as prime materials for a cultural history of selfjustification. The resources that a given culture can or cannot provide to sustain people, or that it provides in conflicting ways, are cast into stark relief in times of crisis like the middle seventeenth century in China.

1

A SURVIVOR

OF BEIJING

"SETTLES HIS THOUGHTS"

LIU SHANGYOU ENTERED Beijing at a truly inauspicious time—midwinter 1643–44. The roving rebel armies that had ranged over most of North China since the 1620s had become uncontrollable, and now, under the leadership of "the Dashing Prince," Li Zicheng, they threatened to invade the capital province, North Zhili (present-day Hebei) for the first time. The Manchus, who had grown in strength since the last decade of the sixteenth century and who had openly challenged the Ming by declaring their own Qing dynasty in Mukden (Shenyang) in 1636, had taken over the entire Liaodong region almost down to Shanhai Pass, just one hundred seventy miles east of Beijing. The Ming government in the North was growing more paralytic by the day.

Apart from what is recorded in Liu Shangyou's own account of his trials from this winter to the next, nothing is known about the author except that he hailed from Jiading County (northwest of present-day Shanghai). Apparently he had gone to Beijing to seek or await formal appointment to some official position. In any case, he was in close contact with Shen Zhifang, a supervising secretary in the Ministry of Rites and also Liu's relative, probably by marriage, and was able to learn a good deal about court affairs secondhand. Typically for a man in the middle ranks of the scholar-official elite, Liu casts the Ming Chongzhen emperor (r. 1628–44) in a favorable light and, conversely, has nothing charitable to say about Li Zicheng or his followers, whom he refers to as bandits.[1] Though unaccustomed to fending for himself among the hoi polloi, Liu abhors only people who engage in armed violence—be they soldiers, highwaymen, or vengeful citizens. He pointedly defends the behavior of Shen Zhifang, who—like many officials who managed to survive the short reign of Li Zicheng in Beijing and later joined the rump Ming court in Nanjing—was indicted for collaborating with the rebel regime.[2] Liu may have written the *Dingsi xiaoji* (A Short Record to Settle My Thoughts) partly as a testimony to Shen's probity.[3]

It is sadly ironic that Liu Shangyou struggled so long and hard to return to Jiading, a county that was mercilessly attacked the following year during the Qing conquest of Jiangnan. The county seat itself was subjected to massacres three times between late August and early October of 1645.[4] Whether Liu survived those ordeals is not known.

. . . I recall that after our boat reached Xingji we had to go by land because the Grand Canal was iced over, and that in the morning when we set out, the beards and eyebrows of our outriders were so completely whitened with frost that we travelers looked at each other and laughed a bit. When staying in the public inn at Jinghai, we saw trees florid with frost, the leaves like layers of jade within jade, all lustrous in the bright sunlight.[5] Some who knew about divination said [the frosty sight] portended combat; others said the death of a ruler. On a clear day in Tongzhou* we heard very heavy thunder and were quite surprised. Upon inquiry, we learned that it was gunfire from the capital. When we drew near Beijing, the walls were so lofty—with parapets like sharp mountain peaks—that without thinking I murmured to myself, "How beautiful—the fastness of mountains and rivers. This surely is conferred by heaven!"[6]

On the road we often heard warnings about bandits, and in all the small neighborhoods and villages we passed through, there were only broken-down walls and ruined chimneys leaning against one another; for several hundred *li*† there was no sign of human habitation. That these northerners seemed unaware of the presence of bandits I took to be lack of concern borne of preparedness, so I thought the situation was very secure. Once inside the city I became busy with social affairs, for the New Year holiday was approaching. . . .

At the early morning audience on New Year's Day [by the lunar

*The northern terminus of the Grand Canal.
†One li is roughly one-third mile.

calendar; February 8], 1644, the drums sounded and the [Chongzhen] emperor went out through the Hall of the Central Ultimate. Although the high-ranking officials had not yet assembled, the emperor remained seated in the Hall of the Established Ultimate waiting for them. Some officials then arrived walking unsteadily and panting as though they were about to expire, and others who arrived later got closed outside the gates. The emperor was indulgent and did not question them. People said that the failure to effect ritual propriety at the first congratulatory court audience of the year was a sign of heaven's indictment. Then, during the night of the second or third day of the year, sounds of combat and crying were heard outside the Great Ming Gate,* as though several tens of thousands of horsemen had gathered on Chessboard Street, and this continued for several nights in succession [map 2]. Also, during the previous half-year no babies were born in the whole city. And in the summer and fall there was a great pestilence: people, seemingly without reason, got virulent cysts and died within hours. It was called the pustule plague, and 40 percent to 50 percent of the capital residents suffered from it. Then in mid-spring there was a blood-spitting sickness, which also killed people in half a day, sometimes taking several together from the same family. At court such anomalies as a freakishly tall man or a horse entering the imperial palace gate were seen, but they were kept secret, and news of such sightings was not passed on. Inside the palace grounds an ancient cypress strangely sprouted four twigs, which the caretaker didn't dare report. Often there were scourges and abnormalities like these.[7] . . .

After Taiyuan [in central Shanxi] fell [on March 16, 1644, to the roving rebel forces of Li Zicheng], the bandits set their sights on what then seemed easy prey—Beijing. Discussions at court, however, were as confused as tangled silk threads, and battlefield defense plans were as feeble as trying to dredge the moon from the water. Our Sacred Ruler above was frayed by work and worry, and his assembled ministers below said yes, yes, just hoping to survive somehow and rarely taking any responsibility. The money addiction grew worse by the day, and selfish factionalism was hard to stop. The minister of revenues [Ni Yuanlu] served fruitlessly by staring at the ceiling, and nothing was done to raise money for military provisions.[8] The minister of war

*The entrance to the compound where the main ministries and agencies of the central government were located.

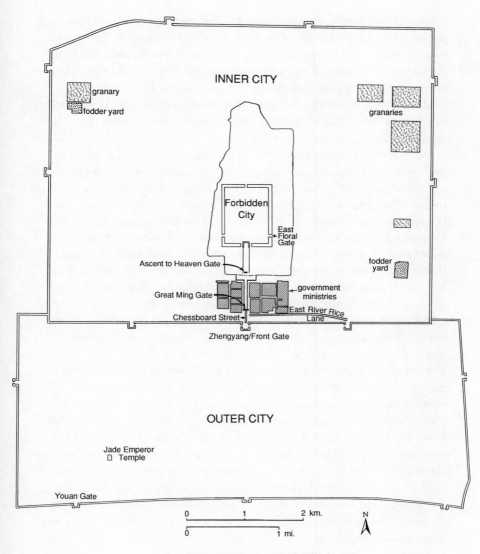

INNER CITY

granary

fodder yard

granaries

Forbidden City

East Floral Gate

Ascent to Heaven Gate

government ministries

Great Ming Gate

fodder yard

Chessboard Street

East River Rice Lane

Zhengyang/Front Gate

OUTER CITY

Jade Emperor
☐ Temple

Youan Gate

0   1   2 km.

0   1 mi.

N

Map 2. Liu Shangyou's Beijing

[Zhang Jinyan] aimlessly responded to official memoranda with empty prose; he proffered no real plan for the military situation. When the bandits were reconnoitering the capital region from Shanxi and their momentum was already toppling the chimneys and burning the rafters of the empire, at court word would go around that the passes had not held or, to the contrary, that the bandits had withdrawn. It was impossible to get either an accurate report or anyone to take even the minor position of provincial courier. . . .

Our Ardent Emperor was heroically perspicacious and firmly decisive, overseeing every matter personally. But his policies were least carried out right there in the hub of the nation. For instance, regarding such things as illicitly casting coins or printing paper money,[9] there would be patient admonitions and promulgations of stiff penalties. But the little people dared to disobey their superiors and in the end were unwilling to accept the aims of the government. Roundups of suspects by the palace secret service were not indiscriminate, but false rumors rose in clusters and became more rampant the more that officials tried to curb them. Manifestos and declarations from the bandits—some going so far as to rebuke the emperor himself—were sometimes tossed into the grounds of government agencies or posted on major thoroughfares. Time limits were set for catching the culprits, but that never worked. The ignorant common people took calamity to be good fortune and rejoiced in disaster, all saying that when Master Li arrived, he would give each poor person five taels. They often seemed to look forward to the rebel leader's arrival as they would to a year of good harvests. The people of the capital were very mixed in type, and identities were impossible to check; all the vegetable peddlers and wine carters were sent by the bandits, so their true business was especially hard to discern. I heard that the emperor in his palace sat alone deep into every night reading and signing documents and that once he sighed, "I am not the sort of ruler who loses his country. How can I have so many country-losing affairs?" and his tears followed his words down, as though in a premonition.

In the middle of the 2nd month the momentum of the bandits became extremely strong. There was a troop mutiny at Changping, so the capital was put on alert, and ample provisions were rushed out to pacify the soldiers. But just as Changping was restored to order, Jurong Pass became indefensible.* On the 29th was the Qingming holiday [when ancestors' graves are tended], so the various officials followed orders and went out to the imperial tombs.† On such occasions in the past they routinely took the opportunity to travel about in the western foothills. But now they all made great haste to return as soon as the ceremonies were over.

At the time some court officials were advocating raising donations to support defense efforts. The donations were to be given according to people's home regions and personal financial capacities. The degree holders from Jiangnan [the rich lower Yangzi region] had gathered in the Four Offices Meeting Hall, and the hall master came with brush in hand to record their donations, but no one was willing to respond with the amount he could afford. Some said that they were impoverished or represented others claiming impoverishment, even sounding like cold beggars and saying things that would never leave the mouths of the most ordinary people. I could have laughed out loud.

This led me to the idea of drafting a memorial to the throne, suggesting that two chests be set up on either side of the Great Ming Gate to urge loyal and righteous gentryfolk from the four quarters and men and women of the capital to aid the resistance as much as they could. One chest would be for donations in amounts from one to one hundred taels, and the other would be for amounts from a tenth to a hundredth of a tael.¹⁰ When the chests were full, then it would be announced to an official comptroller, who would open the chests and report the amounts in a memorial to the emperor. This money could then be kept in readiness so that should the city be surrounded, a unit of dare-to-die soldiers could be raised to burst through the siege. I had the memorial all prepared, but because there were no compatriots who would stand by the gate with me and make tearful appeals and because conditions were already pressing, it was extremely difficult to carry out my idea, so I abandoned it. . . .

On the 17th [of the 3rd month, April 23] artillery fire shook the heavens, and I knew the bandits had reached the foot of the city walls. The guns on the walls were fired empty as often as not—for lack of

*Jurong was the last major pass leading to the capital from the northwestern defense zone, and Changping was the only garrison between that pass and the capital.

†The date is wrong. The Qingming holiday was on the 27th of the lunar month— that is, April 4, 1644.

ammunition. Below the walls the bandits also relied on artillery for their attack; each firing of a cannon was sure to collapse a roof or topple some tiles—anything that got in the way was smashed.[11] Their ammunition was shaped like a man's thumb—keen and shiny, hard and slick, really effective. During past defenses of the city two soldiers were stationed at each rampart on the walls, and they were rewarded generously. The various officials shared defense duties at the gates and made inspection tours around the inner sides of the walls. In this action, however, only one soldier was used at each rampart, and each was given only twenty-four cash—not even enough for satisfying meals. Defense of the gates and itinerant inspections were left to ordinary personnel, and no higher-ranking officials showed up.

On the 18th the siege grew intense. The bandits drove the people who lived outside the city walls to fill in the moat, and they built "cloud ladders" that could be brought to the foot of the wall. Among those who pushed the carts holding the ladders, people who had just recently surrendered to the bandits were placed in front. When felled by arrows or rocks they were immediately replaced, so that not one of the real bandits was injured. Of the generals who were called in from surrounding regions, Wu Sangui didn't make it because he had just entered Shanhai Pass,[12] Tang Tong had surrendered [at Jurong Pass], and Huang Degong[13]—his army isolated and with no prospect of aid—observed the situation but did not advance. In the city there were many bandit sympathizers and collaborators lying in wait, people's hearts were agitated, and the soldiers' spirits sagged even more. . . .

That night my relative Shen Zhifang, [a supervising censor in the] Ministry of Rites, stayed in his office, but he returned to his residence the next morning. I asked him how the news was, and he said: "Not good. Before daybreak I saw some palace people and eunuchs in a flurry, trying to get out. I didn't know why until I learned that the head eunuch, Wang [Cheng'en],[14] had led his housemen in an attempt to storm the gates and leave, but the guards on the wall fired large guns at them, so they came back. And just now, as I was nearing home, I saw two uniformed soldiers on horseback gallop into this lane, cast off their armor, seize the short jackets and small caps of two people on the street, and then flee. How could these incidents be without cause?"

After a short while, the servant on duty came and reported, "The bandits have entered the city!" Shocked and unbelieving, Shen ordered a confirmation. But I said, "It's true. Haven't you heard the gunfire from the top of the wall? For two days and nights, there hasn't been a moment of peace. Now it's quiet." Shen was very upset and anxiously looked for his official robes, intending to return to the court. He said that the emperor had summoned the grand secretaries to an audience that day and that he should be in attendance. His valet firmly held him back and tried to calm him down. Shortly it was reported that the bandits had already entered the Great Inner Precincts [that is, the imperial palace]. Shen then tore his cap and robe and beat his chest in grief, and I, too, sobbed uncontrollably. Because of this news, I got him to change into humble clothing with me and take refuge in a nearby dwelling to watch what would happen. Our luggage was thrown together hurriedly, and we stored just one or two valuable items with the master of the place next door, leaving the rest to be pilfered by the neighbors and servants— no questions asked.

That day the whole mass of bandits entered the Great Ming Gate, and the rebel, ["Prince"] Chuang [Li Zicheng], with a martial flourish, shot an arrow at the Ascent to Heaven Gate,* striking the side of its upper part—wherefrom one of his bogus aides-de-camp divined great auspiciousness. He proceeded to the inner court and sent out a call for all the actors, cooks, official courtesans, and child singers to come and serve him, having the whole Forbidden City scoured so that none got away. But he still didn't know the whereabouts of the emperor. Everyone said that around midnight some soldiers of Regional Commander Wu [Sangui]'s had arrived and taken the emperor, empress, and crown prince to safety.[15] The bandits seized their close attendants and interrogated them under torture, but none knew where they had gone. Then a bill was posted at the entrance offering a reward of ten thousand taels and enfeoffment as a marquis for anyone who could produce the emperor, empress, or crown prince. Not until the next day was it learned that [the first two] had both died on the altars of state.[16] . . .

In the mid-afternoon of the 19th we proceeded toward the residence of someone we knew near the Front Gate [of the Inner City];† bandit horsemen rode turbulently all around us, glancing down at but not confronting us. . . . [The next day] a member of the family told us

---

*The distance from the present location of Mao Zedong's mausoleum to Tianan Gate, the entrance to the Imperial Palace Museum—approximately half a mile.

†Front Gate was the informal name for the Zhengyang Gate, mentioned below. It was the central, southern gate of the Inner City, just south of the Great Ming Gate (see map 2).

of an announcement from the bandits: The higher officials were to appear for court audiences individually, and those who wished to go home to the provinces would be allowed to do so; those who did not show up, as well as those who gave them cover, would be punished heavily. Shen said, "I'll return voluntarily to my residence and not be a burden to my host." He went back only to find the place filled with bandits.

The next day Shen was compelled to go see one of the false [bandit-appointed] officials at court, who, when he heard my relative's name, said, "Master Shen has a reputation for virtue and has long been admired by me and my associates." Then Shen returned with the bunch who had occupied his house and was moved into a small apartment. On the 23rd someone came and told him: "You can be congratulated on escaping death. They want to handle your case with just a demotion and transfer. . . . Your host general requests a meeting." Shen replied, "I know what he has in mind," and then entered his study, found pen and paper, and wrote, "The great affairs of the world have come to this. To recompense my dear ruler, I can only die. A commoner castoff of the Shun rebel court, I am a minister of the Ming." He gave this to his valet and then tried to hang himself. Shen first ordered his valet to prepare the rope, then the valet held on to it, straining until his strength was spent. Not long after the noose had fully tightened and he heard a sound from his master's throat, the valet dropped Shen precipitously to the floor. In about half an hour, however, Shen revived and left the room in a daze. Meanwhile, all his servants, because of their master's decision to die, had hidden in fright; only a young boy in the next room overheard the attempted suicide and told about it later. . . .

On the 25th [May 1] several soldiers came again . . . and everyone was confined in the quarters of a bandit general named Li. Several dozen people were held in one room, suffering in filth and hunger beyond description. Each day they were taken under guard to the court gate, the bandits riding on horseback and the captives on foot. Those who fell behind were thrashed with horsewhips or the backs of swords to impel them forward. Their relatives, friends, and boy servants could only stand nearby and watch, unable to utter a word. After four or five days the bandits separated over a hundred people, Shen among them, and took them to the Ministry of Personnel.

The bandits wanted to employ Shen in his previous official position, but he refused vigorously and was released. . . . When brought back to the bandit general's quarters, [the ones] who had not been taken to the ministry were subjected to cruel beatings to extract any silver they might have. Some were tortured with finger or limb presses more than three or four times. And some implicated others, so that thousands of commoner households were affected, and people were killed in rapid succession. The whole city was in agitation, and people began to lose interest in living. . . .

At first when the bandits entered the city, they restrained themselves and tried to look dignified. When one soldier snatched some merchandise from a silk-goods shop, he was dismembered as soon as it was known in order to deter others. But when the bandit soldiers were not far out of the sight or earshot of their superiors, they cut loose and did anything they wanted. Their generals and soldiers were all domiciled in the homes of officials and commoners, and the well-to-do provided them with fine food and presented them gifts, fearing their displeasure. Not even the humble alleys and grass dwellings of the poor escaped the bandits' footsteps. The men were used as cooks, and the women were violated. If the bandits happened upon anyone in the street who seemed to have a good upbringing, they would seize and flog him, seeking valuables. Those who wore short jackets [that is, people below gentry status] were made to sew and mend or to work as kitchen helpers. If they found southerners, they would always force them to sing songs, and the young ones would be carried back to the bandits' quarters and made into sexual playthings. The destruction outside the city walls was especially severe. So the people of the capital felt that they were having to walk through scalding water or fire, and all kept hoping for the bandits' defeat and thinking back fondly on their former emperor. . . .

[Because of setbacks incurred by Li Zicheng's army at the hands of the combined forces of Wu Sangui and the Manchus to the northeast of Beijing,] on the 24th and 25th [of the 4th month, May 29–30,] the bandits began hurriedly preparing to leave. They rounded up myriads of the donkeys, mules, camels, and horses in the city, and they emptied out everything in the palace, loaded it up, and went westward. Some said they had filled seventeen vaults with gold and silver, each vault holding several tens of thousands of ounces. Jewels, baubles, bolts of satin—all were piled on the court steps in such quantities that they couldn't be completely picked up in several days' time. Also, they ordered that the various ministers come along, greatly alarming everyone who heard this. Of those who had been confined and not released, over half had died of punishments, and now the rest were ordered strangled, causing cries of injustice to reach the outside thoroughfares. . . .

Suddenly it was passed about that on the 29th [June 3, Li Zicheng] would assume the imperial throne. So people then said that the bandits did not intend to return westward—that the intensive packing and transporting of the previous several days had been to solidify their base [in Shaanxi]. Earlier, when the bandits first appeared, some former Ming ministers had risked death trying to return home to the provinces, and sometimes people fanned the flames of alarm by saying, "So-and-so was killed on the road; so-and-so was drowned in the river." Consequently, most officials in the capital hid themselves in the shadows and didn't dare to test circumstances, however lightly. Now the bandit leader actually had the nerve to sit facing southward on the throne, so people were worried for the safety of those few Ming officials who had preferred death to disgrace and had managed to preserve their honor whole by staying out of sight. But the bandits were cowardly at bottom. They took this occasion [the enthronement] to smear everyone's eyes and ears with false impressions and did not bother with anything else.

So at dawn on the 29th Li Zicheng usurped the emperorship, and the following midnight he fled the city, though people did not realize this until daylight came the next morning.[17] The bandit followers made haste to depart with trains of camels laden with packs, and they left eunuchs and other palace personnel scattered outside the Forbidden City. As soon as people got word that "the city gates are wide open, and no common people who want to flee misfortune will be prevented from leaving," pandemonium ensued, with people supporting old and young family members, carrying bundles of dried food, and running every which way. Before long, flames were seen in the fodder yards and granaries, shortly thereafter in the palace, and in no time the whole city was ablaze. Just then for safety's sake I was staying with Zhao Bozhen in Widow Zhang's hostel near the Front Gate. We climbed upstairs and looked around at the flames and smoke that filled the sky in all directions. The Haidai and Shuncheng gates, which flanked Zheng-yang Gate on the left and right, had already burned [fig. 1]. Only the Zhengyang Gate tower, the Great Ming Gate, and the area around East River Rice Lane had not been touched by the flames. Because several dozen groups of bandit spies were still around, residents carrying lances led one another to mount the city wall and defend Zhengyang Gate.

Figure 1. The (inner and outer) Zhengyang Gate, Beijing, with the Shuncheng and Haidai gates on either side of the outer fortification.

Doors, window shutters, and other things were pieced together and lined up to form barricades a few paces apart along the main streets. People with staves stood watch beside the barricades, and citizens with bells and clappers patrolled the avenues constantly. Anyone in the neighborhood whose face was unfamiliar wouldn't be allowed to pass. People were as agitated as if in a boiling cauldron, and both men and women climbed up on rooftops to be lookouts.

Through the whole night my friends Zhao, Zhang, Yan, and I stood together, shouldering packs [of emergency supplies]; we were anxious for our safety every minute. When morning came, those bandits who had set the fires and others who had not left because they had formed some attachments in the city were flushed out one after another. Thereupon a former commander of the military headquarters in the capital, named Yang, was brought forward to sit atop the wall, and over ten former officials took charge of defending the gate tower in rotation. Each time bandits were seized and brought in, after their true identity was determined they were executed forthwith, and bandit leaders were given death by slow slicing. Because several dozen were killed in all, the people were delighted. This day everyone in the streets was ordered to seize bandits, so people from the western provinces [such as Shanxi and Shaanxi] all cleared out with their whole families, even if they had lived in the capital for a long time. And there also were some incidents, which generally couldn't be investigated, of people taking advantage of the situation to settle old scores. . . .

Around dusk clamorous word came that Wu [Sangui] was about to accompany the crown prince into the city, and all the capital residents were ordered to turn out in welcome, wearing mourning garb. Then someone said surreptitiously, "Outside Qihua Gate there's an announcement on a placard with 'The Great Qing Nation' at the top. I don't know what it means." Those who heard this were greatly shaken. The next morning, that is, the 1st day of the 5th month [June 5], the respected elders led one another out several dozen li from the city to welcome the crown prince. A large military unit arrived escorting a man whom the elders led into the city. By the time they reached the East Floral Gate [to the Forbidden City], the authorities had readied the paraphernalia for an imperial procession. Then the one man under escort dismounted from his horse, stepped into the imperial carriage, and said to the common people looking on, "I am the prince regent

[Dorgon].*[18] The crown prince will arrive in a while. Will you allow me to be the ruler?" The crowd, astonished and uncomprehending, was only able to lamely answer yes. Some in the crowd said that he must be a descendant of Yingzong [a previous Ming emperor who had been held captive by the Mongols],[19] and the common people were so apprehensive that they couldn't do a thing.

Thereupon the regent entered the court. At the time the palace buildings had been consumed by fire; only the minor Hall of Virtuous Government had survived. So the regent stayed there with a very small number of accompanying soldiers. They prepared their food in large pans heated in pits dug along the wayside, and they didn't immediately enter any homes. Neither did they prohibit people from going to look at them. But if they saw idlers picking broken things from the rubble, they would vie to run over and get the things themselves. When some women got into palanquins and had themselves carried back and forth in front of the court gate, the soldiers on guard asked them, "If your own emperor were here, would he allow you to go around like this?" As the women's palanquins went by, the soldiers would peer at them and laugh among themselves.

Before long an order came down: All high-ranking officials must report for the court audience tomorrow; all men in the city must shave their heads [in the Manchu style].[20] Thereupon many people wrote open letters requesting that their old [Ming] customs be continued, and the newly appointed vice minister of war, a man from Jiangnan, also vigorously memorialized, urging that in the interest of gaining the people's confidence, head shaving not be considered. The regent said, "I preserved all your heads, and now you cling to your hair?" But to assuage the feelings of the populace, he ordered that people in the city be allowed to wear mourning for their former emperor for three days before being required to respect the new directive to shave the head.[†]
Before this, everyone had passed it around that the Ming crown prince was in Wu Sangui's camp. But only Qing army units entered the city in greater and greater numbers while Wu himself led his forces west-

*The uncle of the seven-year-old Shunzhi emperor of the Qing dynasty. In effect, Dorgon directed the Qing conquest and ruled the dynasty until his death in 1650.

†The order to shave the head was rescinded twenty days later and was not renewed until the summer of the next year, after the Manchus invaded the Jiangnan region. See Chap. 4.

ward in pursuit of the bandits. Several hundred supply wagons were sent back to the capital, but no one heard anything of the crown prince.

Shen, who had been hiding from the bandits, came out when he learned they had gone. When he heard the order that heads had to be shaved by the 9th of the month [June 13], he secretly arranged to meet me at his former residence to plan a return to the South, nevertheless saying, "This will be a life-threatening matter. I don't want to force you to go along." Together we changed into suits of humble clothing, left behind all the luggage we had been using, and on the 6th braved death to depart. I went out the Shuncheng Gate, and Shen went out the Haidai Gate, neither he nor his attendants bringing anything except four or five small bundles in each of two small rented carts. I brought only some essentials packed in a couple of bedrolls. That night we stayed in the Jade Emperor Temple [still within the Outer City walls]— where fear and worry gave me a case of diarrhea—and the next morning we set out through Youan Gate with about a dozen friends from Zhejiang Province [map 3]. People on the streets had said that beyond the gates were only robbers, and they feared that it wouldn't be possible for us to travel, but circumstances didn't permit us to stop.

Having passed several li beyond the Outer City wall, we unexpectedly found a donkey for hire beside the road, so we used it for thirty li at a fee several times higher than usual. After we rested for a short while, Shen came up with another donkey and rode on ahead, the rest of us following on foot. Alongside that stretch of road were thick stands of tall trees, which meant danger in all our minds. We hadn't gone ten li before Shen encountered some robbers ahead.[21] The rest of us, seeing this, gathered and stood close together. One robber raised his bow and arrow as though he were about to shoot me, so I pulled a packet of silver from my sleeve and threw it to him, and he went away. At the outset our Zhejiang friends had been proud of their valor and strength, but at this point not one escaped being robbed, and all the bundles that Shen had placed in the small carts, as well as my packs, were gone.

Ahead we came to a river, where there was a tired old donkey. I had to whip it to cross the river, and the water came up over my ankles, but I didn't care. Having forded the river, we saw on the bank a dozen or so fellows bare to the waist gambling together under a grass tent, and we suspected that they were robbers. After we had gone five or six more li, we saw an old woman at the edge of a grove of trees, who

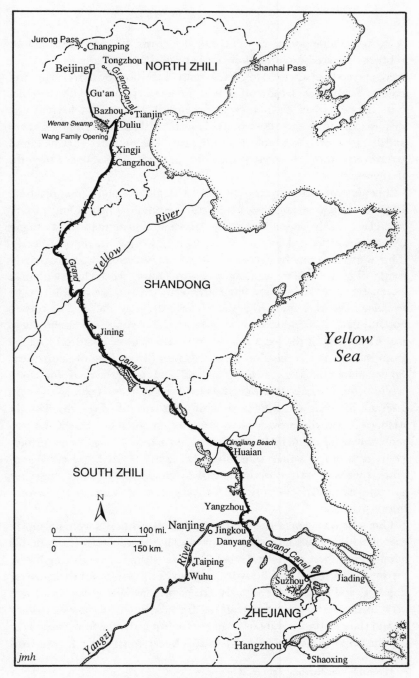

Map 3. Liu Shangyou's Journey Home

spied us coming and then went into the grove. Shortly three or four robbers appeared carrying bows and arrows, knives and pikes, and we were cleaned out again. After a few more li the donkey driver wouldn't go any farther, so I took off a brief linen shirt and a white kerchief with a small silver clasp and gave them all to him. But he still was displeased and eventually left us. Late that night we reached Gu'an, and I was so exhausted that I couldn't eat. The next day it rained, and we traveled thirty li without incident, but my illness took a turn for the worse.*

The day after that we couldn't find a single donkey. Upon reaching Bazhou we saw several dozen soldiers welcoming a new [Qing] circuit intendant and behaving brusquely, so we anxiously made haste to get by them and lodged instead at Su Family Bridge [to the southeast]. That night it rained heavily, and our accommodations were extremely crude. The next day, wanting to go to Duliu, we hailed two small boats. But after traveling a few li the boatman said we couldn't go on because men were lying in ambush along the way ahead. The carters on land had all abandoned their carts and left. My group alighted and made inquiries of the local people, who said that we could take refuge from the bandits at the Zuo Family Manor fifteen li to the northeast. So we floundered along, helping each other through the reeds for a long while before coming to some paths between farmers' fields, and again after a long while we came in sight of what was called the Zuo Family Manor. It was the provincial property of one or the other of the two most powerful eunuchs at court, both surnamed Wang,[22] one of their younger brothers who resided there being called Sixth Master Wang. At first we were barred from entering by an expanse of water, but after pleading earnestly several times, we were allowed to stay in the eastern guest quarters.

Our host was generous, and he saw that all our needs were promptly met morning and night, but I saw nothing commendable about his adopted son. Setting out at daybreak, we saw some men carrying bows, arrows, knives, and clubs hustle on ahead of us. We asked their master about it, and he said, "Yes, today I'm having the best of my housemen serve as escorts to assure your safety." Subsequently we traveled twenty li, and the escorts were about to go back when someone from the manor caught up with us and said, "You absolutely must not take the road

*Probably the diarrhea mentioned above.

ahead; please let me escort you to Cangzhou." After some discussion we agreed to pay him thirty-five taels, for which we wrote up an IOU. Just then, sure enough, we saw the men with bows and arrows, knives and clubs go hustling back. I lay in one of the small carts ready to do whatever our guide directed.

Coming to another river and a place—I don't know where—that seemed like the vast glades of Liangshan Moorage,[23] we managed to get two fishing boats to take us along for half a day, after which we arrived at a town called Wang Family Opening on the border between Bazhou and Dacheng. Everywhere they had been setting up closely spaced palisades and drilling local militiamen for a tight defense. When my group arrived, we couldn't find anyplace to stay. Fortunately, among my friends from Zhejiang was one who was the fellow countryman of a Mr. Hu Yuwang from Shaoxing. He had become a stipendiary student in Shuntian Prefecture [which included the capital],[24] and for a long time his father had run a shop in this place. So Hu had also fled here and had been using a farmer-merchant cover [to conceal his upper-class status]. We happened to mention this relationship, and he happily volunteered to put us up. So we forthwith garnered some security— this being the 11th day of the 5th month [June 15]. . . .

[By the 15th of the 8th month (September 15)] the new Qing dynasty was establishing its officials in the various prefectures and counties [of the North] and was dispatching troops to quell local bandits. All gentry who were present in their locales of registry were ordered to enter the capital, where those who had previously been officials would be employed again in higher posts. Those who didn't go would be penalized. . . . So in the latter part of the 8th month Hu's relative by marriage, Chen Yuanzhu, who had been serving as Ming grain intendant at Tianjin, sent a letter arranging to accompany Hu southward [to join the rump Ming court in Nanjing]. We contracted with a boatman named Yang, and on the 19th we said good-bye to all our friends in the town and were rowed in a long, narrow fishing boat toward Duliu. Water caltrops and lilies covered innumerable acres, and our boat was like a leaf on the rippling expanse of green—it was both frightening and delightful. In the late afternoon we reached shore and at length found accommodations. [Shen Zhifang had already proceeded to Nanjing.]

We had to wait eight or nine days for the party from Tianjin to arrive, during which time I was utterly disconsolate. But when we struck oar and got under way, my mood was lifted by hopes of returning home, even though I knew that frustrating impediments and worrisome difficulties would afflict us every step of the way. My heart chilled at the sight of a military uniform; my face paled the moment I heard any report of soldiers. Toll and dock fees on the canal were erratic, and payments for boat services were ten times higher than usual. It really was trying. Although I was traveling by water, in fact no day passed without taking to land; although a boat was my hostel, in fact on no day did I feel secure. One morning as I was in the middle of a dream a [mere] shout from upstream caused me to leap straight out of my slumber. In the evenings we moored on the canal,* and the men kept defensive watch by shifts all night. But [because I was ill,] Hu always took my turn. Everywhere we eyed any thick underbrush intently. At any given lock three or five ghoulish characters would emerge from behind a tumbledown wall. If what they got after demanding things from us didn't please them, they wouldn't move the planks, and we would have to go the whole night without sleep.[25] At places where the water was shallow, canal traffic was able to get by only by gathering people from a number of boats to emplace movable dikes [fig. 2]. On the boats there were no distinctions of old or young, high-class or low-class; everyone did heave-ho duty. There's a common maxim that says, "Everybody in the same boat has to pull together with a bare back."[†] Because I already was bereft of both servants and luggage, each time I put a hand to this chore, I recited this saying to poke fun at myself. . . .

After the 15th of the 10th month [November 13] we reached Jining [see map 3] . . . and found that the director general of the Grand Canal [Qing collaborator Fang Daxing] had closed the lock to commercial boats. Salt barges under official commission were in the majority, and second in number were those carrying jujubes and pears. All vessels transporting families were held up at the canal banks—over two hundred of them. Hu and Chen hastened twenty li to the Shifo lock hoping as an alternative to buy a small scull in which we could continue, but this was not permitted, either. After several more days Hu said to me, "What they're blocking are just domestic goods and womenfolk. If one is alone with no household, then there's no problem, right? I should see you home and then return for my family members." I was reluctant to reply. So Hu further persuaded me, saying, "Even if they

*That is, not at a city or established moorage.
†Literally, "Board the boat, haul the towline; shirt and pack, throw yourself down."

天津府城

Figure 2. The Grand Canal as it passes a corner of the Tianjin city wall, afloat with the various kinds of private boats that plied its waters.

open the lock today, the canal will soon be frozen and impassable. I
have close relatives here. It wouldn't hurt them to provide enough food
for my family. Once you're home, I'll go back to my own home to
manage things a bit, and around New Year's time I'll return here." So
we decided to set out on foot around sunrise on the 9th day of the 11th
month [December 7], Hu with a small knapsack and me struggling
along behind him. . . .

On the 20th [December 18] we bought a leaflike boat to float down the
canal. It was small, we were heavy, and ice and snow gathered around
us during the three days that it took to reach Qingjiang Beach. Along
the way a friend of Hu's from Hangzhou abandoned our vessel for a
mount, but Hu and I were running low on resources, so we stayed
with the boat all the way. The difficulties and obstructions proved twice
as bad as on the northern route of the canal, but at the time I comforted
myself with the thought that I had now actually entered the South.
From Qingjiang through Huaian and Yangzhou, there was no day
without rain or snow. Because we lacked anything to repel the precip-
itation, our clothes got soaked time and again, and we had to slog
several dozen li through the mire. Resorting to such a small boat had
its dangers in that we were completely exposed [to the human and
natural elements]. Our travel provisions were about gone, and if too
many things came up, we wouldn't have enough to last. On the morning
of the 28th [December 26] when we crossed the Yangzi River, snowflakes
as big as the palm of my hand blurred the line between water and
sky—quite a scene. When we landed at Jingkou, the anxiety I'd felt
up to then seemed to fall away. But it was raining hard and there were
no boats, so we stayed in a small lodging that was damp and narrow,
noisy and messy, and where we couldn't get enough to eat. Because a
bad stretch of water at Danyang was blocking the channel, the next
evening the twelve people on our boat had to stay on board, moored
near the eastern gate of that city. The next day, the 1st of the last
month of the year, Hu and I walked the twenty li to Lingkou along a
narrow path—three or four feet wide—knee deep in mud, with an
escarpment over ten feet high on our left and a steep drop-off to the
water on our right. It's not just the passages into Shu [the Sichuan
Basin] that are hazardous! People traversing this path fell down one
after another. But I tottered along, using my umbrella as a staff, and
eventually got through without injury. I said to Hu, "In my nine-times-

nine difficulties on this trip, this is the eighty-first!"* and Hu laughed in agreement. . . .

First thing in the morning on the 5th of the month we departed from the city [of Suzhou] on a boat for Taicang. Although it arrived at dusk, we crawled on in the dark over the rough terrain of an unfamiliar byway for five, six, or seven more li. When we finally sought a hostel, we had to go to several before one let us in, the doorman having sized us up favorably. The distress and frustration of travel is like this. The old saying "Just one-third of a mile outside one's gate is not as good as at home" was really borne out. In the wee hours of the next morning we walked over ten li to Salt-Iron Opening, where we came upon a small utility boat from my town, so we hired it to go home. When we arrived it was only late afternoon, on the 5th day of the 12th month [January 2, 1645].† When my flesh and blood and I saw each other, grief and joy intermingled, and when I recounted my recent tribulations to them, the past straightaway seemed like another world. . . .

*The number nine was prominent in Chinese numerological calculations based on the *Yijing* (Book of Changes). See Chap. 11, n. 12.
†That is, 205 days after leaving Beijing.

2

"HORRID BEYOND DESCRIPTION": THE MASSACRE OF YANGZHOU

BY THE TIME Liu Shangyou reached his home in Jiading, the Manchu leadership had launched the first stage of their carefully calculated plan to conquer the prosperous, populous lower Yangzi region and eliminate the rump Ming court at Nanjing, presided over by the ineffectual Hongguang emperor. During the winter months they wrested Shanxi, Shaanxi, and northern Henan from Li Zicheng's remaining forces, and in mid-March they were ready to concentrate on the drive into Jiangnan.

The central figure in this drama on the Ming side was Shi Kefa (1601–45), a man of strong character, high principles, and considerable experience in resisting the encroachment of roving rebel armies on Jiangnan. The Hongguang court had appointed him grand secretary and viceroy concurrently to direct the four major Jiangnan defense zones from the headquarters at Yangzhou, a city of great commercial wealth located on the Grand Canal not far north of the Yangzi River (see map 3). The hopes of many in the South had been placed on Shi because of his reputation for uprightness and because he seemed to be the only person of stature who could deal with both the refractory generals in the field and the contentious factional leaders at court.

In the end, however, even Shi was defeated by Ming weaknesses and Qing strengths. He was unable to exempt Yangzhou from the rapaciousness of semi-renegade armies supposedly under his own authority. Just as the Qing armies were advancing through the Huai River drainage and down the Grand Canal toward Yangzhou, Shi was called away from his headquarters to defend Nanjing against a mutiny to the southwest. By the time he got back, morale in Yangzhou had collapsed, and he was unable to rebuild an effective defense before the Manchus arrived at the doorstep.[1]

Conditions were ripe for Shi Kefa to become the greatest martyr of the Southern Ming* and one of the most famous patriots in Chinese history.[2] Because very few near Shi survived the events of his last hours, accounts of his death differ widely, and many rumors circulated long thereafter that he had been seen alive elsewhere. The final blow was most likely delivered at the command of the Manchu generalissimo Dodo, the Prince of Yu,[3] when the captured Shi Kefa refused to submit to him. Shi's body was never found in the immense carnage that ensued.

Shi Kefa's best-known writings are his conscientious memorials to the Hongguang court and his dignified, uncompromising missives to the Qing regent, Dorgon.[4] Below are translated the last words that he sent to his family members, then in Nanjing,[†] as he faced certain death (fig. 3). These letters, though personal, reflect the extremely heavy burden that officials and their families often bore for the state, the acuteness of the sense of obligation they could feel toward even an indifferent "father-ruler," and the awareness on the part of moral and political leaders that even their farewell notes to loved ones would instruct posterity.[5]

The pain of decision for loyalists like Shi Kefa was sharpened by their knowledge that adherence to the principle of nonsurrender on their part would assure terrible consequences for the people under their charge if resistance failed. By repeatedly refusing to open Yangzhou to Qing occupation, Shi made that beautiful, elegant city the first one in Jiangnan to stubbornly hold out against the Qing advance. The Manchu leadership did not hesitate to set an example for the other cities farther on by letting their men, normally under strict discipline, rip loose and reward themselves with the riches of Yangzhou. Having penetrated into the city and destroyed the remaining Ming military forces, Dodo authorized five days of unrestrained killing and rapine.

One lucky survivor of the massacre of Yangzhou was Wang Xiuchu, about whom nothing is known except what is recorded in his *Yangzhou*

---

*Since the latter part of the nineteenth century this term has been used for the collective activities of the four rump Ming governments established by loyalists in the South— those of the Hongguang, Longwu, and Yongli emperors and that of the Prince of Lu (Regent Lu). See Chaps. 4, 7, 8, 14, 15.

†The Shi family ancestral home was in Kaifeng, but because of Kefa's official duties, his close relatives often resided in other cities more proximate to his post.

shiri ji (An Account of Ten Days in Yangzhou), a new translation of which follows the translation of Shi Kefa's last letters home.[6] Wang sees himself as a scholar, and like most urban civilian men in the highly cultured Jiangnan region, he is helpless to resist martial might with any counterforce. His chief resort is mutual aid among family members, the ties among the brothers being especially strong. As for Wang's relation with his wife, readers will note the absence of anything resembling the Western value of chivalry toward women. Wang does his wife great honor, however, in his culture and time by portraying her foremost concern for him, his brothers, and their son and by contrasting her willingness to die for chastity with the looseness of many other women he observed.

Confucian moral injunctions had always included an emphasis on women's chastity, and societal pressures for strict observance of this, among upper-class women in particular, increased markedly in the last three centuries of the dynastic era. Although the social stations and circumstances of Shi Kefa and Wang Xiuchu differed, both men expected their wives to place the honor and well-being of their husbands and families above the preservation of their own lives. Times of acute disruption, such as the Ming-Qing conflict, brought such expectations home to millions of women.[7]

SHI KEFA An unworthy son, Kefa, leaves this missive for his esteemed mother: In eighteen years of official service, I have tasted every bitterness and yet been unable to increase the welfare of the court. I have only been vastly remiss in attending to my parents.[8] Neither effectively loyal nor filial, how can I show my face in the world? Now, even if I die fighting for this city, it will not be sufficient to atone for the wrongs I have done. I hope that Mother will attribute it to fate and not be too sorrowful again. Your son for his part will harbor no hatreds when he lies underground. I have obtained the agreement of my chief military aide, [Shi] Dewei,[9] to finish those matters that should be handled by a son after a father's death, and I hope that Mother will treat him affectionately, like a real grandson.

Written tearfully by unworthy Kefa, 4th month, 19th day [May 14, 1645]

Kefa is about to die. I made a pact with you, my wife,[10] that we would wait for one another in the grave.

Written personally by Kefa, 4th month, 19th day

Kefa leaves this letter for his esteemed uncle, elder brother, worthy third younger brother, and other brothers and nephews:[11] The Yangzhou city wall will fall within a day and a night. Months of toil and strain have come to this end. How could I resent using my one death to recompense the court? I regret only that the death of our former emperor [Chongzhen] has not been avenged. I have obtained the consent of my chief military aide, Dewei, to take care of affairs after my death. He should be accepted into our lineage in the same generation as my various nephews. Do not go back on this, my word.

Written by Kefa in the West Gate Tower of the Yangzhou city wall,
4th month, 19th day

[To Shi Dewei:] Kefa, who received great favor from our former emperor, has been unable to carry out the ultimate revenge for his death. Even though I received great favor from the present emperor [Hongguang], I have been unable to protect his domain. Even though I received great favor from my kind mother, I have been unable to make filial provision for her. I have run upon unfortunate times, in which my will could not be fulfilled. To repay the nation with this one death is surely my destiny. I only regret not having earlier followed our former emperor to the grave.

Kefa's last pen stroke, 4th month, 19th day

Respectfully wishing [my mother] Madam [Shi], [my mother-in-law] Madam Yang, and my wife boundless peace: The Northern [Qing] troops surrounded the Yangzhou city wall on the 18th but have not yet attacked. In any case, the people have already lost heart, and the situation cannot be saved. Sooner or later I must die, and I wonder whether my wife is willing to follow me?[12] In a world like this, life is of no use anyway; one might as well come to this conclusion early on. Mother, in your distress you must rely on Fourth Uncle, my cousins, and others in the family for care. Young Zhao* should do whatever

*Shi Zhaoqing, the son of Kefa's second cousin, Kecheng. Because Kefa and his wife were childless, they may have formally or informally adopted this "nephew" as their

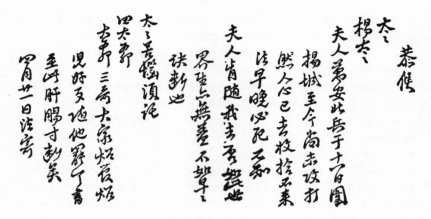

Figure 3. A calligraphic rendering (not Shi's own hand) of Shi Kefa's last letter to his mother, mother-in-law, and wife.

he thinks best for himself. I write no further; my heart* is rent to pieces.

Sent by Kefa, 4th month, 21st day [May 16]

WANG XIUCHU [On the 25th day of the 4th month (May 20, 1645)] one or two persons having told me that Qing troops had entered the city, I rushed out to ask others, and someone said that it was just the arrival of reinforcements from the Marquis of Jingnan, [General] Huang Degong.[†] Soon I saw that the guards atop the city wall were still in disciplined order, but farther on, in the market, people were talking clamorously as a group of disheveled, barefoot people arrived in a trail of dust. Gasping in alarm, they didn't know what to say when queried.

---

son. It is not clear whether Zhaoqing was too young to assume the sorts of responsibilities that Kefa placed on Shi Dewei, whether Kefa did not want to compromise the young man's future by designating him as heir to someone who so prominently resisted the Qing, or whether Kefa was displeased with him for some reason. In any case, Zhaoqing was eventually entered in the Shi lineage record, along with Dewei, as Shi Kefa's successor. It was very common for Chinese men who had no sons to adopt heirs, even from outside their lineages (see Chap. 6, n. 1).

*Literally, "liver and intestines."

[†]In fact, Huang had led his forces southwestward to resist an attack on Nanjing by a renegade Ming army from the middle Yangzi region.

Suddenly a wave of several dozen horsemen was seen galloping desperately from north to south, protecting one man in their midst—the viceroy [Shi Kefa]. They had probably fled to the eastern wall but found the outside troops pressing close, so now, wanting to escape by the southern gate, they had come through here. When I saw them, I had no doubt that enemy troops had entered the city. Presently a single horseman came back, riding slowly with slack reins, his face turned upward, wailing in anguish.* In front of the horse walked two soldiers, who couldn't bear to leave the rider. To this day the sight remains before my eyes, and I regret that the rider's name has not been passed down. When he had gone some distance away, the men guarding the wall came down, making a commotion, and scurried for cover, throwing off their helmets and spears, some even cracking their heads or spraining their ankles. When I looked back at the turrets on the wall, I saw that they were completely empty.

Prior to this time the viceroy had found that the city wall was too narrow to mount cannon on top. So he ordered platforms placed at certain ramparts—the fronts perpendicular to the wall and the backs connecting with the roofs of people's residences just inside the wall—to provide more room for mounting the cannon. But the work had not been finished. When the first enemy soldiers climbed over the wall, brandishing bows and slashing out wildly with swords, the soldiers who'd been keeping watch on the wall jostled against one another, trying frantically to escape. The way ahead being jammed, they all made for those platforms, crawling and pulling, hoping to reach the roofs of the houses. But the new platforms, not yet stable, collapsed underfoot, and people fell like leaves, eight or nine out of ten being killed. Those who made it to the rooftops broke tiles with each step, so that altogether it sounded like swords striking shields in a melee or like a hail of bullets, and the clatter went out infinitely in all four directions. The people in the houses underneath ran forth, startled out of their wits. Soon every room in those homes, from the outer reception halls to the inner apartments, was totally filled with soldiers and people who'd been on the wall and were now desperately seeking any nook or cranny in which to hide, oblivious to the owners' protestations.[13]

In one house after another, people closed the doors to their outer

---

*This lends credence to reports that Shi Kefa was killed near the south gate of the Yangzhou city wall.

rooms and held their breath. Directly in back of the central hall of my home was the city wall, so by peering out through a crack in the window I could see soldiers atop the south wall going westward. They marched in an orderly manner and didn't mind the soaking rain, so I thought they were the well-regimented troops [of the viceroy's command]. But just as I'd regained my composure somewhat, there came an urgent knocking at my door. Some neighbors were organizing a joint welcome for the Qing troops, and they were setting up a bench on which to burn incense to show that they dared not resist. Seeing that things were so far beyond help and being loath to go against the majority view, I lamely uttered a string of OKs. Then I changed into another style of clothing and waited, neck craned, watching apprehensively.

When quite a while passed and no troops came, I again peered through the back window to the top of the wall, where the military unit was spreading out, some soldiers walking on and some stopping. Suddenly I saw some women dressed in the Yangzhou fashion being bundled along among them, and for the first time I was taken aback. I turned to my wife and said, "Enemy soldiers have entered the city. If things go awry, you should cut short your own life." "Yes," she said, "Let me give you my few pieces of silver to keep." And then she sobbed, "Women like me in situations like this no longer think to live in the human world.". . . Just then someone from the countryside rushed in exclaiming, "They've come! They've come!"

I ran out and saw several cavalrymen approaching from the north, all leading their horses by the reins and walking slowly. . . . At this point people were looking out for themselves, and there was no communication among neighbors. Although we were only feet apart, not a sound could be heard. When the soldiers got somewhat closer, I began to see that they were going from door to door soliciting silver.[14] But they weren't being greedy, and they let people alone after getting small amounts. If someone refused to give anything, the soldiers would raise their swords threateningly, but they still hadn't struck anyone. (Later I learned that someone had donated ten thousand taels, but goaded by some Yangzhou natives, the Qing soldiers had killed him anyway.) When they got to my door, one horseman pointed to me and said to another, "Get something for me from this one dressed in blue." But before the second horseman could let go of his reins, I was in flight, so he gave me up and rode away on his steed. I wondered why they had wanted to get me even though I was wearing coarse clothes like a villager.

When my younger and eldest brothers arrived, we put our heads together, saying, "All those who live near here are wealthy merchants, so they look on us as wealthy merchants, too. What can we do?" The upshot was that I relied on my two brothers to brave the rain and hurriedly take the womenfolk through back-alley shortcuts to my second elder brother's house. It was located behind the He family graveyard, and close by on either side lived only very poor people. I alone stayed behind at my place to keep an eye on developments. But in no time my eldest brother came back and said, "Blood has been spilled on the main streets. What are you waiting here for? If all four of us brothers face life or death in the same place, then whatever happens, we'll have no regrets." So, respectfully carrying our ancestral tablets, I accompanied him to my elder brother's house, where we hid along with his wife and son, our youngest brother, my own wife and son, two of my wife's sisters, and her younger brother.

By dusk the sound of Qing soldiers slaying people had penetrated to the doorstep, so we climbed onto the roof for temporary refuge. The rain was heavy, and several of us huddled under one blanket, so every strand of our hair got soaked. The sounds of lamentation and pain outside struck terror from the ears to the soul. Not until the stillness of late nighttime did we dare let ourselves down from the roof by the eaves, light the stove, and cook something to eat.

Fires had started all over the city—more than ten close by and innumerable ones farther away. The red glare was reflected in the sky like lightning; the crackling of the fires bombarded my ears incessantly. Faintly one could also hear the most pitiful sounds, and the mournful aura was extremely chilling—horrid beyond description. When our rice was ready, we just looked at each other, so anxious and tearful that we couldn't use our chopsticks, nor could we think what to do. My wife took the silver that she had given to me previously and broke it into four portions, one for each of us brothers to keep, and we hid the pieces in our topknots, shoes, and waistbands. She also found a tattered robe and a pair of old shoes. After I changed into those, we lay wide awake till dawn. . . .

On the 26th [May 21], the force of the flames abated somewhat, and the sky also gradually cleared. So again we ascended to our rooftop hideout and found more than ten people already concealing themselves in the rain gutters. Suddenly a man emerged from a chamber to the east and climbed straight up the wall with a saber-wielding soldier in fleet pursuit. But when the soldier saw my group, he let that man go and began chasing me. Terrified, I fled downward off the roof, followed by my brothers, and we ran more than a hundred paces before stopping. After this incident I was separated from my wife and son and no longer knew if they were alive or dead.

The shrewd soldiers, fearing that many were in hiding, tricked people with a "warrant to assuage the populace," which stated that no one who came out voluntarily would be executed. So those who'd been hiding vied to comply, and soon fifty or sixty people had gathered, half of them women. One of my elder brothers said, "If the four of us alone run into fierce soldiers, we won't be able to avoid calamity. It would be better to cast our lot with that group, for larger numbers make it easier to evade harm. Even if the worst happens, we'll have been together in both life and death and have no regrets." Because our minds had become muddled and we had no better idea for saving our lives, the other three of us perfunctorily agreed, and together we joined the larger group. The three Manchu soldiers in charge searched my brothers and got all their silver, but they didn't search me.

Some women came up, and two among them called out to me. I recognized them as the concubines of my friend Zhu Shu, and I anxiously stopped them. The two concubines' hair had fallen loose, they were partially naked, and they stood in mud so deep that it reached their calves. One was embracing a girl, whom a soldier lashed and threw into the mud before driving her away. One soldier hoisted a sword and led the way, another leveled his spear and drove us from behind, and a third moved back and forth in the middle to make sure no one got away. Several dozen people were herded like cattle or goats. Any who lagged were flogged or killed outright. The women were bound together at their necks with a heavy rope—strung one to another like pearls. Stumbling with each step, they were covered with mud. Babies lay everywhere on the ground. The organs of those trampled like turf under horses' hooves or people's feet were smeared in the dirt, and the crying of those still alive filled the whole outdoors. Every gutter or pond that we passed was stacked with corpses, pillowing each other's arms and legs. Their blood had flowed into the water, and the combination of green and red was producing a spectrum of colors. The canals, too, had been filled to level with dead bodies.

We came to the residence of the police chief, the Honorable Yao Yongyan, and went straight in the back entrance. The place was spacious, and there were piles of corpses everywhere. I thought that this would be my place of death. But we wended our way through to the front door, out onto the street, and to another house—that of a merchant from the west named Qiao Chengwang—which was the lair of the three soldiers herding our group. Upon entering, we saw a soldier who had detained several young women and who had been rifling the chests and hampers, making mountains of varicolored silks and satins.

When he saw the other three soldiers arrive, he laughed heartily and then drove the few dozen of us men into the back hall. The women were put in a side room wherein were two small square tables, three dressmakers, and a middle-aged woman, who was also working on some garments. She was a local person, heavily made up and gaudily dressed, who gestured, talked, and laughed smugly. Every time the soldiers ran across some good item, she would beg them for it, brazenly using her fawning charms. One of the soldiers at one point remarked, "When we campaigned in Korea [1627 and 1636–37], we captured women by the tens of thousands, and not one lost her chastity. How is it that wonderful China has become so shameless?" Alas, this is why China is in chaos. Then the three soldiers stripped the women of all their wet clothes, from outer to inner wear and from head to heel, and they ordered the middle-aged woman to take measurements and make alterations so the others could change into fresh new gowns. Needless to say, the women, relentlessly forced to expose their naked bodies, felt so ashamed and awkward that they wanted to die. After the women had finished changing clothes, the soldiers cuddled them while drinking wine and eating meat, doing all sorts of things with no regard for propriety.

Then one of the soldiers jumped up, drew his saber, and bellowed, "Come on, you southern savages!" By the time we got near the front of the hall, some of us men were being tied up, including my eldest brother. My elder brother said to me, "Things having come to this strait, what more is there to say?" Desperately clasping my hand one last time, he went forward, and my younger brother followed him. The men who'd been captured now numbered over fifty. If a soldier so much as raised a sword and shouted, our souls expired, and not a single one of us dared make a move. I, too, followed my eldest brother from the hall and saw that outside they were killing people; the men in the group awaited their fate in turn. At first I thought that I'd just as soon be bound up, but all at once my heart quickened as if aided by some supernatural force, and I slipped away through the hall to the rear without anyone knowing.

In the western room of the quarters in back of that hall, some old women were still holding out, so I couldn't hide there. I went straight through to the back and found there nothing but corralled camels and horses. Unable to jump over them, I began to panic. But then I stooped down and crawled under several of the animals' bellies to get out. If anything had spooked the camels or horses and caused them to lift their hooves even slightly, I would have been mashed. . . .

I rushed to a door that led to an adjoining alley and clutched the bolt of the lock in both hands beseechingly. Although I shook it a hundred times, it wouldn't budge. When I attacked it with a rock, the sound echoed as far as the outer courtyard, and I feared detection. Having no other recourse, I began joggling it again, bloodying my fingers. Then the lock moved abruptly, and I pulled on it with all my might. With the lock in hand I anxiously tugged at the crossbar, but it, being made of hibiscus wood, had become swollen in the rain and was jammed twice as badly as the lock. I was desperately applying all my strength to raising the crossbar when the hinges broke, and the whole door and surrounding wall collapsed thunderously. My panic-stricken body fairly flew over the rubble—I don't know where the power came from. I dashed madly out the back gate and found myself at the foot of the city wall. . . .

In the neighborhood to the left of the Qiao residence I squeezed through the back door of a house and found all the hiding places already filled with people. Because they definitely wouldn't allow me to stay, I went toward the front—through five areas, all just as crowded—and didn't stop until I reached the front door. It opened onto a main street, where troops went back and forth in endless procession, so it had been abandoned as too dangerous. But I hurried in and found a bed with a canopy. I climbed one of the bedposts and squeezed myself into a hiding place above the canopy. Just as I'd caught my breath, through the compound wall I heard the voice of my younger brother shrieking and the sound of a saber hacking—three strikes, and all was silent. After a short while I also heard my elder brother say pleadingly, "I have silver at home in an underground vault. Let me get it and bring it to you." One strike, and again silence. By that time my spirit had left its lodging, my heart was like burning lamp-oil, my eyes were parched and tearless, my bowels were in knots, about to split, and I no longer could control myself. Shortly a soldier entered with a woman under his arm and wanted to lie down with her on the bed. She refused, but he forced her. Then she said that it was too close to the marketplace to stay for very long, so in a little while the soldier took her somewhere else. I barely escaped detection!

The room had a false ceiling, apparently made of straw matting. It couldn't sustain a person's weight, but one could use it to reach the rafters. I grasped each rafter with both hands and made my way up them until I could prop my feet on the center beam. Below, the matting shielded me from view, and in between, it was as black as lacquer. Soldiers still came and thrust their spears up through the ceiling. But finding the space empty, they thought there was no one up there. So I was able to go a whole day without encountering any soldiers. Below me, however, I don't know how many people were run through with swords and spears. . . .

After a long while, the horsemen thinned out, and on either side of me I heard only people's mournful cries. Because half of us brothers had been killed, and I had no way of divining whether my eldest brother still lived, I thought that I should try to track down my wife and son, even though I didn't know where they were, and perhaps get to see them again. So, using the beam, I slowly got down and crept stealthily to the street out front.

There in the street, severed heads lay cushioning one another, and in the gathering darkness one couldn't tell whose was whose. I stooped over the corpses and called out all around but got no response. At a distance to the south I saw a swarm of people coming toward me carrying torches. I quickly evaded them and fled along the city wall, where I tripped repeatedly on the piled-up bodies. Each time something alarmed me, I lay flat on the ground and pretended to be a stiff corpse. At length I reached a small street, where people were startling and bumping into each other in the dark. By contrast, on the main thoroughfares torches were so ubiquitous that it was like broad daylight. I walked from early to mid evening before reaching my elder brother's house. The door was closed, and at first I didn't dare knock. But momentarily I heard a woman's voice—my sister-in-law's—so I tapped lightly and my wife answered the door. My eldest brother had returned earlier, and my wife and son both were there. I sobbed with my eldest brother, but I couldn't bring myself to tell him right away about our other two brothers' being killed. My sister-in-law questioned me, but I didn't tell her the truth about her husband.

I asked my wife how she had avoided trouble, and she told me: "When the soldier came at us and you fled, everyone else did the same except me. I held our son Peng in my arms and tried to kill myself by jumping off the roof, but it didn't work. My younger sister, having tripped and injured her foot, was lying there with me when a soldier came and took the two of us into a room. Inside were several dozen people all tied together like a string of fish. The soldier, ordering me and the other women to keep an eye on the rest and not let anyone get away, then went out carrying a saber. Another soldier came in, seized my sister, and left. After a long while, I didn't see any more soldiers come, so I tricked the other women and got out, whereupon I ran into Old Lady Hong. We helped each other back to our former place, so I fortunately escaped the fate of the other captives. . . . "

On the 27th I asked my wife where she'd hidden [with Old Lady Hong, a relative of the wife of my elder brother], and she took me circuitously to a spot behind a coffin, where no one ever went and where there were only some old tiles and worthless bricks. Squatting in the overgrowth, I placed my son on the coffin and covered him with a reed mat. My wife crouched toward the front end of the coffin and I toward the other end. If we lifted our heads or stretched out our legs, then the tops of our heads or our feet could be seen. We took shallow breaths and packed ourselves in by tucking in our hands and feet.

Just as I'd calmed down somewhat, the sound of killing pressed in on us. Wherever sword hilts clattered, a din of sorrowful cries arose, and several dozen—sometimes over a hundred—people would plead for their lives in unison. Whenever a soldier appeared, the southerners—whether few or many—would all hang their heads and grovel, or stretch out their necks to receive the sword, and not a one would dare to flee. It goes without saying that there were droves of orphaned children and widowed women, crying in hundred-voice choruses, their lamentations verily shaking the earth. By afternoon the stacks of corpses had grown mountainous, but the killing and pillaging just grew more intense [fig. 4]. When evening came, we emerged hesitantly. My son Peng had lain contentedly on the coffin and had neither cried nor spoken nor wanted anything to eat all day long. When he'd been thirsty, we'd

Figure 4. A late-Qing artist's visualization of the massacre of Yangzhou.

used a piece of tile to give him some gutter water, and he'd then gone back to sleep. Now we woke him up and carried him with us.

Old Lady Hong appeared and informed us that my sister-in-law had been abducted, too, and that my nephew, still in swaddling clothes, was missing. What terrible anguish! In just two days I'd lost four loved ones—my elder and younger brothers, a sister-in-law, and a nephew. Together we looked to see if there was any rice left in the mortar, but there was none. So my eldest brother and I lay pillowing each other, bearing our hunger until dawn. That night my wife again tried to kill herself and would have succeeded if Old Lady Hong hadn't intervened.

On the 28th I said to my eldest brother, "We don't know who might be killed today. You fortunately are still unharmed. Please take my son Peng to keep him alive a bit longer." My brother tearfully consoled me and then, taking little Peng, fled to another place. Old Lady Hong said to my wife, "Yesterday I hid inside the coffin and was fine from morning to evening. Today I should change hiding places with you." But my wife insisted that she didn't want to and, as before, concealed herself with me behind the coffin. Before long, several soldiers came in, opened the coffin, and snatched out Old Lady Hong. Although she was beaten a hundred times over, she never divulged where anyone else was, and I was very grateful to her. Soon more and more soldiers came near our hiding place, one on the heels of another. But when they happened to come into the area behind the house, they just saw the coffin and left.

All at once, more than a dozen soldiers came into the house yelling and acting fierce. I saw someone approach the coffin, and when he poked my foot with a long bamboo pole, I flinched in alarm and came out. He was a Yangzhou man—whose face I knew but whose name I'd forgotten—who was guiding the others around. I begged him to have mercy on us, and after taking some of my silver he released me, though he still had the gall to say, "I'm letting your wife off cheaply." He went back into the house and told the soldiers to let us go for now, so they dispersed.

Before I'd caught my breath, a young man dressed in red came straight at me with the point of a long sword. I gave him silver, but he also wanted my wife. She, in her ninth month of pregnancy, was crouching on the ground and absolutely refused to rise. So I lied to the man, saying, "My wife has been pregnant for many months. Yesterday she slipped and fell from the roof, causing a miscarriage. There's no way the child can be born alive. How can you expect her to get up?" But the man in red didn't believe me, so he opened her dress to look at her belly, and what I had said was further confirmed by her trousers, which we had previously daubed with blood. So he paid no more attention to her. He had already taken a young woman, her daughter, and little boy captive. When the boy cried to his mother for something to eat, the soldier grew angry and bashed in the child's skull with one blow. Then he carried the mother and daughter away.

I told my wife that the place had become too well known, so we couldn't be safe there and should change to another location. But my wife was now determined to kill herself, and I, too, was at my wit's end with fright. So we both went into the house and tried to hang ourselves together from a rafter. But the rope, which was slung over the rafter to make two nooses, quickly broke under our weight and dropped us simultaneously to the floor. We hadn't yet gotten up when soldiers again filled the gate. They headed straight for the reception hall and didn't take time to pass through the two side corridors. So my wife and I had a chance to dash feverishly outside and into a thatched hut. It was occupied by some peasant women, who allowed my wife to stay but rejected me. I ran hurriedly into another thatched hut to the south of that one and found straw piled to the ceiling . . . in which several people were hiding. Within the piles I also spied several square tables completely surrounded by straw but with enough empty space underneath for twenty or thirty people. I forced my way in under the tables and thought I'd hit on a good stratagem. But unexpectedly the decayed wall gave way and opened a hole two or three feet high, through which some soldiers quickly detected me and the others. From outside the hole they jabbed us with long spears, and everyone closer to the outside was severely wounded, whereas I was injured in my thigh. The former were all nabbed by the soldiers, but those farther in, like me, crab-crawled out and got away.

Going back to where my wife was, I found her and the other women all lying on a woodpile, their bodies smeared with blood, gobs of excrement in their hair, their faces powdered with ashes. They looked like phantoms, and I could tell which one my wife was only by her voice. I begged the women to let me hide under some straw while they lay in a bunch on top. Holding my breath and not daring to move, I almost suffocated. But my wife gave me the end of a bamboo tube, through one end of which I could get air from above, so I was able to survive. . . . As it grew dark, the women all got up, and at last I emerged from the straw, dripping sweat like rain.

That night we returned to the Hongs' house and found both Old Lady Hong and her husband there. My eldest brother also came and said that he'd been taken and made to carry loads, after which he'd been tipped a thousand cash and released with a flag to assure his safe return. . . .

The next day was the 29th—the fifth day since the slaughter began on the 25th—and I was beginning to think that by some good fortune I might be spared, when the rumor flew around that everyone in the city was to be exterminated. Of those in the city who were still left breathing, over half then risked death to lower themselves down the outside of the city wall and make a run for it. The old official moat, which had grown clogged and no longer admitted a flow of water, became a broad, flat road [via which people were escaping]. But in so doing, they also ran into peril, because those who tried to save themselves by fleeing the city carried all their valuables with them, and this had led groups of thugs to enter the moat at night and rob people of their gold and silver. No one could do anything about it. We [my wife, son, and I] didn't think we could escape through that gauntlet, and my eldest brother couldn't bear to leave me and go by himself. So we mulled over the idea until dawn and then put it to rest.

Because we couldn't stay in the place where we'd been hiding, and because my wife had been spared harm several times because of her advanced pregnancy, I alone hid in some water plants at the edge of a pond while my wife and son lay pitifully above me. Although several soldiers came, and a few accosted them, each time the soldiers left after being paid off with small amounts. But subsequently a vicious soldier came, looking very evil with a mouselike head and hawkish eyes, and he wanted to seize my wife. She crept forward feebly and told him she was pregnant, but he didn't listen. When he tried to force her up, she rolled on the ground, refusing to rise even if it meant death. He then beat her with the back of his sword until blood soaked her clothing all the way from the inner to the outer garments. Prior to this my wife had warned me, saying, "If I meet misfortune, then I'm determined to die. Don't plead for me on the ground that we are husband and wife, because not only you but our son, too, will be implicated." So I hid at a distance in the pond grass as if I didn't know [what was happening]. But I really thought she was going to be killed. The evil soldier, not content to leave her injured, bound her upper arms with her hair and dragged her sideways, cursing and beating her vilely. From the path in the field through a deep lane out onto the main street, the route curved over the distance of an arrow shot, and he was bent on thrashing her several times every few steps of the way. Suddenly, however, he ran into a group of horsemen, one among whom spoke several sentences to him in Manchu, so he let my wife go and left. Only then was she able to crawl back to me and have a big cry; not a patch of her skin was unbroken.

Then fires broke out again all around, and the numerous thatched dwellings on either side of the He family graveyard were engulfed in flames as soon as they ignited. The very few who had slipped through the dragnet by hiding in undiscovered nooks and crannies, once forced out by the flames, ran straight to their undoing—not one in a hundred avoided this fate. There were those who just closed their doors and let themselves be burned to death—from several people to as many as a hundred in one house. Later it couldn't be discerned how many people's bones were massed in a given room. . . . My wife, son, and I lay together toward the back of a tomb, covered with mud and dirt from head to toe, looking scarcely human. As the force of the flames mounted, the tall trees in the graveyard caught fire: they blazed like lightning flashes and sounded like a landslide. The hot wind roared angrily, and the bright sun itself appeared pale and dim. Before my eyes I seemed to see countless [Buddhist] guardian demons driving a million souls to their deaths in hell.[15] When not trembling with fear, I quite lost my senses and, on the whole, no longer knew whether I was still in the human world.

Out of nowhere I heard loud, heavy footsteps and desperate, heart-stopping shouts. Turning to look toward the graveyard wall, I saw at a distance my eldest brother struggling with a soldier who had grabbed him—the same one who'd seized and then released my wife the day before! My brother, being a strong man, got free by shoving the soldier, who then hastened away. For a short interval my heart was palpitating. Then my brother, naked, his hair disheveled, dashed toward me with the soldier in close pursuit. As a last resort he asked me for some silver to save his life. Although I had only one ingot,[16] I took it out and gave it to the soldier. But, not satisfied with such a small amount, he became enraged and attacked my brother with his saber. As my brother writhed on the ground, blood flowing over his whole body, my son Peng (then four years old) tugged at the soldier, tearfully begging him to stop. But the soldier just wiped his sword on the boy's clothing and continued his attack until my brother was near death.

Then he turned on me and pulled my hair, demanding more silver and striking me indiscriminately with the back of his sword. I pleaded that my silver was gone and that if he'd accept nothing but silver, then I'd gladly die—but what about other valuables? The soldier hauled me by the hair into the Hongs' house, where my wife's clothing and accessories had been placed inside two urns. I emptied them under the stairs and turned out everything for him to choose from. He didn't pass up any of her jewelry, but of her garments he took just the nicer ones. Seeing that my son wore a silver chain around his neck, he used his saber to cut it off. As the soldier left, he looked at me and said, "If I don't kill you, somebody else is sure to." So I knew that the rumor about wiping out everyone in the city was true, and I fully expected to die.

Leaving our son in the house, I rushed back outside with my wife and saw that my brother's neck had gashes about one inch deep in both the front and back and that his chest was even more grisly. The two of us helped him into the Hongs' house, but in querying him we realized that he was already beyond feeling pain and was only semiconscious. Having tried to make him secure, my wife and I again hid out near the tomb, where all the neighbors, too, were lying in the clumps of weeds. Suddenly what seemed to be a human voice said to me, "Tomorrow they're going to scour the city and kill absolutely everybody. You'd better give up your wife and make a run for it with me." My wife also urged me to go. But how could I leave my eldest brother in such a perilous state? Besides, I had relied before on still having some silver left. Now it was completely gone, so I didn't see how I could survive. I passed out from sheer misery and didn't come to for a long while—by which time the fires had subsided.

From far off, we heard three bursts of cannon fire, and the numbers of troops going back and forth gradually diminished. My wife, holding our son in her arms, sat in an excrement pit, where she was joined by Old Lady Hong. Several soldiers had captured four or five women, the older two of whom were crying dolefully while two of the younger ones were smiling, laughing, and enjoying themselves. From behind, two other soldiers raced up and tried to steal some of the women, and a fracas ensued. One soldier in the group tried to break it up, speaking in Manchu. Suddenly one of them hoisted one of the younger women and crudely copulated with her under a tree. Then the two other younger women were sullied while the two older ones wailed and begged to be spared. The three younger ones shamelessly thought nothing of it when about a dozen men took turns raping them before handing them over to the two soldiers who'd run up later. By that time one of the younger women couldn't even get up to walk. I recognized her as a daughter-in-law of the Jiao family, which in ordinary times could be said to have deserved this. But under such shocking circumstances I couldn't help but sigh regretfully.

Just then I saw a man dressed in red with a rapier at his waist wearing a Manchu-style hat and black boots; he was under thirty years of age and of nobly handsome and forthright bearing. He was followed by another man, clothed in yellow with armor on his torso, who was also very imposing. And close behind them were several Yangzhou people. The man in red scrutinized me and said, "It seems that you're not like the rest of this lot. Tell me your identity truthfully." Thinking that some had gotten off because they were scholars and that others had been executed immediately for the same reason, I didn't dare blurt out the truth but instead made up something to tell him. He also pointed to my wife and child, asking who they were, and I acknowledged them candidly. He said, "Tomorrow the venerable prince [Dodo] will order that all swords be sheathed, and you three shall live." He had those behind him give us a few articles of clothing, as well as one ingot of silver. He asked how long we'd been without food, and I replied, "Five days." So he ordered us to follow his group. My wife and I were simultaneously trusting and suspicious, but we didn't dare refuse to go. [With Old Lady Hong] we reached a house where goods had been gathered in great profusion, fish and rice completely filling the place. The man in red said to a woman there, "Treat these four persons well," and then took leave of us.

After dusk my wife was distressed to learn that her younger brother had been seized by a soldier and that his fate was unknown. Soon Old Lady Hong brought out some fish and rice for us to eat, and because our house was not far from the Hongs', I took some to feed my eldest brother. His throat was so badly injured, however, that he couldn't swallow, so I stopped after a few tries with the chopsticks. As I dressed my brother's hair and washed the blood from his wounds, my heart felt as though cut out by a knife. . . .

The next day, the 1st of the 5th month [May 25], the violence of the soldiers was not severe, but some killing and pillaging continued. . . . On the 2nd, we heard that [Qing] officials had been placed in all administrative units in the region and that assuaging placards had been carried out among all the common people, declaring that they should not be alarmed. Also, it was decreed that monks in the various monasteries were to begin cremating bodies. (No small number of women had hidden in the monasteries and then died of fright or hunger.) The book for recording cremations, when checked later, was found to list eighty thousand[17]—not including those who threw themselves into wells and rivers, those who closed their doors and immolated or hanged themselves, nor those who died in captivity.

On the 3rd, relief measures were announced, and we accompanied Old Lady Hong to Quekou Gate to receive some rice. . . . All those who came to carry off sacks of food had scorched pates, pulpy foreheads, and broken or otherwise injured arms and legs. They had sword gashes all over their bodies, the blood from which had clotted in patches, and their faces were streaked with trickles of blood like tears from burning red candles. In grabbing for rice, people didn't look out even for their own friends or relatives. The strong went and came back again, but the old, weak, and hurt were unable to get a scoop of grain all day.

On the 4th the sky cleared. A hot sun cooked the city, and the smell of corpses became staggering. Front and back, left and right, everywhere were pyres, the combined smoke from which was like a fog, and the rancid odor went out several dozen *li*. On this day I burned some cotton and human bones together and used the ashes to treat my brother's wounds. Tears fell from his eyes as he nodded to show his appreciation, but he couldn't speak. On the 5th . . . the sword gashes burst open and he died. Such grief!—pain beyond expression. Especially when I recalled that in the beginning of this catastrophe, there were eight of us, not counting my wife's sisters and younger brother—my elder and younger brothers, sister-in-law, nephew, niece, wife, and son—and now only three of us remained.

I've discursively recorded only what I experienced personally or saw with my own eyes from the 25th day of the 4th month to the 5th day of the 5th month—altogether ten days. . . . All I intend is that people of later generations who are fortunate to live in a peaceful world and to enjoy uneventful times, but who neglect self-cultivation and reflection and are inveterately profligate, will read this and be chastened.

3

"THEY APPEAR MORE HUMAN":
A MISSIONARY
DESCRIBES THE MANCHUS

AFTER SUBDUING THE POPULATION of Yangzhou, the Qing army's next major objective was to cross the Yangzi River at its juncture with the Grand Canal. This feat, and the consequent collapse of Ming forces immediately south of the river, was witnessed not only by Chinese but by at least one "Western barbarian" as well—Father Martino Martini (1614–61). His records, and those of other Europeans who visited China in the Ming-Qing era, provide us with alternatives to Chinese points of view and detailed, straightforward descriptions of many things that seldom, if ever, are mentioned in contemporaneous Chinese writings—such as what ordinary Manchu soldiers were like.

The decline of the Ming dynasty in its last half-century coincided with the arrival in China of some astute observers—Christian missionaries from Europe, priests of the Society of Jesus, commonly called Jesuits. This rigorously disciplined religious order had provided shock troops for the papacy in the Catholic Reformation of the middle sixteenth century, and by the end of that century the Jesuits were leading a great wave of Catholic missionary enterprises not only in East Asia but also in the Americas. The insistence of this order that their members be accomplished in some branch of the sciences (such as astronomy or cartography), as well as have an aptitude for letters, and the expertise that many Jesuits developed in the manufacture of artillery were important factors in the acceptance they found among Chinese scholar-officials and rulers. Strongly committed to the extension of Christian teachings to all parts of the world (especially to populous countries like China), the Jesuits were remarkably flexible in adjusting to the cultures and politics of foreign lands. Indeed, Jesuits managed to ingratiate themselves with all three of the major protagonists in the seventeenth-century Chinese dynastic upheaval—the Ming, the Qing, and the roving rebels. They were concerned mainly that they be allowed to stay and proselytize, but they also hoped that the favor of autocrats would lead to mass conversions.

Martini, an Italian by birth, was fascinated by China and inspired by Jesuit accomplishments in that country from an early age. He entered the Society of Jesus in 1631 and, after several years of training (particularly in mathematics, geography, and cartography), was dispatched on the perilous sea voyage to East Asia. He arrived in Macao in 1643 and proceeded immediately to Hangzhou, which had been a center of Jesuit missionary activity since the days of his great predecessor Matteo Ricci (1552–1610). Within three years of his arrival, Martini witnessed the establishment of the rump Ming court in Nanjing and the Qing conquest of the Yangzi delta and central Zhejiang regions. Partly because of his knowledge of cannon and other firearms, he was treated well by both the Ming and the Qing authorities. From 1647 until he temporarily returned to Europe in 1651, Martini was allowed to establish a church in Hangzhou and to travel widely in China. After barely surviving a hazardous voyage back to East Asia from Europe, Martini reestablished his ministry in Hangzhou in 1658. Weakened by years of unremitting exertion, he died of cholera just two years later at the age of forty-six.[1]

Martini had been eager to promote European knowledge of China and enthusiasm for the Jesuit work there through his writings. Three of his books became influential: the *Novus atlas Sinensis*, an atlas of China; the *Sinicae historiae decas prima*, a history of China since antiquity; and the *De bello Tartarico*, a history of the conflict between the Ming and the Manchus and of the Qing conquest of China through the 1650s. The last was enormously popular and appeared in at least twenty-five editions (in Latin and nine other European languages) by the end of the seventeenth century. The quotations below, from an English translation by John Crook published in 1654, reflect the generally positive attitude of the Jesuits toward the Manchus, as well as their hope that the "Tartars' " success in state building would lead to greater Catholic success in converting the Chinese to Christianity.[2]

The Tartars . . . doe shave both the Head and Beard, reserving only the Mustachoes, which they extend to a great length, and in the hinder part of their heads they leave a Tuff, which being curiously woven and plated, they let hang down carelessly below their shoulders; they have a round and low Cap, which is alwaies garnished round with some pretious skin three fingers broad, the Castor [beaver] or Zibellin [sable], and serveth to defend their Temples, Ears, and Foreheads from colds and other Tempests. That which appears above the skin being covered over either with curious red silk, or else with black and purple horse-hair, which they die and dress most curiously; so as their appurtenances being handsomely joined together, makes the caps both commodious and handsom. Their Garments are long Robes falling down to the very foot, but their sleeves are not so wide and large as the Chineses use; but rather such as are used in Polony [Poland] & Hungary, only with this difference, that they fashion the extremity of the Sleeve, ever like a Horse his Hoof.* At their Girdle there hangs on either side two Handkerchiefs to wipe their face and hands; besides, there hangs a Knife for all necessary uses, with two Purses, in which they carry Tobacco, or such like Commodities. On their Left side they hang their Scymiters, but so as the point goes before, and the handle behind, and therefore when they fight they draw it out with the right hand behind them without holding the Scabbard with the other. They seldom wear Shoes, and use no Spurrs to their Boots, which they make either of Silk or of Horse-skin very neatly drest; but they often use fair Pattins,† which they make three fingers high. In riding they use Stirrups, but their Saddles are both lower and broader than ours; their faces are comely, and commonly broad as those of China also have; their colour is white, but their Nose is not so flat, nor their eyes so little, as the Chineses are; they speak little, and ride pensively. In the rest of their manners they resemble our Tartars of Europe, though they may be nothing so barbarous [figs. 5 and 6]. They rejoice to see Strangers; they no way like the grimness and sourness of the Chines gravity, and therefore in their first abords [that is, on first approach] they appear more human.

.   .   .

*The sleeve is drawn together at the wrist, and the cuff that extends down over the knuckles flares like a horse's hoof—a style that derives from hunting and battle dress.
†Thick-soled boots that protected the foot from mud or wetness.

Figure 5. Frontispiece from a Latin edition of Martini's *De bello Tartarico*. Unlike the book's content, this illustration and title emphasize the barbarousness of the "Tartar" conquerors. The presumably Manchu horseman looks thoroughly European, and, incongruously, he appears to be slaying men who exhibit the Manchu queue and shaven pate.

Figure 6. Europeans who had seen Manchu noblemen knew that they could cut striking figures. This portrait, by the Jesuit missionary Giuseppe Castiglione (1688–1766), is from happier days in the eighteenth century.

Under eight colours [that is, flags] are comprehended all the forces of the Kingdom of China, whether they be Natives or Tartars; the first of which is White, called the Imperial Banner; the second is Red, the third is Black, the fourth is Yellow; and these three last are governed and Commanded by the Uncle of the Emperour.[3] . . . Of these four colours by several mixtures, they frame four more, so as every Souldier knows his own colours, and to what part of the City to repair, where they have ever their Arms and Horses ready for an expedition; so as in one half hour they all are ready; for they blow a horn just in the fashion of that, which we appropriate usually to our Tritons, and by the manner of winding it, they presently know, what Companies and Captains must march, so as they are ready in a moment to follow their Ensign, which a Horse-man carries tyed behind him, though commonly none but the Commander and Ensign knows wh[i]ther they go: this profound secrecy in their exercise of War, has often astonished the Chineses; for many times, when they thought to oppose them in one part, they presently heard they were in another Quarter; and it is no wonder they are so quick, for they never carry with them any Baggage, nor do they take care for Provision; for they fill themselves with what they find, yet commonly they eat Flesh, though half rosted or half boyled; if they find none then they devour their Horses, or Camels; but ever when they have leasure, they go hunting all manner of wild Beasts, either by some excellent Dogs or Vultures, which they bring up for that end, or else by incompassing a whole Mountain, or large Field, they beat up all the wild Beasts into a Circle, and drive them into so narrow a Compass, as that they can take as many as they please and dismiss the rest. The earth covered with a Horse-cloath is their Bed; for they care not for Houses and Chambers; but if they be forced to dwell in Houses, their Horses must lodge with them, and they must have many holes beaten in the Walls; but yet their Tents are most beautiful, which they fix and remove with such Art and dexterity, as they never retard the speedy march of the Army. Thus the Tartars train their Souldiers to hardness for War.

·   ·   ·

Now to give the Reader a little touch how the Tartars stand affected to Christianity, it deserves to be reflected on, that in the Metropolitan City of Quangcheu [Guangzhou, alias Canton], which as I now related was utterly destroyed, there was a venerable person, who had the care and superintendency of all the Christians, whose name was Alvarus Semedo a Jesuit;[4] this man they took and tyed hand and foot, for many days, and threatened to kill him every hower, unless he would deliver the Christians' Treasures; but the poor man had no Treasure to produce; so as he suffered much, till at length the King,[5] hearing of his case, took pity of his venerable gray Heirs and comely person, and gave him not only his life and liberty, but a Bible and Breviary, which is their [Catholic priests'] Prayer Book, together with a good sum of Mony for Alms, and finally a House to build a Church for Christians; and this is less to be wondered at from him, who heretofore was a Souldier under that famous Sun Ignatius[6] . . . where he knew what belonged to Christianity, and also had seen the Jesuits in the Camp, from whence he fled to the Tartars. Nor is it only this Tartar that loves us Christians, but in a manner all the rest do love, honour, and esteem those Fathers, and many have embraced our Religion, nor do we doubt but many more would follow their example, if we could enter Tartary, as now it is projecting, where doubtless many great things might be performed, for the reducing of that Nation to the Faith of Christ; and perchance as God has opened away to the Tartars to enter China, to give Christianity a passage into Tartary, which hitherto to us have been unknown and inaccessible.

4

"THE EMPEROR
REALLY HAS LEFT":
NANJING CHANGES HANDS

MARTINO MARTINI ALSO TELLS us that "the Chineses all ran away, as Sheep use to do when they see the Wolf," when the leading units in the Qing campaign into Jiangnan crossed the Yangzi River and then concentrated their attention on Nanjing, the Southern Capital. Nanjing had been established as the main capital of the Ming dynasty by the "Great Ancestor," Zhu Yuanzhang, in the 1360s and early 1370s, and it had functioned as such until Beijing was designated the main capital by the third Ming emperor, Zhu Di, in 1421.' Thereafter, it had been maintained as the auxiliary capital by a skeleton staff, largely composed of sinecure holders. In the spring of 1644 the shocking loss of Beijing, and of the Chongzhen emperor, had prompted a wrenchingly fast re-conversion of Nanjing into the hub of Ming government. In late June of that year a reluctant imperial prince had been enthroned as emperor there with the reign title Hongguang.*

Nanjing was strategically located for effective defense within a great bend of the Yangzi River (see map 3), and throughout the Ming period it was the most heavily fortified city in South China. It proved easy prey for the Manchus nevertheless, largely because of the demoralization that had overcome the Hongguang court, the military establishment, and the citizenry of Jiangnan between June 1644 and June 1645. Contributing to alienation and indifference were incompetence on the throne, fierce factional conflicts between the "pure element" (with which

---

*In earlier dynasties, auspicious or inspiring two-character slogans officially designated successive periods—of indeterminate length depending on circumstances—within a given emperor's reign. Beginning in the Ming, however, there was just one slogan per reign, so in Ming and Qing history the slogan is called the reign title.

Shi Kefa* was identified) and the "pernicious clique" (epitomized by Grand Secretary Ma Shiying and Minister of War Ruan Dacheng),[2] frictions and open breaches between civil and military officials, and failures to deliver supplies—the last of which worsened the rampancy of Ming regular troops. In the early spring of 1645 a young man who claimed to be the lost crown prince (that is, the eldest surviving son) of the Chongzhen emperor was summarily imprisoned and declared to be an impostor whose real name was Wang Zhiming. By that time the people of Nanjing were in a mood to declare the Hongguang emperor bogus instead.[3]

The first account below is from the *Mingji riji* (Daily Jottings from the End of the Ming) by Yao Wenxi, a scion of the old and prominent Yao lineage of Tongcheng County in western South Zhili (present-day Anhui Province).[4] He was about twenty-one years old in 1645. Like many families of means in Jiangnan north of the Yangzi, the Yaos gradually moved most of their family to the relative safety of Nanjing as waves of social disturbances—revolts by field tenants and indentured servants, attacks by home-grown desperadoes, and invasions by roving rebel armies—crested in their home locales.[5] Since 1634, Yao Wenxi and his father had managed to survive a series of hair-raising, often grisly events in Tongcheng. It was not until mid-1644, when they heard of the emergency in North China, that they joined other relatives in Nanjing.

Although Yao Wenxi numbered among his paternal uncles the chief minister of the Seals Office of the Hongguang court, as well as the magistrate of Dongyang County in Zhejiang Province, he evinces little remorse over the demise of the Nanjing court. Indeed, his memoir— apart from lamenting the imposition of the Manchu-style queue[†]— displays a jaded attitude toward Ming authority, and fear tempered by curiosity toward the Manchu-Qing leadership. When the dust settles, he is glad to be able to return home under any regime that can keep public order.

The second, appended account—of Nanjing in more stable condition eleven years later—is from the *Het gezantschap der Niêderlandtsche Oost-Indische Compagnie aan den grooten Tartarischen Cham. den tegenwoordigen Keizer van China* (A Legation of the Netherlands East India Company

*See Chap. 2.
†See Chap. 1, n. 20.

to the Great Tartar Khan, Now Emperor of China), which was widely read in Europe after its first publication in Amsterdam in 1665.[6] The author, Johann Nieuhof (1618–72), was secretary to an embassy of officers from the Dutch East India Company, who made their way northward by river from Guangzhou through Jiangxi to Nanjing, again northward via the Grand Canal to Beijing, and then back again by the same route in 1655–57.

Concomitant with the arrival of Christian missionaries was the extension of European mercantilist enterprise into the East Asian maritime zone. Leading the advance of this potent combination of capitalism, imperialism, and navigational technology into Chinese waters were the Portuguese, who established a trading center at Macao as early as 1557. But in the early seventeenth century, Portuguese dominance was effectively challenged by the Dutch. From its head-quarters at Batavia (present-day Jakarta, Indonesia), the Dutch East India Company tried unsuccessfully to dislodge the Portuguese from Macao and to establish regular commerce with China after about 1620. Frustrations led to violence on some occasions, and mutual distaste and distrust formed between Ming officials and Dutch traders.[7] As was the case with the Jesuit missionaries, the disruptions caused by the Chinese civil wars and the initial openness of the Manchus to foreigners allowed entry where such had not been possible before. The ambassadorial mission in which Johann Nieuhof participated arose from Dutch optimism that the new rulers of China would permit free trade with Europeans—an optimism that was soon squelched by reimposition of the usual ceremonial strictures of the Chinese system of foreign diplomacy.[8]

Nieuhof's detailed observations of everything that his group encountered are a valuable record of material, social, and political conditions in China in the middle 1650s. For instance, he corroborates that active Ming-loyalist resistance and serious banditry had been quelled in the areas along his mission's route of travel but also indicates that although large metropolises recovered rapidly from the destruction of the Qing conquest, small and middle-sized urban centers remained devastated much longer. His observations also confirm that at this early point in the Qing period upper-class Manchu women were considerably more casual and forward in male company than their Han-Chinese counterparts. His description of the former Ming palace grounds within the otherwise unharmed city of Nanjing suggests how surgical the

Manchus could be in their use of force, but Nieuhof could not have known to what extent that ruination had been perpetrated by the citizens of Nanjing themselves.

YAO WENXI   When Ma [Shiying] and Ruan [Dacheng] heard that Yangzhou had been crushed and that news from the north was urgent, on the 6th day of the 5th month [May 30, 1645] they had three [of their political enemies], Guang Shiheng, Zhou Zhong, and Wu Su, executed in the marketplace at Bamboo Mat Bridge. Two others, Zhou Biao and Lei Yinzuo, after drinking together one last time, both hanged themselves with lengths of silk that had been conferred on them in prison.* At that time Zuo Liangyu's whole army had come down the Yangzi River to Jiangnan [from Huguang Province] to punish Ma and Ruan for their crimes. So Ruan Dacheng, with Huang Hushan [Degong], installed watchtowers along the riverbanks at Taiping and Wuhu [see map 3], and they had mounted cannon on a cordon of warships stretched across the river to block Zuo's advance. All day long, their troops and Zuo's had been killing each other.

Inside the Southern Capital no one was permitted to talk casually in the teahouses or wineshops or at the corners of streets or lanes. The police went out in all directions on patrol, and they straightaway grabbed anyone they saw conversing in public. Toward evening every household tightly closed its front door and didn't dare light any lamps. In sum, one couldn't utter one word about the situation to the north.

Ma and Ruan had clearly said that if the Tartars came, everyone should scatter. At that time I'd been tutoring students in my home. But because things in general didn't look good, and I couldn't concentrate on my reading, I went out walking in the streets. On West Floral Gate Boulevard on the 9th of the month [June 2] I saw some eunuchs dressed in military garb and armed with knives. They were transporting under guard a number of very small crates—so heavy that two or three men were needed to carry each one. They went out West Floral Gate toward South Gate Boulevard [map 4].[9]

----

*The presentation of a length of silk to a prisoner indicated that he had been given the privilege of committing suicide, rather than suffering the indignity of dying by the hand of an executioner.

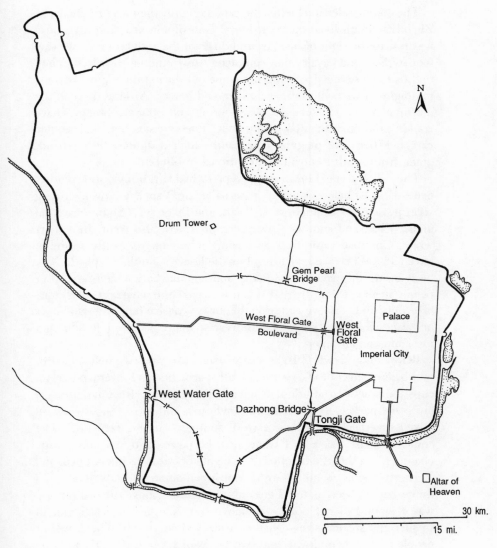

Drum Tower

Gem Pearl
Bridge

Palace

West Floral Gate

Boulevard

West
Floral
Gate

Imperial City

West Water Gate

Dazhong Bridge

Tongji Gate

Altar of
Heaven

0   30 km.

0   15 mi.

Map 4. Yao Wenxi's Nanjing

The commander in chief of the capital guard, the Earl of Xincheng, Zhao [Zhilong], lived on West Floral Gate Boulevard, and my house was just to the right of his. Around dusk on the 10th [June 3], we saw foot soldiers and cavalrymen completely surrounding the place. They told us to close our doors and not come out during the night. Toward midnight all we could hear were men and horses. Around three in the morning we heard some people shouting and others sobbing, so we couldn't but open the door and go out. Then we saw men and women carrying their sons piggyback or leading their daughters by the hand, going from south to north in a continual hubbub.

They all said the [Hongguang] emperor had left, but we still couldn't believe it. Just before dawn my paternal uncle [Yao] Zhongwen's young servant, named Chunbao, said, "Wait, and I'll go see." So my maternal uncle, Zilai, and another young servant, Liuxi, also went. In a short while, Chunbao came back and said, "The emperor really seems to have left." When we asked him how he knew, Chunbao replied, "I've been inside the palace, and going and coming back I saw no end of people stealing things there." When we asked him what sorts of things, he groped in his sleeve and brought out two palace fans and two boxes of palace incense, saying, "There were so many people, I couldn't get my hands on any more."

Before long, Uncle Zilai also came back, carrying two bolts of satin, four bags of silver beads, two small satin garments, and several porcelain cups and bowls. In addition, he felt around inside his sleeve and brought out some packets of roasted rice, soybeans, and bits of aloeswood all mixed together and half of a fresh summer squash. He said, "The emperor really has left. I went into the palace and saw three large chambers. In the middle one lay an eight-foot gold-lacquered bed, and in the two side chambers were cool [open summer] beds. The good things had all been looted; I got only the satins. Above the bed canopy was a mound of red boxes—similar to one another in design but in smaller and smaller sizes—that were stacked very high. The crowd of people pulled them down, and two boxes of silver and pearls and one box of aloeswood bits spilled onto the floor, where the aloeswood got mixed up with some soybeans and roasted rice. I brought some of that home in the two packets in my sleeve. This half of a summer squash was on the windowsill of one of the chambers. These two small garments had been thrown on the floor, so I took them, too. When I went back in, there was nothing left—only a white parrot. I tried to cage it in my sleeve, but by the time I'd walked to West Floral Gate, my hands hurt from carrying so much stuff, so I dropped it."

Before dawn, sometime between three and five in the morning, countless court ladies carrying gold and silver fled from the palace. Some went back to their natal families, some were taken in by other families, and some went with men who were fleeing. When the looters had emptied the interior of the palace, they pillaged the eunuchs' residences. In taking knives from the palace armory, some got their hands or feet cut off. The silver, the fine satins, and the bronze and pewter utensils were first seized by some and then grabbed away by others, so that the original looters got nothing.

Also pilfered and brought out were various kinds of wine drunk in the inner quarters. Among those coming and going were two men who drank to one another as they went along the road, hoisting a crock of wine. When they got onto the bridge outside West Floral Gate, the two men—who'd been drinking the wine by grasping the mouth of the crock on opposite sides—finally fell asleep, and the crock was spirited away by others. The onlookers all got a big laugh out of that. After noon Liuxi returned. He'd grabbed a *yuanbao*,* but a bunch of people had divided it up, leaving him only two ounces.

During the night of the 10th the Hongguang emperor fled into the camp of Huang Degong at Taiping. So for three days in succession—through the 11th, 12th, and 13th [June 4–6]—there was no emperor. Zhao [the Earl of] Xincheng had his troops surround and secure his headquarters, and cannon were mounted on either side of the entrance. Throughout the city common people killed soldiers from Sichuan,† and they seized the residences of Ma Shiying and Ruan Dacheng. Shiying's son and daughter-in-law were nabbed and paraded around in the streets with their hands tied behind their backs, their captors carrying knives and yelling, "These are the son and daughter-in-law of the traitorous minister Ma Shiying!" It was the same when they got their hands on the son and daughter-in-law of Wang Duo.

On the afternoon of the 12th I saw a bald man with a beard wearing a long commoner's gown of blue cloth in front of the Drum Tower. He was being marched along, hands tied behind his back, by a crowd

---

*Yuanbao were ingots of fine-grade silver cast in the shape of horse hooves or of "shoes," which weighed from forty-five to fifty-five ounces.

†Especially fierce fighters from the native tribes of the western provinces had been brought to Nanjing to serve under the command of Ma Shiying.

of people who were shouting, "This is the traitorous minister Wang Duo, who wouldn't recognize the crown prince of our master, the Chongzhen emperor." One by one, these captives were taken under citizen's arrest into the headquarters of the Old Master, Commander Zhao [Zhilong], who said, "All of them should be put to death. Let me keep them here to be gradually killed off." But that bunch wasn't fated to die then; they made use of Zhao's ploy to keep themselves alive.

By that time the other civil and military officials had hidden even their shadows. On the afternoon of the 11th I saw [the Earl of] Chengyi, Liu [Kongzhao], who was wearing a four-cornered scholar's cap and lined gauze garment, riding through the streets on horseback.* But on the morning of the 12th the rumor went around that his whole family had disappeared.

Inside the city walls every household piled up meat-chopping boards, damaged desks and stools, or broken vats and crocks to barricade their doorways. During the night a lantern was lit at every front door, and someone in each household kept guard there holding a weapon.

On the afternoon of the 12th a lot of beggars and ne'er-do-wells plucked Wang Zhiming out of the Central Ward jail and carried him in a throng into the Imperial City. From there he issued an official edict calling on the Earl of Xincheng to attend his court, but the latter stayed in his headquarters. All anyone saw were the soldiers who'd been in defense positions along the river running toward the city out of formation with spears, knives, and guns slung on their backs and saying, "The Qing troops have come!"

On the morning of the 13th [June 6] the Earl of Xincheng put out a notice, which read: "I am already in communication with the supreme commander of the Great Qing, who will have his own way of handling matters. You common folk need not be alarmed." Everyone vacillated between belief and doubt until noontime, when another long, itemized notice was posted throughout the city. It read in part: "The Great Qing army is approaching the foot of the city wall. You citizens are not to fight against it, thereby bringing on regrettable consequences." At this,

---

*Liu was an earl in the military aristocracy who was commander in chief of river control. He was the most outspoken of the military nobles to clash with civil officials who resisted the militarists' encroachments on bureaucratic authority. Yao's comment underscores how nonmartial the demeanor of the military nobles had become.

everyone in the whole city realized that the Qing troops had actually come.

All the civil and military officials, holding their calling cards, went outside the city wall toward the Altar of Heaven to meet the Prince of Yu [Dodo],* and everybody else in the city, including us, went out to watch. The Prince of Yu turned out to be a fine specimen of a man. His face was like a full moon, and his lips looked as if they had been daubed with vermilion. He hardly seemed to have just come through the wind and dust of a military campaign. Tall and broad-shouldered, probably not over forty years of age, he wore a large purple python-robe† with clusters of flowers in the fabric design. He sat on a mat on the ground, and to his side sat several men of high rank, including one Chancellor Wu,‡ a man of very small stature who spoke smartly, saying, "We are members of one family; you common folk should not be afraid."

[The former Ming officials'] calling cards lay in a pile as big as a hillock. Having seen the emperor leave, each man had looked to his own fate and hidden out. But when the Prince of Yu arrived, they wanted to be officials again, so they came out in greeting. The Earl of Xincheng, Zhao Zhilong, met with the prince inside the Qing camp, and the prince favored Zhao with a seat and some tea.

Straightaway, Chancellor Wu was deputed to lead several dozen horsemen into the city to inspect the granaries. After Wu got inside the Imperial City and looked around, Wang Zhiming was brought out, the others hanging around were driven away, watchmen were assigned, and Manchu soldiers replaced the Ming soldiers who had previously kept guard atop the gates of the Imperial City.

During the three days after the emperor left, everything had been held together by the efforts of Zhao Zhilong. . . . When the Prince of Yu had reached the foot of the city wall, Nanjing was handed over without his having to expend one iota of energy. So the next day, when

---

*See Chap. 2, nn. 3, 4.

†The most formal attire of high-ranking officials, the "pythons" of which were writhing, embroidered dragons. Use of this type of ceremonial robe had increased gradually during the Ming dynasty, and in the Qing period it was authorized for titled noblemen and officials down to the seventh rank.

‡The Manchu nobleman Udari, of the Nara clan, who was a chancellor of one of the Three Inner Departments, the highest advisory and secretarial bodies of the Qing court at that time. His position was the formal equivalent of chancellor of the Hanlin Academy in the Ming and later in the Qing period, though Udari's duties in this period were clearly more martial than those of the usual Hanlin academician.

word went around that military officers were to shave their heads,* the first one to do so was Earl Zhao—inside the Qing camp. The Prince of Yu conferred on him a white horse with golden saddle, bridle, and stirrups, a Manchu hat and boots, and a white python-robe with a clustered-flower design.

When the Qing came into the city, everyone said that only military officers and soldiers needed to shave their heads, so before long quite a number of Nanjing military men deserted. After a few days an edict was issued notifying all civil and military officials, soldiers, and civilians that every male was to shave his head within three days and cultivate a coin-sized rat's tail [a queue]. Anyone who didn't conform was to be killed. The common people were afraid to die, so within three days the men had shaved their heads shiny clean.

Among the civil officials the first to shave his head was Zhang Sun-zhen.[†] Upon seeing the Prince of Yu at West Floral Gate, Zhang also told his circle that his own ancestors had been Tartars and that he still had a portrait of them in Manchu costume in his home, so it was fitting that he shave his head. I don't know how they [Zhao and Zhang] got employed as officials in the first place. That the two of them had now slipped through the net of circumstance was something to be decried for thousands of years.

We young men cherished our hair,[‡] and when we saw people with shaven heads, they didn't seem human. At first some of us hid out, unwilling to shave; but later we didn't see anyone on the streets unshaven. We *had* to shave. Old Master Sheng, who'd been in charge of the imperial hunting park, lived not far from my family. But we saw only his butler, carrying a net cap[§] and sobbing as he walked back toward Master Sheng's home. We asked him why, and he said, "The old master of my household was unwilling to shave his head and concealed himself in another old gentleman's home. But today, having heard that everyone—big and small—in the whole capital city had shaven, he had no recourse but to shave as well. I saw him there crying,

---

*See Chap. 1, n. 20.

[†]A strident but corrupt censor identified with the Ma-Ruan clique who was responsible for hounding key self-styled "righteous" figures out of office.

[‡]As part of one's body, gotten whole from one's parents. Preservation of one's hair was an expression of Confucian filiality.

[§]A thin summer cap of open-weave silk that clung to the head and incidentally reduced the appearance of baldness—or having a shaven pate, in this case.

heartbroken, with the other old gentleman. And later when I saw him shaven, indeed, he looked very ugly. I can't help but shed tears, too." When he finished speaking, he walked on, carrying the mesh cap and sobbing.

On the 17th [June 10] the Prince of Yu deputed Chancellor Wu to go into the city with some soldiers. They demarcated the whole area north of Tongji Gate and Dazhong Bridge and west of the place called Small Camp near Gem Pearl Bridge [for exclusive occupation by Qing bannermen], and they ordered everyone to move out of the dwellings in that area within three days. The common people again were not very happy, but neither did they dare fail to accede. From the northeast of Nanjing to the southwest is a distance of twenty to thirty *li*. How could anyone move much at all? In some cases, one family teamed up with another to use a carrying pole—one member of each family at each end—lugging first an item for one family and then an item for the other. And the pawnshops didn't even want silver for redemptions; people were told just to identify and take back their own things. Weeping and wailing, people moved until breakfast time on the third day, when the whole Qing army entered the city. . . .

Each day I saw women who had been captured in Yangzhou being brought into the city several dozen at a time.* Manchu troops drove them from behind with leather whips, lashing them pitilessly, as though they were driving pigs. Also, I saw a woman, about fifty years old, whose hair had been cut off to a length of just four or five inches, sitting on an unhinged door,† crying loudly and cursing vehemently. Four people came and swiftly carried her away [on the door], followed by some Manchu soldiers who were taking her into custody—I don't know why. Every day I went into the Qing camp to look at the captured women. Some had disheveled hair and dirty faces and cried in anger; others used makeup and emollients and laughed with delight. Every day there were fathers ransoming their daughters, and husbands ransoming their wives. There was one woman who didn't want to go back and who wouldn't go until the Manchu soldier in charge of her got mad.‡ Each woman had a price tag stuck into her hair. The best were going for only three or four taels. Those wearing clothes worth more than

---

*See Chaps. 2, 5, and 6.

†Chinese doors could easily be taken down and used, for instance, to cart goods and people.

‡For a variation of this story, see Chap. 5.

ten taels were being sold or ransomed for no more than a few tenths of a tael.*

Inside the camp velvets, pongees, and silk garments of various colors were piled up as high as the hillsides. The best rhinoceros-horn goblets had been chiseled in half and drilled with holes so the soldiers could fasten them to their belts for drinking tea and eating rice. When the Prince of Yu first entered the Imperial City, some who had looted yuanbao but not gotten a fair cut turned themselves in, and resentful bystanders turned in others. Numberless people lost their lives because of that. Then one day word went around that things pilfered from the Imperial City were going to be confiscated. So during the night people everywhere threw python brocades and armory knives into the levees, wells, and ditches.

In the autumn, when Hong Chengchou† came to relieve the Prince of Yu and the latter went back to Beijing, several hundred of the women who'd been captured—the ones between fourteen or fifteen and thirty years of age, not too fat or too thin—were taken along. As they went out West Floral Gate toward West Dryland Gate on horseback, they knew that the North was not as good as the South, and the sound of their lamentations shook the earth. No one among the onlookers could keep from shedding tears.

From this time forth, the Chinese world was at peace. Those who'd been living temporarily within the White Gates [of Nanjing] daily left the city and returned to their native places.

JOHANN NIEUHOF [On May 4, 1656] we came in sight of that Renowned and Royal City of Nanking [Nanjing; fig. 7] . . . ; we came to Anchor in the Harbour, and lay with our Vessels before the Gate Suisimon [Shuiximen], which signifies the [West] Water-Gate. The Embassadours went the next day to visit the three Governours of this City,‡ and were carried in Palankins, and their Followers waited upon them on Horseback. . . .

*The author implies that the soldiers were so unsophisticated that they didn't know the worth of what they had.

†See Chap. 9.

‡The identities of these men are uncertain. At that time the governor of Jiangning (as the Qing then called Nanjing and the coextensive prefecture) was Zhang Zhongyuan. The administrative commissioner for Jiangnan, with particular responsibility for the Jiangning circuit, was Liang Fengming. And the Manchu general with the highest military authority in Jiangnan—Jiangning in particular—was Hahamu.

Figure 7. The outskirts of Nanjing in the 1650s, viewed from the west. Like most Chinese metropolises, Nanjing was horizontally, not vertically, extensive, with few buildings over two stories high. Although Nanjing was protected to the north and west by the wide Yangzi River, it still relied on stout city walls for security from attack, as did most Chinese cities in broad, level agricultural regions.

The chief Governour shewed the Embassadours his withdrawing room and made them, after accustomary Complements to sit down next to him: He was a Chinese, born in the City of Leaotung,* but of a very civil behavior; the Embassadours shewed him a Letter of the Presents which were designed for him, but he would not receive them, they having not yet seen the Emperour. After they had discoursed a while with this first Governour, they took leave and went to the second, also a Chinese, and born at Leaotung; who shewed himself no less courteous then the former: he caused the Embassadours to sit down with (almost) the same Complements, and received the Letter with great civility from them, which nominated his allotted Presents; but he illiterate himself [as were many military men, even high-ranking ones], gave it to one of the Commanders to read, and on the former account refused to accept them.

From hence we went to the third, who dwelt in the wall of the old Imperial Palace; he sent for the Embassadours, who came to him in his Chamber, having his Wife with him: The Apart[ment was] four-square, with Benches round about covered with Silk, and a Stove to warm the room in Winter, in which they burn Reed, Wood there being very scarce. This Governour was by birth a Tartar, a young well-set Man, but understood not the Chinese Language, therefore his Sons were Interpreters. His Wife, a proper and comely Dame, spoke more then her husband, and [was] strangely inquisitive about Holland; she was not dismayed at our strange Arms, but like a bold Virago drew out our Swords, and discharged our Pistols, which much delighted her. . . .

.   .   .

As we were riding out one day to take the air, and to view the City, we passed by the Gate of the Old Imperial Court, where sat a great Tartar Lady, with her servants waiting upon her, about forty years of Age: She very civilly sent to our Interpreter to invite the Embassadours into her House; Jacob de Keyzer hereupon lighted, and the Lady then made towards him: She was very debonair and free, looked upon our Swords, and much admired their bending without breaking: She took the Embassadours Hat, and put it on her own Head, and unbutton'd

*Present-day Liaoyang, in Liaoning Province.

his Doublet almost down to his Waste: Afterwards she led the way into the house and desired him to follow, appointing one of her Attendants to conduct him, who brought us into her apartment, where we found her standing with her Daughter about half her age, waiting our coming, in great state.

The Daughter was clothed in a Violet-coloured Damask Gown, and the Mother in Black Damask, and had both of them their ears hung with Rings; their Hair braided and twisted about their Heads with Strings of Pearls, but over their Hair they wore little Caps made of Reed, with a Tassle upon the Crown of Red Silk. Their Cloths reached down to their Heels, tyed about the middle with a broad Ribbon, and buttoned down from the Neck to the Waste: Their Shooes were of Black Leather, their Faces unmasked without any Painting. They had us into a large withdrawing room unfurnished, only a few Benches covered with Silk, upon which they desired us to sit: They drank to us several times in their liquor made of Beans, which is very strong, but agrees wondrous well with their constitutions. They set before us also some of their Sweet-meats, much intreating us to Eat, excusing the meanness of the Entertainment, her husband being absent.

.   .   .

This stately City, without parallel, is the Diadem of all China. . . . Her situation is most Pleasant, the Soil Luxuriously Fruitful, [because of] the River running quite through this City, whereof some Streams are Navigable for great Vessels. Here formerly was kept the Court of the old Chinese Emperours, the residence of the Kings [of] U [Wu, 222–80 A.D.], Cyn [Eastern Jin, 317–419], Cung [Song, 420–77], Ci [Qi, 479–501], Leang [Liang, 502–56], Chin [Chen, 557–87], and Tanga [Southern Tang, 937–75]: Here also reigned many Lustres [illustrious figures], the Race of Taiminga [the "Great Ming" dynasty, 1368–1644], till they removed to Peking, the better to prevent the Invasions and Designs of the Tartar. . . . [10]

Where this City borders on the River Kiang [the Yangzi], it hath a broad and deep Graff [canal], into which you come out of the Kiang up to the Town, about half a Mile from the River toward the Land [see fig. 7]: they pass over on a Bridge of Boats, which brings them conveniently into the City, whose East-side, which runs far into this Countrey, covers a Flat, with Several Navigable Channels running through so that you may come with large Vessels up to the Town on that side. Over these Channels are several Stone Bridges, very rarely Built. According to all Chinese Geographers, this City exceeds all the Cities of the whole World," not only in bigness, but also in beauty and handsome decorements, and is at least five hours going about, being round, close, and well built; but the Walls [alone are] at least six Dutch miles* in length, the suburbs excepted, which run out much farther; besides this, the City hath another strong Wall for the better defence and safety of the place. The Chineses describe the circumference of this Wall by two Horse-men, who in the morning set forth at one and the same Gate, parted, riding contrary, and they say, met not until the close of the evening; by which they would have us guess at the vast circumference of the Walls of their City. The first Vesture [outward fortification] of the City is above thirty feet high, built Artificially of Stone, with Breast Work, and Watch Towers.

There are thirteen Gates in this Wall, whose doors are Plated with Iron, and guarded day and night with Horse and Foot; some of these Gates rest upon four or five Arches, through which you pass before you come into the City. We lay with our Vessels before the . . . Water-Gate; so great a number of people pass daily to and again through this Gate, that there is no getting in or out without much crowding: The Chief Streets of the City are twenty eight paces broad, very neatly paved, and strait: In the night there is such good order observed for the pre-venting of House-breaking, or disturbance in the Streets, that there is not the like in any part of the World. The ordinary Burgers Houses are but mean, built without any convenience, and stand all with the cross-ridges next to the Street; they have but one door to go in and out, and but one room to Eat and Sleep in: Next the Street over the Window (upon which those that drive a Trade, expose their Com-modities to Sale) appears only a four-square hole to let in light, which is commonly covered with Reeds, instead of Glass, to prevent Gazers that walk in the Streets from looking in. The Houses are but one Story high, they are covered with white Pan-Tiles, and the out-side are made White with Chalk.

Such as dwell in these ordinary Houses, drive very mean Trades;

*The Dutch mile may have derived from the ancient Germanic *rasta*, lengths of which could range from three to over six English miles in regions of northern Europe, including Scandinavia.

Figure 8. A commercial street in Nanjing in the 1650s, showing poles
bearing symbols of the various trades.

but the Shops of the chief Citizens and Merchants, are filled with all
manner of rich Chinese Wares, as Cottons, Silk-Stuffs, China Dishes,
Pearls, Diamonds, etc. Before each Shop stands a board, upon which
is inscribed the name of the Master in Gold Letters, as also what Goods
they sell; beside these boards, stands (as is expressed in the annexed
Print) a high Pole, which reaches above the House, upon which they
hang Penions and Flags, or something else, wherein they (as we in
Europe with our Signs) make known their Habitations [fig. 8]. They
have here, as through all China, no coined money,[12] but they pay for
such Commodities they buy, small pieces of Silver, which are of different value and weight; and though you buy never so little, yet you
must always have a pair of Scales about you, if you will not be cheated
in the weight of the crafty Chinese, by weighing in their own Scales;
for they have commonly two sorts of weights by them, and are so
nimble and deceitful in their balancing, that you had need of Argus
eyes when you buy any thing of them.

Besides the vast number of People, there lyes a Garrison of forty
thousand Tartars [that is, Qing bannermen, who were not all Manchus]:

Here resides also the Governour of the Southern Provinces,* in the name of the Emperour. This City exceeds likewise all others, for stately Idol Temples, Towers, Rare Edifices, Triumphal Arches: But the Emperours Court or Palace formerly exceeded all the rest of the Buildings, wherein the Emperour of China was wont to reside, with the same State and Pomp, as now at present the Great Cham at Peking. This Palace was situated on the South-side of the City, built four-square, surrounded with a Wall, which contains the greatest part of the City: Each side of the square, wherein this Palace was included, contained in length one Italian mile[†] . . . ; and as much as can be discerned by the decayed Walls, and known from the Inhabitants, this Court, or Palace, with all belonging, was as big as Harlem in Holland. Within the first great Gate lay a large Court which led to the four-square, and was paved with fine smooth stone. . . . The buildings are all of a hard sort of Stone, which the Natives have most curiously Painted with a Yellow Colour, that when the Sun reflects on them, they shine like Gold.

· · ·

And though the Tartars in the last War did not much deprive and impair this City of its former Lustre and Splendour (no City escaping better then this Nanking) yet however the stately Palace of the Kings, was totally destroyed by them. It is supposed that the Tartars did this for no other end or cause, but out of a particular hatred or grudge which they bore to the Family of Taiminga, who Governed till the Court was removed from thence to Peking.

---

*There was no such official position. The author may be referring here to the viceroy of Jiangnan and Jiangxi—then Ma Mingpei.

†The Italian mile was approximately the same length as the Roman mile, that is, about 1,618 yards. The standard U.S. mile is 1,760 yards.

5

CHANGSHU IN
CHRONICLE, STORYBOOK,
MEMOIR, AND ROMANCE

EVEN AS SOME UNITS of the Qing army were taking over Nanjing and capturing the Hongguang emperor, others were establishing control as quickly as possible over the major prefectural seats in Jiangnan south of the Yangzi River, such as Suzhou to the southeast and Ningguo to the southwest. From these centers they proceeded through the summer of 1645 to gradually place Qing governments in all the lesser administrative units of the province. This thorny process was made even more difficult by the order, issued from Nanjing on July 21, that all male citizens were to demonstrate their allegiance to the Qing by shaving their heads and cultivating the queue in the Manchu style—to be enforced on pain of death beginning ten days after receipt of the order in each locality. This was the catalyst for several months of resistance in the Jiangnan region, especially in the east between Tai Lake and the seacoast (including Jiading) and in the southwest between the Yangzi River and the Tianmu Mountains (including Ningguo).

Typically many local officials abandoned their posts when they heard of the collapse of the Hongguang court and the occupation of Nanjing by the Qing. Confused strife then ensued among various armed elements that wished to either support or desert the Ming cause or to take advantage of the power vacuum for short-term gains. The first agents whom the Qing sent to take possession of local tax and property records (usually Chinese collaborators) generally were not openly opposed by the populace until the head-shaving decree became known. Then the vanguard Qing agents, as well as local notables who had cooperated with them, were often killed or chased away as grass-roots armed resistance coalesced. Such violent expressions of noncompliance elicited

massively destructive and brutal suppression campaigns by various
Qing armies, many of which were commanded by erstwhile Ming
generals who had surrendered to the Qing only recently. Cities and
their surrounding populations were hit fast and hard to clear the way
for the assignment of Qing officials and the stationing of some Qing
troops. Eliminating significant armed resistance in a given county often
took much longer.' Changshu followed this general pattern (except that
the commander in charge of the massacre and pillage of the city was
a Qing bannerman). The selections translated below are from the middle of a narration that began on May 17 and ended on November 3,
1645.

Unusually, the same sequence of events in Changshu has been recorded in four different subgenres of Chinese unofficial, provincial, or
"rustic" histories.² One is a straightforward chronicle, in the "outline-
and-detail" (*gangmu*) form, entitled *Haijiao yibian* (Surviving Chronicle
from the [Yangzi] Cape). The unknown author is chiefly concerned to
cover the main actions and actors within his chosen frame of time and
space. Though not loath to use a colorful story here or there, he seeks
to set down the events so that lessons in political morality can be learned
from them. Another work, the *Qifeng yibian* (Surviving Chronicle by
the Seven Peaks [Recluse]), takes precisely the same events treated in
the chronicle, adds interesting details, and organizes them into a sixty-
unit story sequence that could serve as material for professional storytellers. As in the traditional Chinese *xiaoshuo* (novel or novelette),
each unit (*hui*) opens with one or more catchy quatrains (with varying
meters and rhyme schemes) that aim to entertain, mainly with irony
and sarcasm. A favorite practice is to show people's true colors in times
of crisis—ridiculing the cowardice and stupidity of those who pretend
to superiority and praising the loyalty and valor of those who usually
go unsung.

A third work, the *Haiyu beibing ji* (Record of Military Subjugation
in [the Land of] the Yu Hills and the Sea), is a memoir—what in Chinese
is called a *jianwen lu* (record of what someone saw and heard)—written
by an unnamed elderly gentleman of modest means who lived in Changshu city and whose ancestral home was in a nearby village.* Like many
authors of this sort of account during the conquest period, he wrote

*Even families of middling resources commonly maintained both urban and rural
residences.

mainly to explain things to himself—especially his own survival, when so many died—under the pretext of explaining them to others. An important part of his explanation is predestination, the chief means by which ordinary people of his time dealt psychologically with terrible events, reducing their shocking quality by putting them in a long perspective of fated occurrences; people nowadays place recent calamities in a wider context for the same reason—to reduce their relative magnitude. In the middle of his memoir the old gentleman consciously enters into the fourth subgenre, which he calls *yesheng* but which goes by a variety of names in Chinese and sometimes is lamely called historical romance in English. The stories related in such works may well have occurred, but they are chosen and rendered to titillate—with elements of the sensational, the unexpected, the supernatural, and the ribald, among others. Below, passages from all of these four subgenres have been alternated to give readers some sense of the different modes through which cataclysmic events were preserved in the historical memory of the ordinary people of a typical locality in late imperial China.

Changshu County, bordered by the Yangzi estuary to the north and by several lakes to the south, was a land of waterways, as were most counties in the Yangzi delta region, and the county seat itself was both surrounded and crossed by numerous artificial waterways (figs. 9 and 10). Even more than in Yangzhou, boats and bridges, like walls and gates, were ubiquitous physical entities that conditioned events of the conquest and the resistance, as well as the survival efforts of people caught in the middle.[3]

CHRONICLE [*Haijiao yibian*] [7th month] 13th day [September 2, 1645]. Qing troops arrive at the channel outside South Gate.* Shi Min abandons his battalion and flees. Hu Laigong closes the six city gates to defend his own. Yan Zizhang leads his forces to engage the enemy at Councillor Chen Bridge and at South Altar.[4]

Shi Min, . . . acting on his own, had his battalion encamp in the

*This text, like most published under Qing rule, observes the formality of referring to the Qing armed forces as the Great Army or the Great Troops, even though the account of their actions is not complimentary. Throughout this translation, "great [*da*]" in this usage is rendered Qing. "Northern troops" also means the Qing.

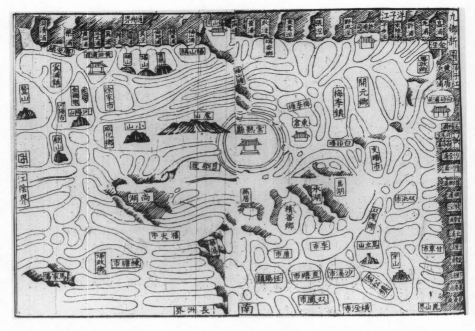

Figure 9. A map of Changshu County showing how its very low altitude within the Yangzi delta rendered it almost half land and half water.

second zone of land outside South Gate. But his idea was not to resist the enemy; rather, it was to directly intimidate and kill off the people of that ward to avenge their arson of his residence.*
On the morning of the 13th, when he learned that the Qing army was about to arrive, Shi prematurely led more than eight hundred men under his command on a purported inspection tour and became the first to desert. Remaining in that battalion were only a hundred old or weak men, who broke ranks and scattered as soon as the Qing army came. All their firearms, ammunition, other weapons, food, and equipment thus were obtained by the Qing army, which then sped right to South Gate.

*Shi Min was very unpopular with the common people of his ward because he had allowed his servants to exploit them. When Beijing was seized by Li Zicheng's army, Shi surrendered to the "roving bandits," and news of this additional perfidy incited the local people to set fire to his residence. That blaze reached even the coffin of Shi's mother—an offense against his ancestors—so his hatred for the citizens of that area was intense.

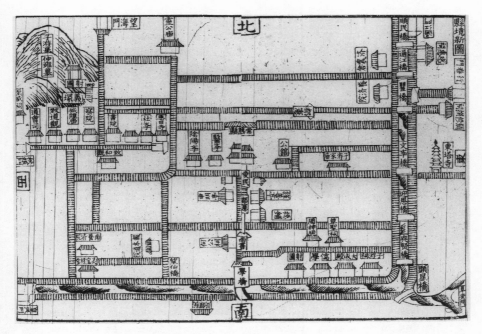

Figure 10. A map of Changshu city showing several of the many bridges spanning the canals that ran through the city.

STORYBOOK [*Qifeng yibian*]
Transfer troops when pressed by the enemy—
That's the traitor's evasive specialty.
Guns and ammunition are all grabbed away.
Shi Min will be called a bungler [*shi ji*] probably.

CHRONICLE   Yan Zizhang was just returning from an inspection tour. But Hu Laigong, within the city walls, hurriedly ordered that all six gates be tightly closed. He assigned large numbers of men to guard them closely and check the flight of anyone inside. Outside South Gate the bodies of people who had succumbed to lances and arrows already lay pillowed on one another. The Qing forces set fire to West Manor at the western end of the Bridge of Bounty and Happiness, but Yan Zizhang stopped them at Councillor Chen Bridge with about equal casualties on both sides. From that it could be seen that the enemy was very strong, but Com-

mander Hu would not come out to Yan's aid. Yan and his son
needed to retreat into the city, but South Gate was closed, so they
withdrew their men to South Altar, with the enemy right on their
tail.

STORYBOOK
West Manor is set afire—gathering clouds of enemy power.
Our strong men, spears in hand, are ready to devour.
Too bad Hu Laigong, with thoughts of turning coat,
Shut all the gates in order to within the city cower.

CHRONICLE   A drill sergeant under Yan's command, He Yunpeng,* tore forward to fight the Qing hand to hand and took two
armored soldiers' heads before returning. The Qing force was
somewhat deterred by this, which enabled Yan and his son to
avoid annihilation. At that time it was the county jailer, surnamed
Du, holding Canal Route Bridge who set tactics for He, and together they decapitated a member of the enemy's vanguard. But
soon bullets and arrows were raining down, and their unit suffered
heavy losses. Commander Du could not hold out, so he led his
unit in an orderly retreat from Sweet Font Lane over Welcome
Spring Bridge. . . .

STORYBOOK
Lifting stones, wielding knives, his strength was of the best.
Always fond of chivalry, he loved the combat test.
At South Altar bloody sabers clashed one on one,
And our local bravo's name stood out among the rest.

A lowly jailer with an unknown first name
With the country in chaos could have left with no shame.†
At the bridge he stanched the foe with his pikes
And showed that fierce loyalty with his life's breath came.

CHRONICLE   After the Qing troops crossed Canal Route Bridge,
they plunged ahead, killing their way to the foot of Welcome

---

*The text indicates here that He Yunpeng was from Taicang Subprefecture (to the
southeast of Changshu). A stipendiary student in the military curriculum, he was known
as a brave fighter who could lift three thousand catties.
†Du had not left his post when the Changshu magistrate fled in the 5th month, nor
had he gone along when the assistant magistrate surrendered authority over the city to
the Qing in the 6th month.

Spring Bridge. But when they saw the stout defense preparations of the heroic-looking militia of Noodle Seller Zhu and others, the Qing pulled back their troops to West Manor. Hu Laigong feared that the enemy would come from the east and then turn north, cutting off the route back to his lair [at Fushan]. Knowing also that those troops from the east would again turn southward, he took advantage of that interval to surreptitiously open Small East Gate and have all the people's houses south of Welcome Spring Bridge set on fire. That night the wind happened to be up, so the conflagration illumined the sky and radiated over several dozen *li*. Of all the people's homes and palanquins, not a whole beam or half a pole remained.

STORYBOOK
Everyone in Changshu was sure to meet his end
With cowardly Commander Hu the city to defend.
Fearing only the enemy like tigers or wild bears,
Concern that homes were turned to ash he did not pretend.

MEMOIR [*Haiyu beibing ji*] In the evening of the 12th day of the 7th month, 1645, my son, Lin, leading my grandson, Kui, came into the city and warned me, saying, "I'd been planning to return for the sacrifices to our ancestors on the Ghost Festival [15th day of the 7th month]⁵ when this morning in a dream someone warned me not to enter the city because a lot of killing would take place there. I woke up alarmed and puzzled and just thought it best to come early."

On the morning of the 13th day spirits were high in the city. Toward dusk we heard that troop boats were coming from the south but that Yan Zizhang had leapt onto his horse, gone out of the city, beheaded one of the enemy, and returned. So the populace felt very safe. Yan and Shi Min were jointly leading local defense corps, and Yan's concern truly was to protect the city. But Shi, because of the arson and pillage of the previous year, let his hatred of the commoners show through fairly often. Yan paid no heed. That night a northeast wind roared like thunder, and flames lit up the sky.

CHRONICLE 14th day, early morning. The city is broken into and the stipendiary student Xu Shouzhi and others die in the carnage.

The Qing army regrouped below the south wall and picked up all the firearms and ammunition obtained from Shi Min's battalion. These they placed to the west of Islet Cloister and commenced firing toward the southwest corner of the city. From daybreak through early morning, cannon fire blasted the sky, and lead bullets flew wildly without pause. When they directly fired on the temple of the city god, and the city wall had already collapsed in several places, Hu Laigong stationed his unit on Lingjia Hill and sat there, observing whether the enemy would succeed or fail, without releasing a single arrow. He merely ordered his men to keep the gates tightly closed and not allow any of the common people to escape from the city.

STORYBOOK
The heavens shook as over the west wall cannonballs flew.
Men and women of the town were in a barbecue.
Laigong, his one technique (pretension) out of place,
Just waited for the wall to—any moment—be pierced through.

CHRONICLE   Yan Zizhang was going back and forth outside the city wall, unable to get in any of the gates. And inside, the local volunteer soldiers, leaderless, did not know what to do. So the Qing troops took doors, window shutters, and other boards from people's houses and made a big raft, on which they crossed the city moat. Some swarmed up like ants through the collapsed parts of the wall, and after they beheaded the people who had been holding South Gate, the rest were able to enter at a more leisurely pace. There was a certain Jin Laojiang, an old actor in the household of an official named Lu. Sporting a stiff woven hat with a fringe around the wide brim and a blue-green gown with large sleeves, he led a group of people holding incense to kneel in welcome. The first horseman to arrive asked him in the barbarian language, "Do you southern savages have any money?" Laojiang didn't understand, [so, indicating some silver or coins,] the horseman said in [Wu-dialect] Chinese, "This kind of thing [ve]." Laojiang then jokingly replied, "The Buddha [ve] is in the East Pagoda Monastery." Before he finished speaking, his severed head had dropped to the ground. An actor so accustomed to sarcastic talk doesn't change even at death. The others, seeing this, ran away, and those who were a little slow got killed.

STORYBOOK
The Qing troops came not on a routine day,
But Jin Laojiang his usual clever words did say.

Not expecting to become a specter by the sword,
He still thought, to the very end, that he was in a play.

CHRONICLE   Feng Shu, a master at the Confucian school, was
learned and put on airs. At the time he was staying in the home
of Administrative Commissioner Sun Guangfu. When he heard
that the city was coming under siege, he barely managed to get
out South Gate before it was closed, and he was forthwith taken
captive by the Qing army. He was tied up in a troop boat, but
when the person assigned to watch him grew a bit lax, Feng used
a combat knife from the storage rack to cut off his bindings and
got away by swimming to the channel bank. His younger brother
Zhishi, a stipendiary student, was also captured, but he was killed
for refusing to bow [to Qing authority].

STORYBOOK
The elder Feng was widely called most wise.
Beneath his gaze, none thought to criticize.
For the latest on the war he had no need;
To rumors and alarms he paid no heed.

He railed at them for bringing down the gate
And squeezed out underneath the falling grate
Just in time to see horsemen arrive.
He got captured and was lucky to survive.

MEMOIR   Early in the morning of the 14th, we heard the sound of
artillery but still thought it was from the ranks of Yan and Shi. Then
my old servant, Liu Man, came in trembling and said, "The enemy
has attacked the city, and the wall is about to be broken through!" My
son anxiously urged me to leave. But besides being set in my ways, I
also had no way to lock my living quarters. As soon as I left, my several
rooms would be robbed of everything. While I procrastinated, my son
lifted my grandson and went out the door. Dazed, I didn't even know
which way they went. Then I took my wife, my younger brother,
Zaiyin, and the seventy-year-old wife of my elder brother to North
Gate. Finding that gate closed, I parked them to one side and headed
back home through a rainstorm, planning to gather a few things. As I
was passing Shao Lane, just ahead of me at eye level a cannonball flew
across and hit the door of Painter Chen, dashing it to bits. It was from
the cannon outside South Gate, and if I'd been walking slightly farther
ahead, it would have struck my brow. Pretty dangerous!

When I'd almost finished gathering up some essentials and was about to lock the front door, several men and women appeared. Two of them, with horsehair hats and shoulder bags, were agitated and wanted to enter my compound. I made haste to motion them away, saying that I was just about to leave. One in a horsehair hat asked, "Where are you going, sir?" When I replied, "North Gate," he said, "I just came from North Gate. The enemy has already occupied the tower, and arrows are raining down like a deluge. How can you go there?" I said nothing but closed the door to [my own rooms] and therein held my breath with my elder brother, Tiyin.*

In no time we heard the sound of Tartar pipes coming from the north, going from house to house in a great commotion. When the sound got to my front door, someone wearing iron armor and wielding a pike burst in. I gulped another cup of strong liquor and lay down to wait [in one of my rooms]. But after a few minutes it was quiet. I wondered to myself, "Could he possibly be behaving like a proper guest, waiting for the host to come out and greet him?" I got up and peered out, but he was gone. Again, I'd locked the door and was holding my breath when suddenly soldiers came house to house a second time—and then a third time—until finally all was quiet.

CHRONICLE   The next day dead bodies filled the main streets in front of the temples, and below the bridges the water was red. Among the dead were over ten who had crouched behind a fence and gone forward bent down step by step. When they saw a man in barbarian dress going through the Land-God Temple, they sprang out to kill him. But his buddies were right behind, and wielding sabers, they annihilated the dozen citizens. The local volunteers at North Water Gate, led by Fat Yao and others, pooled their strength and fought bravely, but all were killed. At Moon Wall Inlet and below the suspension bridge, corpses were piled five or six feet deep. . . .

When the wall had earlier given way, the common people who had wanted to run for their lives were blocked from leaving the city by the soldiers that Hu Laigong had deputed to guard the gates. . . . Cordoned off by the soldiers' swords, they packed the streets with their cries and milled indecisively in the filthy mud produced by the heavy rain, which fell from noon to night. After

*On the layout of traditional Chinese homes such as this one, see Chap. 2, n. 13.

the gate guards from Hu's camp dispersed, those still waiting
scrambled to escape. But those who didn't manage to get out of
the city—whether upper-class or common, old or young, male or
female—all were prey to the Qing soldiers, who took people by
surprise and killed them at will along the streets. Everywhere—
in through streets and small lanes, on bridge walkways and canal
banks, in dilapidated buildings and abandoned wells—corpses lay
in masses. The total number was over five thousand, not counting
the men and women who were taken away as captives.[6]

STORYBOOK
South of town firing starts—armies in a fray.
In the town common people vie to get away.
Incensed at facing death before a shutdown city gate,
A drove of men and women this policy berate.

CHRONICLE   At North Dryland Gate over a thousand towns-
people, with family members in their arms, wanted to escape from
the city but were stopped by Hu's guards. Just as they were pacing
back and forth between two perils, Ding Jingsu came riding up
on a horse and told the guards that he had been ordered by Sir
Hu to leave the city on official business, so they should open the
gate quickly. Thereupon the gate was opened, but Jingsu waited
patiently while the thousand-plus men and their families got out
before he gave his horse its head and departed. Jingsu . . . had
directed the military commission at Chuishan* in remitting supplies to Banzi Wharf [serving Nanjing]. . . . He was an old ac-
quaintance of Laigong's and had been taken on as one of his
personal aides, so the soldiers guarding the gate believed him.

STORYBOOK
"Jingsu leaves the city on a public charge!"
He raised his whip and shouted in a voice so large.
Then with slackened reins, he waited for the feet
Of a thousand people to be fleet.

MEMOIR   On the morning of the 15th I peeked into the back room
of my compound at the dozen or so people [who had taken refuge there the
day before] and saw that the two with stiff, woven, wide-brimmed hats
and shoulder bags were gone. Among the ones left, three told me, "Last

*To the northwest from Changshu, in Zhenjiang Prefecture.

night we sneaked out, hoping to get through West Gate. The two with
hats, ahead of the rest of us, ran into some soldiers and were killed. In the
moonlight the soldiers opened their shoulder bags and divided up all their
possessions. So we three had time to get away." Around noontime there
again was the big commotion of going from door to door, I again lay down
and waited, and as before, it became quiet.

Toward evening we heard rustling sounds near the neighbor's wall,
and then two stout fellows came down on our side via the eaves of a
two-story building in the Zhu family compound and a parasol tree.
My brother Tiyin, startled, said, "Do you suppose they're Qing
troops?" I gestured and said no. Upon asking, we learned that their
names were Jiang and Qian and that they'd been generals subordinate
to Hu Laigong separately assigned to hold the southern city wall. When
the wall had been broken through, they'd concealed themselves in the
moat until the middle of the night. Then they'd crept out, hoping to
get to North Hill, but they'd encountered some enemy soldiers and
had quickly run into the Zhu family's pavilion. They had gotten into
my place from there. The two gallant young men's anguish and fear
showed clearly in their faces. . . .

Late that night I tossed and turned, thinking about my flesh and blood
having been scattered on the wind and wondering where they had
ended up. Before dawn I dreamed that I was casting dice and that six
pieces had landed end to end like a strong cord. I interpreted it to mean
that father and son, husband and wife, grandparent and grandson all
were unharmed.

CHRONICLE   Hu Laigong flees to Fushan.*

When Laigong saw from his headquarters at Lingjia Hill that South
Gate had been lost and that Qing troops were surging in like a
tide, he led his men to take valuables like gold, silver, and silk
fabrics—passing up staples like grains and beans, which were left
at the base of the hill. Then he got out by lowering himself down
over Mount Yu Gate.[7] Riding on horseback through the wind and
rain, he fled to Fushan harbor and then . . . out to sea. . . .

STORYBOOK

A fox plays the tiger, ready to swallow a steer.
Jade belt on crimson suit, who could be his peer?

*A strategic military site north of Changshu city on the south bank of the Yangzi
River.

The wall is taken, the enemy looks for a fight.
Pikes and mail are cast away; his perfidy we jeer.

CHRONICLE   Local volunteers kill Shi Min.

When the more than eight hundred men whom Shi Min had led
away from the battlefield heard that the wall had been broken
through, they scurried away in all directions. With just five or six
household servants Shi concealed himself in Tang Market.* At
that time volunteer fighters in the countryside were at their peak.
Regardless of whether they knew [Yan, Shi, or Hu], they all said
they would gladly follow Yan Zizhang, and they all gnashed their
teeth and cursed Shi Min and Hu Laigong. From his boat, moored
at Tang Market, Min heard some residents vociferously con-
demning him for sending ammunition and guns straight to the
Qing soldiers and thereby helping them to crush Changshu. Feeling uneasy, he skulked away and went to stay in the home of Mao
Jin.† When the local volunteers heard this, they surrounded the
Mao residence in great numbers, caught Shi Min, and exposed his
severed head on a pole at Seven Star Bridge.

STORYBOOK

Eight hundred sets of claws and fangs guarded his bungalow.
His arrogance smoked up the sky, but his brain had turned to
    dough.
The wall being smashed, his battalion about-faced and split.
His lone boat went back and forth but found no place to go.

Flaunting power's avarice in the first place was not smart.
When war drew nigh he played around; his unit fell apart.
The day his head was hoisted on the Bridge of Seven Stars
To then regret his dirty tricks it was too late to start.

CHRONICLE   Sixteenth day. The Qing withdraw their troops to the
prefectural seat [Suzhou]. He Fengxiang and others arrive with their
forces but, having missed the enemy, return [to Fushan].

It was rumored that the commander of the Qing army was a nobleman named Tong from Liaodong.[8] While razing the city, he had all
the gold, silks, and captive men and women loaded onto huge ships
outside South Gate. This continued for two days, from the 14th

*At a distance to the southeast of the city.
†One of the most famous and productive publishers of the seventeenth century. See
ECCP, II:565–66.

through the 15th, until the ships were full, or so one heard. Then, at daybreak on the 16th, a horn sounded, signaling that he was about to gather in his army and return to the prefectural seat.

STORYBOOK
Door by door they gathered up all our pearls and gold.
The seizure of young boys and girls we cannot redress.
Under sail, victors withdraw, our treasures in their hold.
Today their leader will report his army's big success.

CHRONICLE   The leader of the volunteers at Canal Route Bridge—Thousand-Pounds Zhu—and the man called Noodle Seller Zhu, hearing that the enemy was about to leave, got together a large group and proceeded stealthily to Land-God Altar. There they saw a soldier dressed in Manchu garb standing under the tower having a smoke. They shot him in the abdomen with an arrow, and the man hollered in pain. Soon another man jumped down from an upper level of the tower and charged straight toward them brandishing a saber. Thousand Pounds shot him down, too. Suddenly over forty more men wearing armor came forward, and they were about to have a go at the volunteers with swords when the horn at the South Gate levee was blown urgently. The forty or more men looked back with angry faces and then retreated in defensive formation.

STORYBOOK
With awe-inspiring mien into the fray he bounds.
His name is Zhu, but people like to call him Thousand Pounds.
Not one arrow does he waste; the fearsome foe retreats.
Changshu has its heroes too!—the news afar resounds.

CHRONICLE   At this time the Fushan local commander, He Fengxiang, arranged with various volunteer forces from the countryside to meet his garrison troops outside the city wall, intending to engage the Qing troops in a life-or-death battle. But by the time he arrived, the enemy had cast off and sailed away—several li or farther—leaving behind a ruined and empty city with streets full of corpses. The garrison and volunteer troops had no place to get victuals, so they returned to their base.

MEMOIR   After sunrise on the 16th I heard Changshu voices at the end of the street, and only then did I dare to open the front door.

Some Fushan troops suddenly appeared. When a large unit passed my door, they asked, surprised, how I'd gotten back into the city so easily, for the Northern troops had just left. I laughed and said, "I've been here all along. The troops have been gone quite a while. How come you've entered so tardily?" The soldiers moved on without saying anything.

That evening the son of a bondservant came from my family home in the countryside and, thinking I was dead, walked in crying mournfully. Reassuring him, I asked about the others and at long last learned that my son and grandson had gotten out by lowering themselves down the outside of the city wall, that my wife and younger brother had gotten out North Gate, and that they had all been in East Village for two days.

That morning I went out on the streets to look around. Not a single family had been left whole, nor had a single home escaped damage. At the end of the lane a seductively beautiful woman lay dead by the wayside. From north to south, corpses were in disorderly piles; [before the people were killed] all of them had either been bound hand and foot or had their hands tied behind their backs as they knelt or crouched. It was heartbreakingly cruel. In small winding lanes there were suicides, including husbands and wives who'd hanged themselves side by side. Of the dogs and pigs that had been slaughtered, some had no heads and others only half a body, and their remains were mixed in with those of the dead people. The vaporous stench of the filth was so overpowering that one couldn't walk. So on this day, too, there were very few people out and about. . . .

Returning homeward, I met up with Ye Jisun. His elder brother, Daodeng, a truly good man, had met death, and this caused me great anguish. But Jisun said, "It's fortunate that he was killed at home, because at least he can be properly encoffined. The rest [of the dead] are all strewn about the street corners among lots of other corpses, which have become so bloated that one can't tell them apart. Who could ever put them in coffins or dress them for burial?"

Passing in front of Shining Wisdom Monastery, I saw three people probing with staffs. They recognized a corpse in a cluster of bodies and cried out grievously, "It's him!" I asked who it was, and one of them said, "My younger brother, Zhou Erguan. On the morning of the 14th, he'd already left the city. But he became separated from our father, so he braved the danger of reentering the city to look for him.

Who would have thought that our father would reach our country home and my brother would be the one to lose his life?" How hurtful it was!

On the morning of the 17th it was rumored that troops were coming again from the south, so the whole city roiled like a cauldron. I wanted to go out North Gate, but my nephew, Wanru, forcibly held me back. As we left via South Gate instead, all I could see was a burned expanse where not so much as a simple hut remained. The large clan of Pu Zhiting's had lived together near the wall, but when the Qing troops attacked the wall, the first rounds of cannon fire had completely wiped out all thirty Pus. In the middle of the scorched waste was a big cabinet that was half in ashes. Someone pointed to it and said, "This was the cabinet in a pawnshop. The wife in the family had just given birth, so when the troops came, she couldn't make it away. In haste she got into this cabinet, and someone locked it as usual [inadvertently trapping her inside]. When the fire reached here, the cabinet and the woman both were incinerated."

Wanru, on his way to South Village, found every rice paddy filled with the corpses of children—some in sitting positions, some with their heads down, some with their heads thrown back; their flesh having been sucked clean by mosquitoes and gnats, only their white bones remained. Meanwhile I had run, heedless of anything, to East Village. Someone came there from North Gate and told me it had been so crowded that a total of seven people had been trampled to death. There must have been some lingering element of the disastrous Ghost Festival day. Again, I'd been fortunate to avoid it—to the credit of my good nephew! . . .

That night I heard that Shi Min had been killed by the people at Seven Star Bridge and that his death had been brutal. Even without Shi Min's wrongdoing, events [of the Qing conquest] had come to such a pass that nothing could have made Changshu anything like an impregnable fortress. Anyway, how could his one life be worth enough to make up for the myriad names of the slain? On the other hand, those who had burned and pillaged Shi's home were not necessarily the ones who suffered his revenge. [Though apparently senseless, it is] a delayed punishment for the bad deeds of people's ancestors and relations.[9]

I entered the countryside to make myself inconspicuous near the graves of my ancestors. Several in my family came and went, still unsettled; morning and night we were together only intermittently.

Every night in the rural area we had to protect ourselves against robbers. Having packed their young sons and daughters safely into small boats, my family members would swish in among the shoreline reeds. Just we old people were left under the thatched eaves to watch the head of the ford through the phosphorescent glow of will-o'-the-wisps. Right before daybreak those in the reeds would return, their heads affected by exposure to the wind and rain. Everyone in the household was afflicted with malaria. I, too, became sick on the 12th of the 8th month and didn't recover until the beginning of the 9th month.

CHRONICLE [8th month, 13th to 16th days.] Hong Yiwei, appointed the Qing magistrate of Changshu, comes to assume his post but is cornered at the drill levee.

.   .   .

17th day. The Qing provincial commander in chief, named Wang, arrives [in Changshu County] with his troops. Yan Zizhang leads his men to defend Huadang,* but they are scattered, and Yan escapes.†

.   .   .

The Qing magistrate, Hong Yiwei, and the assistant magistrate, Chen Risheng, assume their posts and issue notices to calm the people.

MEMOIR In the middle of the night on the 23rd of the 8th month, seventeen boats carrying men whose mouths were muffled for a sneak attack moored in front of my family's graveyard. The whole village ran and hid, trembling, in the grass at the water's edge. The soldiers, however, surrounded the home of Zhang Wangyun looking to catch Zhang Tianrui. He had previously been a Ming military official, and the Qing troops had reason to dislike him. . . . So Wangyun's house, along with the neighboring abodes of wealthy families, was pillaged and burned into oblivion. That night the flames lit the village like daylight. The chickens and dogs were so terrified they didn't make a sound.

Some soldiers, crossing a small stream, tied the gunwale of their boat

---

*A wide point in the main waterway to Suzhou, southwest of Changshu city.

†Yan, wearing heavy armor, is said to have been rescued from drowning by some miraculous astral force. He managed to conceal himself among fellow clansmen in a rural area for five or six years, after which he was employed as an officer under the very commander who defeated him in this action.

[to a mooring] and sang out, "Why is it so quiet?" When a little boy
in the reeds along the shore piped up in response, the boy, his father
and mother, elder brother, and aunt were killed. Seven or eight people
fell into the water and drowned in the front and back of the village,
too.

I happened to be ill at the time and hid in a cluster of bamboo plants
with my infant grandson. Fortunately he didn't cry, but I couldn't
suppress my groans. Suddenly I heard men in the lead unit say, "That's
all," as though they were about to gather in the troops. At daybreak
the seventeen boats cast off and left, and the villagers inched out like
worms from the water reeds and bamboo groves and looked at each
other as if decades had passed. . . .

On the morning of the 21st I returned to the city. The four walls
were in ruins, but the green hills hadn't changed. Only a scattered few
of my old acquaintances were there, but the scene was affecting. So,
on the spur of the moment, I wrote out some of what I had seen and
heard in the form of a rustic history, as follows.

ROMANCE [*yecheng*] Mid-morning on the 14th of the 7th month,
Qing troops broke into the city. Over half of the residents were able
to escape before this, but those who did not—poor or rich, old or
young, whether they hid, came out, or bowed down welcoming the
invaders—all were killed. Those who met death did not number fewer
than ten thousand. The deaths by rape were terribly cruel. And more
than three thousand men, women, boys, and girls were taken away as
captives.

Xiao Zhengxiang's sister-in-law, surnamed Xu, was beautiful. When
captured, she refused to submit [to sexual demands], so they killed her
husband to further intimidate her, but she stamped her feet and begged
for death even more insistently. They carried her into a boat and tried
to rape her under the points of several knives, but in the end she would
not submit. The soldiers were so angered that they killed her and cut
out her liver, saying, "This is the liver of a chaste woman martyr!"
and they vied to eat it.[10] . . .

A man named Tao in South Market had been intimate friends with
a business partner named Wu from Suzhou. On the 14th, three men
wielding swords entered Tao's gate, Wu among them. Tao cried out,
"Elder Brother Wu, save me!" But Wu, feigning surprise, said, "Who
knows you?" They hacked around with their three swords, bagged

everything he owned, and went out. Tao was just heaving a sigh of amazement that anyone could be so unfeeling as that when Wu returned and jabbed him several times with a spear until he was dead. . . .

Guo Zhangsun's wife had been kidnapped, so Guo made inquiries and learned that she was in the home of a certain general. With silver in hand, he sought to ransom her. The general took the silver and had the woman sent out, but she hated her former husband and was unwilling to go. The general returned Guo's silver and then cursed the woman, saying, "You couldn't help being captured, but what sort of heart refuses to go back when ransomed? What use have I for such an unrighteous woman!" He killed her on the spot. . . .

In the fall of 1643, Cao Wanwu fell ill and [in his delirium] entered the netherworld for three days. When the judge there was about to send him back, Cao kowtowed and asked how many more years he had to live.[11] The judge picked up a short, foot-long ruler from his bench and showed it to Cao, whereupon the latter came to. Cao often told his relatives that because there are ten inches to a [Chinese] foot, he had been given ten more years! In fact, he was killed this year on the 14th day of the 7th month—only three years since his visit to the netherworld. Someone explained this by saying that colloquially we refer to being killed by decapitation as becoming one foot shorter. Aha! Isn't this an exact correlation? So it is that life and death are predetermined, and the judge in the netherworld proved clever indeed.

At Huadang Opening there was a middle-aged woman who was still attractive. When some soldiers forced her onto a boat for a gang rape, she said, "I have a beautiful daughter-in-law who lives on the other side of the confluence. I'm willing to have her take my place. One soldier said enthusiastically, "Could you take me?" She said, "Sure." Looking out over the confluence, she started to cross it by wading in up to her ankles. She pointed to the side of some reeds and said, "The water is shallow here." So the soldier walked over [what turned out to be a drop-off]. As he sank and floated, sank and floated, he yelled to the woman to save him. But she just smiled as she stepped ashore and then ran as though she had wings while the soldier drowned. In a nearby boatload of captives who'd witnessed this, no one could help laughing. This angered the other soldiers so much that they killed everyone, leaving only a boy with knotted hair who came back and told of this incident. . . .

MEMOIR   [When everything from] fish in the deep to pheasants aloft is afflicted by calamities, the common people suffer. Although this is naturally the case, there is also evidence of predestination. After sightings of sharks and tigers a city is destroyed. This was calculated by the fortune-teller Zhou Wuyang. In the middle of the 5th month I also divined that the city surely would be threatened, and I went about telling all my relatives and friends that on the day of the Ghost Festival no family would be able to carry out its ancestral sacrifices. My son's dream on the morning of the 12th was uncanny, too. . . .

Although I live in the heart of the city, that old house which was my grandfather's is quite humble. Inside the door is a garland chrysanthemum. That the soldiers came several times but then unexpectedly left again surely is attributable to the power of that chrysanthemum! In fact, among my relatives and friends whose homes are even more humble than mine, none escaped harm. I heard that when slaying poor scholars, the soldiers always cursed them, saying, "You rich people have just borrowed these tumbledown rooms to hide yourselves." Truly, mine was the pinnacle of good fortune!

6

From Orphan
to Princess:
The Story of Liu Sanxiu

AMONG THE MANY WOMEN who were taken captive in Changshu and other places during the conquest period, very few were able to transform adversity into blessing as successfully as Liu Sanxiu from the small town of Renyang near the southeastern border of Changshu County (see fig. 9). She was born into a respectable scholarly family in somewhat reduced circumstances. After losing her mother when she was six and her father when she was ten, Liu was reared by her two elder brothers until she was fourteen. She was, we are told, a lovely and intelligent girl. Through the greed and chicanery of her second eldest brother, she was virtually sold to a widower three times her age, the master of the one wealthy household in Renyang: Huang Lianggong, a notorious miser who had married his previous wife for her wealth and then treated her shabbily. Huang doted on his new wife, however, and by him she bore a daughter, Zhen, to whom she was devoted. Because no male progeny seemed forthcoming, Liu sought to adopt one of her eldest brother's sons, called Qi, into the Huang family to continue her husband's line of descent.[1] But Qi turned out to be a bad sort, who lusted after Zhen and became violent when she was betrothed to someone else, so he was expelled from the family. After Huang Lianggong's sudden death, Qi first unsuccessfully demanded an inheritance and then unsuccessfully schemed with ruffians to rob the household of the new widow. From this point the story below continues, revealing some typical problems of widowhood in late imperial China under exacerbating circumstances.[2]

Liu's life experiences were originally told by an old woman, surnamed Zhang, who served successively as her nurse, governess, and maidservant—accompanying her from natal to marital household, as was common in the society of that day. Such an intimate companion could hardly regard her mistress objectively, and Liu was obviously the apple of her maidservant's eye. But circumstances suggest that Zhang's high estimation of Liu was largely justified. In 1673, having grown too old to serve her lady any longer, Zhang returned to her own family in a locale not far from Renyang. There she related—both orally and in writing—what Liu had gone through to a female cousin and her husband.* The latter harbored a deep antipathy for the high-handed, exploitive Huang family and had derived great satisfaction from its complete ruination in the late 1640s. In 1676 the cousin's husband, using a pseudonym, combined Zhang's account with things he himself knew about and composed the *Guoxu zhigan* (Feelings Aroused on Passing by Ruins).[3]

Although the text of this story bears no obvious earmarks of a fictional (or purposely fictionalized) tale, many passages must have derived from hearsay, if not active imagination. So much in the *Guoxu zhigan* corresponds to what is definitely known about the period that it cannot be dismissed as a mere fabrication. But the identities of key figures in the story have not yet been corroborated in firm historical sources.[†] These factors naturally cast some doubt on the factuality of the account. Indeed, Liu's struggle with adversity and her extraordinary destiny could be read as a variation on the numerous Chinese romantic stories and plays about "talented men and beautiful women," which in late Ming times tended to emphasize sagacity and accomplishment in heroines. On the other hand, we may have here a case of life imitating art, which was not uncommon in the dramatic events of the Ming-Qing transition.[4] The *Guoxu zhigan* is incontrovertibly true to the times, and though hardly the work of an abstemious historical intellect, it offers a rare view of the conquest period from the (albeit male-mediated) perspective of a woman.[‡]

---

*The cousin, a Wu, was not the man's formal wife but his concubine, or "new wife," a status appropriate to someone on Zhang's lower social level.

†See, for instance, n. 13, below.

‡The full work is written in the third person. Only those parts that relate directly to Liu and are presumably narrated by Zhang are presented here, so all references to Zhang have been changed to the first person. Correspondingly, most references to Liu Sanxiu as "Liu" have been changed to "Mistress Liu."

Mistress Liu, having been frightened by Qi several times in a row, knew that the enmity between them would continue. She became depressed as she thought over many possible ways to deal with the situation. Then she abruptly said, "I'd better put the dead to rest," and proceeded to have [her recently deceased] husband, [Huang] Liang[gong], buried in his family's ancestral graveyard near Mao Lake. As soon as the burial sacrifices were over, she said to her son-in-law, Qian Shenkun,[5] "I cannot live here any longer. I wish to rely on you for the rest of my life."

So the biggest and heaviest items in the Huang household were loaded up and transported to the Qian residence in Zhitang using over a hundred hired laborers.* When, in five days' time, this process was complete, my mistress sent her daughter, Zhen, on ahead to the in-laws' home. Handing Zhen a record book, she said, "This lists 120 sacks of white rice and 200 sacks of brown rice; each sack holds two *yuanbao*† for safe transport. Various other amounts of silver have been stored under the clothing in over twenty large trunks and more than ten medium-sized trunks. There are twenty-seven chests filled with copper cash, and those with certain markings on them also hold silver. All these items are very important, so I've listed them in this notebook, which I'm entrusting to you. With this record there should be no losses." Within four days the silver, cash, and clothing were also transported.

Mistress Liu then had the chickens and pigs slaughtered, and she summoned all the poor farmers in the village—over two hundred came. After feasting them with wine and meat, she called them forward, took the documents that recorded the debts they had accrued to the Huangs over many years, and burned them, saying, "I want to aid the fortunes of the deceased [her husband] in the netherworld." The crowd was very happy. In addition, she opened the storehouses and had each guest given two pecks of rice and one peck of wheat, five pounds of raw cotton, and five pints of legumes. So the crowd was even happier, and they spontaneously surrounded her and bowed.

They all said that "Mother Huang" had always extended kindnesses

---

*A small town immediately to the east of Renyang.
†See p. 61*n*.

to them and canceled the debts of the poor, even though her creditor's hand never had been heavy. "Now," they said, "you have done these other magnanimous things. How shall we repay you?" Mistress Liu said, "I'm not looking for repayment. What I wish to ask is that you cart over two thousand piculs of rice to Zhitang. The rich wine and fatty meat would be yours; you could take your fill." Everyone said that they were willing to do as she said, and in the course of four days, all that grain was transported. . . . Thus, everything that the Huangs had accumulated over three generations, valued at not less than several hundred thousand taels, was transferred in a short time and without incident to another family's home. It was as marvelous as the changes wrought by the Creator, and the intricate way that Mistress Liu carried things out was also very clever.

Qian Shenkun came soon to formally invite Mistress Liu to his home, and she planned to depart within days. Consulting a calendar, they determined that she should not move immediately; she would have to wait three days for a favorable astrological augury.* After two days and half a night, trouble arose.

A General Li Chengdong had surrendered to the new [Qing] dynasty during the Hongguang period. Every city or town he'd gone through had been arbitrarily ravaged, and the women who were seized filled more than ten boats. When he passed through Jiading,[6] his boats were burned by people in the countryside, and over half of the women perished. When he reached the garrison city of Luodian, Li vowed that he would seize the most beautiful women of the Wu [Suzhou] area as compensation. He went on to subjugate Songjiang, where he chose a large house for his own residence and therein kept many courtesans and concubines. Subsequently, when he was ordered to campaign in Guangdong Province, he directed his younger brother to stay there and look after their mother. And he ordered his most trusted lieutenant, in command of a thousand soldiers,[†] to protect Songjiang—truly a thoughtful householder!

Among Qi's bunch of rascals was a soldier in the personal guard of

---

*The editor's note asserts that this prognostication was mistaken, because the favorable star in question was in fact unfavorable to women in that particular configuration.

†The text repeatedly refers to Li's forces as "banner troops" (*qi bing*). However, Li's army, like most of those that surrendered to the Manchus after the latter entered North China, never was integrated into the famous Qing banner system. The main reason for this is exemplified in the recklessness and lack of discipline described below.

the general in charge of protecting Songjiang. . . . Qi told the soldier that if the services of a hundred troops from his camp could be procured, then a lot of silver, coins, rice, and other grains could be brought there all bundled up [from a raid on the Huang household]. The soldier replied that it would be better to take the less dangerous route of clearing the job first with the commanding general. If the take was big, then Qi would earn merit. He would get an official position or at least a substantial reward. Qi clapped his hands and gave a big laugh, saying that he wanted to be an official!

So they cleared the matter with the general, saying that Liu, who controlled a million taels' worth of goods, bit people like a tigress and was hated to the marrow by the villagers. It would be very convenient if Qing troops could in one fell swoop get rid of a scourge on the people and take possession of the million in goods to build up military stocks. The general agreed and forthwith ordered one of his subordinates to lead a thousand men via the Liu River through Kunshan to Qiputang, whence they would advance on the Huang residence.

At the time Mistress Liu was locking the two-story buildings in the compound, busily admonishing the caretakers from morning to night, and, with me, setting finer matters in order. Wearing a plain gown and light makeup, she then sat down to await the dawn and plan her departure.

Suddenly, outside the gate the sound of guns blasted the sky, the doors in the outer wall collapsed, and a thousand troops surged in. They opened the granaries—empty. They opened the storage cellar—empty. They searched through the chests and cabinets—not a single utensil or item of clothing was left. The lieutenant was very angry. He watched as Qi and several others brought Mistress Liu to him, and he was about to interrogate her when he saw her features in the torchlight. His gaze remained fixed for a long time before he abruptly said, "We have to rely on this woman. Otherwise, we have nothing with which to compensate the head of our unit [Li Chengdong]." So they took Mistress Liu away as a captive, and I followed along.

By this time the thousand soldiers, who'd labored but gotten nothing, were in a turbulent state. Without waiting for any order from the general, they wildly stabbed Qi with their knives and set fire to the offices, pavilions, granaries, and pantries of the Huang residence. Within minutes everything was a huge inferno. The crowd threw Qi's corpse into the fierce blaze, plundered the residences of a few dozen families in the nearby village until their grain supply was somewhat replenished, and went back [to Songjiang].

When Zhen heard about this incident, she was alarmed, and sobbed until she didn't know morning from night. Having given birth by that time, her milk ran dry. The old Mr. Qian became so worried that to assuage Zhen's worry about her mother, he ordered Qian Shenkun to go to Songjiang and make inquiries. But when Shenkun got to Songjiang, he found that Li Chengdong's family had been taken into custody* and that all the women Li had seized had been consigned to banner units in Nanjing.[†] So he went back and asked Second Brother Liu to accompany him there.

When they arrived at the banner commanders' headquarters [in Nanjing], they saw a posted set of orders from a certain [Manchu] prince, among which was the stipulation that relatives be permitted to take back any women who had been abducted by the traitorous Li Chengdong. Qian and Liu were overjoyed and eager to go in and report Mistress Liu's case, but they didn't know how to proceed. A low-ranking officer happened to come out of the headquarters just then, so Qian took him aside and asked whether the language of that particular item in the posted orders was credible. The officer replied that three women had been sent home the day before. Qian told him their situation, and the officer said, "From your accent you seem to be a man of the Wu region. I, too, am a man of Wu, though I've joined a Qing banner. Out of friendship toward someone from my home area, I cannot but be truthful with you." He led Qian by the hand to a place where no one else could overhear and said to him, "The prince's order is firm, all right. But with Headquarters Director Hei, such things aren't possible without dough." Qian asked how much they wanted, and the officer said it depended on the age and appearance of the woman, the young and pretty ones going for as much as a hundred taels. Qian asked what could be done if he couldn't come up with that much right away, and the officer told him that if he hurried home and got the amount needed, the matter could be accomplished in five or six days.

Qian Shenkun then went back with Second Brother to get the ransom money. Zhen unreservedly emptied out all she'd saved and sent the

*Because of Li's revolt against the Qing and his reversion to Ming allegiance in Guangdong in May 1648. See *SM*, pp. 121–29.

[†]Nanjing had been renamed Jiangning by the Qing government.

two men back, ordering Qian Shenkun to spare no expense if anything could truly secure her mother's release. So they went back to Nanjing with one thousand taels in hand to find the officer they'd met. After telling him that they had prepared what was desired, they also offered to reward him with fifty taels for completing payment of the ransom. He was pleased and told Qian Shenkun to provide Liu's age, features, and place of origin. He also said, "Inside the official compound it's the second lady housekeeper who actually looks after the captive women. With every hundred taels in ransom fees, it's understood that she be given ten taels. Otherwise, she's sure to raise difficulties and obstruct matters." Qian Shenkun said he'd do anything he was told. So the officer took the information about Mistress Liu, entered the compound, and had the second lady housekeeper search for someone who matched the description. After a long while, he came out waving his hands vigorously and said, "There's no such person here. What can I do?"

Qian Shenkun was stunned. He recounted how Mistress Liu had been taken captive by a certain general on a certain date in a certain place and how he and other relatives had made inquiries in Songjiang and had confirmed that the general in question had given Liu over to Commander Li's household. How could she not be in there? . . . Tearfully he said to Second Brother, "When I, your nephew-in-law, return home this time, your niece will surely die; and when she dies, I swear I will not live without her." Then he sobbed heavily. Second Brother said to him, "Crying is no help. It would be better to continue our search. . . . Perhaps we can get definite proof of whether this is so."

Qian Shenkun stepped forward and grasped the officer's lapel, saying, "I beg you, sir, to show us one piece of evidence to confirm or disprove this, and we'll surely reward you." Thereupon he raised up the fifty taels they'd promised, and presented them to the officer, who hesitated a long while, unable to think of any recourse. Then he said, "I've got it," and dashed back into the compound. In a moment he returned with a booklet in his sleeve and said to the two men, "Here is your definite proof. . . . But do me the favor of keeping this secret and not leaking word of it to anyone else. My head still wants to go on eating for a few more years. Don't get me killed."

Qian and Liu hastily opened the booklet and scanned it carefully to the last page where, sure enough, they found the two names Ms. Liu-Huang and Maidservant Zhang marked with a red circle. A note alongside indicated that they had been chosen to enter the prince's mansion.

... Qian cried, not knowing what to say; and Second Brother said, "There's nothing we can do but go home." Only a few days after they returned to Changshu, a letter from Mistress Liu arrived.

Prior to this, Mistress Liu had been abducted to Songjiang and had entered the Li household. Li's mother had liked her at first sight and said, "You must be the daughter of a famous family! How did you ever become so beautiful? If you're willing to serve me as a daughter and take sleeping and living quarters near mine, then I'll soon have you escorted back to your home area."

But before long, Li Chengdong revolted in Guangdong, and his mother and younger brother were both taken in fetters to the capital. His courtesans, concubines, and other women—Mistress Liu among them—became subject to dispersal among members of the ranking banner unit [in Jiangnan] and were relocated to Nanjing under the supervision of the commander in chief, a [Manchu] nobleman named Hei.[7] An area was cleared behind his official compound in an empty yard beside the horse stables, and there a crowd of over three hundred women were domiciled in several tents made of matting. It was almost like living in the open. The stench of horse manure and urine was so pervasive that one could hardly stand it for more than a quarter-hour. So the women wailed tearfully, unwilling to live any longer.

After a day and a night, a Manchu lady came—the head maidservant in the prince's mansion. She was over seventy, with white hair and a dark complexion. Her hair was drawn back in a chignon, and she wore a flower clipped at one temple. Her garments and shoes were all masculine in style.*[8] She spoke Chinese very well, showing a quick wit and much savvy. When she arrived, all the commanders knelt in greeting, and the second lady housekeeper kowtowed. Then they led her into the mat tents to look around. In Chinese she said, "Sisters, have no fear. I am the official who confirms blessings from heaven. But I do not yet know who among you is blessed."

Then she sidestepped through the troop of women, selecting those who struck her as appropriate. Tugging on certain lapels and then walking on, she picked over thirty women, whom she had line up in front of her in a separate place. She looked them over from side to side,

---

*Manchu women did not bind their feet into tiny stumps or wear correspondingly small booties, as had long been the fashion among Chinese women. Later in the Qing dynasty, many Manchu women emulated the Chinese practice in spite of prohibitions.

and after some time she culled that group by pointing and saying, "There she's a bit too long; here she's a bit too short." In this way she eliminated half of the thirty or more women. Then she called about a dozen of them forward and scrutinized their hair, arms, palms, and fingers; and she eliminated another seven by feeling their two breasts through their upper garments. The remaining five she had sit in a row for tea service. Courteously she questioned them and carefully judged their intonations, besides listening patiently and attentively to their answers. Among the five was one woman whose voice was somewhat poor, so she, too, was eliminated. Then the old Manchu lady stood up again and said to the four remaining women, "Don't move; sit quietly. I just want to observe the form of your shoes." Thereupon she parted the front overlap of their skirts and stuck in two fingers to measure their footwear [fig. 11].*[9] Then she jokingly said, "I have to be rude like that. Otherwise, I wouldn't get to see true talent, and you wouldn't be able to pass the test!"[†] So she took only four women—including Mistress Liu. The old Manchu lady said of her several times in Manchu, "*Saileng, saileng*," which means "the best."[10] Again she spoke to the four women, asking if any had handmaidens—if so, they could come along. . . .

Soon the four women were lifted into a carriage bound for the prince's mansion. Mistress Liu clutched me and sobbed painfully, saying, "Once I enter this place, there'll be no chance in ten thousand to see Zhen again, and my life will come to an end." I put my arms around her and cried, too.

Toward sunset the prince had a banquet and ordered that the four women should serve the wine. The old Manchu lady instructed each of the four to kowtow before the prince and remain prostrate, head down, until he commanded them to rise. And she warned them strongly against crying, lest the prince be angered and have them whipped. So three of the women did as they were told and crawled forward on their knees. After knocking their heads on the floor, they stayed down, holding their breath, not daring to make a sound. Mistress Liu, however, came along only gradually and stood near a pillar with her face turned toward the left wall, her eyes seeing nothing. In the lamplight the radiance of

*The ideal length of the bound foot was three inches—about the length of a woman's middle finger.

†She lightly draws an analogy between this selection of women and the men's civil service examinations.

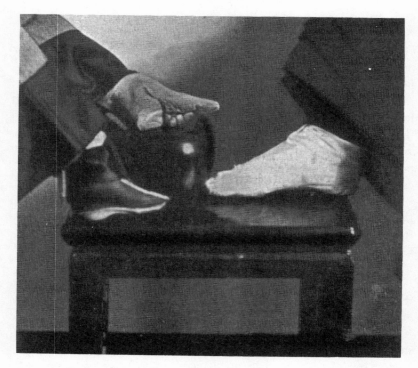

Figure 11. A comparison of the Chinese elite woman's bound foot with the normal foot, which Manchu women were supposed to keep unbound.

her forehead was striking. The tears on her eyelashes and the slight red glow in her cheeks made her twice as alluring.

The prince noticed her unusual demeanor and asked her where she was from, but Mistress Liu didn't respond. He asked her age and again got no answer. He asked whether she had a husband—again no reply. Then she burst into tears and said, "I'm a commoner widow who was taken captive by Tartar troops. Because of my attachment to my only daughter, I didn't seek death right away. But now that I've reached the point of eternal separation from her, what use is there in living? Why don't you kill me quickly? I'm a woman of good family who'll never be a female slave in a Tartar household!" And she dashed her head against the pillar. The old Manchu lady made haste to restrain my mistress in a bear hug. But she went on struggling and wailing until her coiffure came undone and her hair, more than ten feet long, fell to the floor. Seeing this, the prince thought her even more unusual and began to have feelings of love. He directed the old Manchu lady to give her very good care and support and not to let her grow weak from distress. So the old lady used a hundred clever phrasings to get Mistress Liu into the lady's own sleeping quarters and calm her down.

Morning and evening my mistress was brought ginseng,[11] and every kind of edible fruit and porridge was stacked on her table, but Mistress Liu didn't taste a single piece or spoonful. Whether sitting or lying down, all she did was cry. I became very worried and spoke with the old Manchu lady on my own, saying, "Mistress Liu has weakened this much from grief because she misses her daughter terribly. . . . I think that if she had a chance to put through an inquiry about her daughter and ease her mind, perhaps then she would take a little food and drink." The old Manchu lady agreed and broached the matter with the prince, who said to have her write a letter at once and dispatch it by fast runner. When the old Manchu lady told Mistress Liu, her face cleared, and she said, "I haven't wanted to hear anything you've said for all these days. Only this commands some interest." Then she wrote a letter to Zhen[12] as follows.

My life has been ill starred; repeatedly I've suffered hardships. That day when I sent you off at the river's edge has now become the point of our permanent separation into different worlds. So painful, how can I bear to say it? So painful, how can I bear to say it?

After Beast Qi indulged his villainy and I was abducted to Songjiang, I was luckily favored by [Li Chengdong's] kind mother. She provided me with sleeping and eating quarters close to her and promised to send me home to Changshu so that mother and child could be together. Unexpectedly I was affected through the fault of another: When the Li household was confiscated, I was dispatched to the provincial capital, where, moreover, I was chosen to enter a royal harem and join the ranks of the odalisques. So I have come to be like one who has fallen from a precipice—trying to fly with no wings.

Alas, my daughter Zhen, your mother has been reduced to this. How can she go on bearing it silently to preserve her life? As I have said to Maidservant Zhang, you are my sole small vein of life's blood [that is, her only descendant]. If I should fail to get in touch with you and die in obscurity, you would be infinitely lonely. This is why I've lamely prolonged my feeble breath and repeatedly endured distress and frustration without dying.

Earlier in Songjiang I was alarmed to hear that all the villages in the Zhitang area had been gutted by the soldiers. I thought that Beast Qi, having failed to get what he wanted [at Renyang], may have set the soldiers loose again in your direction. Considering the situation, I feared that your home might have become one of the smashed eggs in the nest [of Zhitang]. I've been unable to determine whether this is true or not. Now if my letter arrives and you write back in your own hand, then I will know that fortunately you have not been killed by Beast Qi. If my letter arrives and I receive no letter back in your hand, then I will know that unfortunately you ended up being killed by Beast Qi. Life or death will be decided by a piece of paper. Only keeping vigil for the migratory goose [that is, for her return missive] shall comfort my saddened heart.

If indeed I am to be a desolate widow in service to a barbarian court, then I have long since decided what to do. If the prince insults me as an underling and tries to order me around with a whip, then my refusing mouth will spit in his face until my head butts his chest, and I will not recant even if they grind my bones to powder. By nature I am high-minded and uncompromising, unwilling to subordinate myself to others. If I stake everything and lose, what will death matter to me?

My Zhen, my Zhen. For my sake, do not worry.

Mistress Liu sealed the letter and gave it to the old Manchu lady, who showed it to the prince. He, in turn, ordered one of the generals in his personal guard to send out a fast runner, setting a time limit of two days and nights to Changshu and two days and nights back to Nanjing.

Zhen cried when she received her mother's letter . . . , as did Qian Shenkun when he read it. . . . Looking at Zhen, he said, "The matter simply is this: According to the most important rules of propriety, a widowed wife must not take a second husband. But according to our truest emotions, a daughter cannot bear to contribute to her mother's death. At this juncture it's extremely difficult to put anything into words. You'll have to think very carefully in writing back."

Just then Second Brother arrived. He opened the letter and perused it several times. Then, with a knit brow, he said to Zhen, "Your mother is stubbornly recalcitrant and heedless of advantage or disadvantage. The prince referred to is none other than the paternal uncle of the present emperor. When the emperor came through [Shanhai] Pass, he was the most meritorious of the accompanying officials. On the way to Jiangnan he forced the surrender of Hongguang and both eastern and western Zhejiang Province. He is an imperial relative of high attainments.[13] His power and prestige are this great, but she wants to spit in his face and butt his chest and be uselessly mangled in the tiger's fangs. If by chance she provokes powerful repercussions, you and I will disappear from the human race. The matter leaves us no option. In writing back, you should urge her to be more accommodating." But Zhen replied, "For a daughter to urge her mother to lose her virtue would be unprincipled. All I know is that in my heart of hearts I don't want her to die."[14]

Then Zhen wrote a letter, opening with an assurance that she was unharmed and proceeding to say that as long as her mother lived, she would live. If her mother died, then she also would die. She expressed strong feelings of affection and admiration but refrained from using words that would induce one choice or another. . . .

Second Brother, however, privately composed his own letter without the knowledge of Qian Shenkun or Zhen. Therein he wrote grandiosely about His Excellency's magnanimous selection, including even the coarsely adorned women of poor, insignificant families; he wrote that his younger sister, being an exceptionally intelligent woman, would not, of course, hold the simplistic loyalties of ordinary women and that she should keep in mind the words of the [fortune-teller from] Bear's Ear Hill*—his sister's union with this prince might well be the extraordinary good fortune she was to receive. He concluded by telling her that the Huang home [in Renyang] had been completely destroyed and that even if she returned with her virtue intact, she would have no place to stay there, and it would be difficult for her to depend perpetually on the outside [that is, affinal] kin of her son-in-law's family. It would be better for her to establish herself in the prince's household so that her two brothers might receive patronage. Then he signed First Brother's name at the end and appended his own.

Earlier, when Mistress Liu learned that the prince had dispatched her letter, she felt grateful and took some ginseng and porridge. When the return letters arrived, she anxiously unsealed them and spontaneously smiled when she learned that Zhen was all right. But as she

*The fortune-teller had predicted that Liu would be closely associated with the governmental power of a royal family and would have two sons of high status, but had said that the future of her husband, Huang Lianggong, was very inauspicious.

delicately sensed the implications in the subtle words of the letter from her daughter and son-in-law, she couldn't help shedding tears. After reading the letter ostensibly from her two elder brothers, she thought deeply for a long while and then unconsciously made an angry face and said, "This is not First Brother's letter; these are the words of Second Brother Liu. He didn't get the forty taels he wanted [for betrothing me to Huang Lianggong],* so now he's even more keen on selling me into a [Manchu] banner as a maidservant-concubine!" And she ordered me to burn it.

Not long thereafter, the prince's chief consort, of the Hula clan,† died in Beijing, and when the announcement of her death arrived, [a memorial tablet] was positioned in the central hall. All the women who received sustenance under the prince's own banner were to approach it ceremoniously and cry in mourning each day for three days; those outside were merely to wear plain white clothing—this apparently being one of their state regulations. . . . The old Manchu lady suggested to Mistress Liu and me that we should respectfully comply with this practice. Mistress Liu said, "I certainly am one who has eaten the food of this household. How could I violate its most important rituals?" So she put on a mourning headdress of coarse linen, a white dress of raw silk with a softer raw silk trim, and plain shoes. Then she went out at a leisurely pace to participate in the ceremonies. She was so attractive, even unadorned, and had such underlying composure that the soul of anyone who saw her would take flight. The prince happened to run into her on the central walkway and immediately asked, "Isn't this the woman whose long hair fell to the ground?" and he followed her with his eyes for a long time. Then he discreetly ordered the old Manchu lady to take especially good care of that woman with the extraordinary bearing and not make her join the host of female servants. From this occurrence onward, the old Manchu lady always knelt and touched her forehead to the floor when she saw Mistress Liu and followed her orders, fearing only her dissatisfaction.

*Once the betrothal had been concluded, the miserly Huang typically not only halved the bride payment to the Liu family and the go-between's fee for Second Brother but further deducted 10 percent from both amounts.

†Probably the Ula tribe. The word *fei*, which usually means "concubine," can also mean "wife," especially of a first-degree prince. It has the latter meaning here. To reduce confusion, this position is rendered "chief consort" or "principal consort" in this translation.

Before long, an assortment of gifts came one after another: first, a trunkful each of Chinese-style and Manchu-style garments; next, ten pounds of ginseng from Beijing and a hundred eastern pearls;* then a box of jewelry, two fans from the imperial palace, two handkerchiefs, four clutch bags, and one tray each of silver and gold ingots. All were arrayed neatly on Mistress Liu's table. Each time the old Manchu lady presented these things, she knelt and said, "Gifts from our master, the prince." But Mistress Liu wouldn't look at any of them.

The old Manchu lady said, "When the prince bestows gifts, one should kowtow before him personally and extend thanks." But Mistress Liu instead flopped down on her bed and wouldn't get up. That night the prince ordered Mistress Liu to accompany him to bed. Hearing this, she wailed loudly and cried, "He wants to keep me like a maidservant-concubine after all. I'm a woman born and reared in a good family who's simply plagued by misfortune. What crime have I committed that I should be sent into penal servitude to do the bidding of others every morning and evening?" When the prince heard of this, he let the matter drop.

The old Manchu lady sought me out privately and said, "Since Mistress Liu entered the prince's mansion, he's treated her with special courtesy. He hasn't ordered her to take responsibilities for his meals, ablutions, or any other such things, and his gifts to her have been substantial and repeated—truly an unusual augury. The prince's intentions cannot be called ungenerous. Now his principal consort has died, but he still has no male heir. Among all the other concubines there's absolutely none whom he especially favors; rather, he's interested solely in Mistress Liu. This is a time when great good fortune can come. Why does she have to be so disagreeable? She may dislike being a widow [and taking a new mate]. But in our Manchu banners, according to established regulations, when a woman's husband dies, she is remarried in order to keep expanding our male population. What repugnance is there in that?"† I replied that Mistress Liu was high-minded and uncompromising by nature. In her own home she liked to

---

*From the rivers of northern Manchuria, in present-day Heilongjiang and Jilin provinces. They were especially large and round and pure white.

†The matter of widow chastity was one of many areas in which Chinese and Manchu social attitudes differed at this early point in Qing rule. Another example is the period of mourning for a deceased parent. Three years was standard for the Chinese, but the Manchus found it impractical to spend that length of time in relative inactivity.

be in charge, and all her female servants followed her dictates without a peep. All at once they wanted her to bend her back and knees in front of the prince—it was understandable that she would have none of it and would prefer to die.

The old Manchu lady keenly sensed my meaning. After a few days had passed, the prince suddenly bestowed on my mistress a golden phoenix crown and the gown of a wife of highest official rank.* I said to Mistress Liu, "Since you've received such respectful, formal treatment, you'd best go along. Heaven did not make you so beautiful only to let you sink into loneliness for the rest of your life." Mistress Liu said nothing, but she did accept the crown and gown with her own hands. The old Manchu lady, peeking through a crack in the screen, saw that her attitude had changed. So she had lanterns and colorful decorations hung everywhere, and she had lively music played, making sure that Mistress Liu heard it. Then she seized the hour to approach Mistress Liu again, saying close to her ear, "It's the established practice of our court that whenever a principal consort unfortunately dies and a secondary consort bears a son, it's permissible to memorialize and have the latter declared the succeeding principal consort. The gown presented today is only for a first-rank official's wife, but later there could be more exalted ones."

When night came, the prince was having Mistress Liu guided to his sleeping quarters with an imperially bestowed wax torch when Mistress Liu called the old Manchu lady to her and said, "How could nothing be forgotten except the worshipful expression of gratitude for the emperor's benevolence?" The prince thereupon had the torch placed upright in the middle of the central hall. Mistress Liu stood behind him to the left, and in unison they performed the ritual of nine kowtows. When they reached the prince's bedroom, Mistress Liu removed the gold phoenix crown and the gown of highest rank and performed three bows and three kowtows to the prince before rising. He was pleased that her actions were so fitting—those of a paragon of beautiful and virtuous court ladies.

So that night Mistress Liu bedded with the prince, and the next day he was ecstatic. He rewarded the old Manchu lady with sixty strings of copper cash, and she led the three hundred or more men and women

*That is, the highest rank for the wife of a civil service official, as distinct from a member of the imperial clan or honorary nobility.

who served in the prince's mansion to kowtow and express congratulations to Mistress Liu. The latter took out four hundred taels' worth of silver and distributed it among them in greater and lesser amounts according to their statuses. So everyone in the whole mansion was very happy.

The prince commanded two eunuchs named Chen and Liu—who had served the former [Ming] court and who both were over seventy years old—to follow Mistress Liu's direction. She wrote a letter and ordered Eunuch Liu to deliver it to Zhen in Changshu. Therein she said:

> Your mother's fate has worsened, and she has lost her body to a militarist from the northern regions. This wrong is not of my doing—"I appeal to heaven in asserting my innocence."[5] In my whole life I have never uttered despondent words, but now I must. The shame is unbearable, but I cannot refrain from telling you this.
>
> Mother and child originally are one body; moreover, you alone carry the bloodline of the Huang family. You cannot eschew your responsibility to your parents, so I herewith explain my intention to you: When your father was alive, in truth he scarcely spoke to me, and the private disharmonies between husband and wife in our case surpassed the norm. I cannot say that I am like Gui, the marquise of Xi, who could not cease harboring fond memories of her first husband and bore her self-pity in silence. But hungry were the ghosts of the Ruoao [clan, which was totally extinguished].[6]* [Huang Lianggong] probably feels anger in the grave and cannot close his eyes in repose. Now I think that there would be nothing more fitting than to establish some young man from the Huang lineage to be his male descendant and to set aside ten thousand taels for the long-term sustenance of that line. It would both satisfy the living that they had done all they could and bring peace to the soul of the departed one. Sympathize with my innermost feelings. I sincerely look to you to accomplish this.†

Sir Liu is a court eunuch from the previous dynasty who has joined the

---

*Ghosts that harbor some dissatisfaction from when they were living persons were popularly believed to remain restless. Also, if not "fed" with sacrifices from (male) descendants, they roam in "hungry" or "starved" condition.

†After extensive searches, no suitable or willing male relative could be found. Later, because Zhen bore three sons, her mother persuaded her to give the second and third sons the Huang surname and designate them as Huang Lianggong's descendants, but each boy died after being so designated. In the mind of the author-editor, this confirmed that the Huang lineage was doomed because of its prolonged niggardliness and malfeasance.

prince's banner. Be sure, now, to treat him with special courtesy. When he departs, give him two of the yuanbao I left in your keeping as a parting gift. [Besides expressing thanks,] it will also let him and his fellow eunuchs know that you are not the daughter of a poor and parsimonious family.

The ten eastern pearls can be used by my son-in-law as cap ornaments. When you wear the Beijing-style bracelet, I hope you will look at it as though looking at your mother. I cannot thoroughly express my unsettled feelings to your two uncles [Liu's brothers] or your husband. It's not that I do not want to but that my words would be disgraceful.

Alas, my daughter Zhen, neither now nor hereafter can I live with you again. What else is there to say?

.   .   .

Not long thereafter, the emperor summoned the prince back to the capital. When the prince's entourage reached Jining,* Mistress Liu became nauseated and would vomit as soon as she mounted her carriage. So the prince raised the pennon to halt their procession and ordered the provincial governor to search Shandong for good doctors to treat her. They all said that she was not accustomed to the [more arid northerly] environment and that she should take a purgative to dry her system. When Mistress Liu saw their prescriptions, she tore them up and burned them, excoriating the doctors and calling them wild oxen. The prince didn't understand what she meant and seemed angry. So Mistress Liu forced herself to sit up, holding the coverlet around her, and she pulled on the prince's clothing to get him to sit down on the couch where she'd been lying. Then, stroking his back with her hand, she leaned toward his ear and told him, "My illness is pregnancy, but they want to kill me off with their purgatives!" When the prince heard this, he was delighted and comforted her extravagantly. After a few days Mistress Liu began to feel better and was able to travel again.

When the prince reached the capital and had an imperial audience, Emperor Zhang [the Shunzhi emperor] asked him[17] how it could be that he was forty years old but still had no son. The prince replied that in Jiangnan he had gotten from his banner a woman named Liu, who now was happily with child—it was said to be a boy. Straightaway this was reported to the Imperial Household Department, and before long Mistress Liu indeed had a boy. When the emperor learned this,

*In southwestern Shandong Province on the Grand Canal. See map 3.

he bestowed on the prince a hundred pounds of princely-grade ginseng, and the empress dowager[18] also bestowed a million "coins for washing a baby boy." The prince then showed his respect for precedent by requesting of the emperor that Mistress Liu be officially elevated to the position of Succeeding Principal Consort.[19]

On the empress dowager's birthday Mistress Liu, as the chief consort of a prince, [had the privilege of] leading the wives of lower-ranking Manchu noblemen into the palace to offer congratulations [fig. 12]. As soon as the empress dowager saw Mistress Liu, she said, "I've heard that the succeeding consort of a certain prince is absolutely beautiful. You must be the one! How old are you?" Mistress Liu said that she was thirty-five, and the empress dowager said, "Your face still has a young woman's glow." She asked further about my mistress's place of origin and how she had advanced in life, and Mistress Liu pleased her by replying fully and candidly. When the congratulatory ceremony was over, the empress dowager looked into Mistress Liu's eyes in part-ing and said, "I never thought there were such extraordinary women among the common people." And the next day she presented her with sacrificial-grade fruits, tributary fans, a cake of moxa shaped like a tiger, and other things in praise of her exceptional qualities.

At that time Emperor Zhang was emphasizing the civil service ex-aminations. When the time came in the autumn for another round, he ordered the education officials to present to the prince's mansion copies of the examination papers that had been submitted by students in the National University. A eunuch brought them to Mistress Liu's quar-ters, and when she happened to run her eyes over the names, she saw that of her son-in-law, Qian Shenkun. He had entered the capital as a tribute student to further his learning,[20] but, abiding by Mistress Liu's previous admonition, he had not tried to see her again. Mistress Liu then noted the place of registration and the calligraphy and concluded that there was no mistake. The next time she bedded with the prince, she told him of this. The prince said nothing, but in that examination it turned out that Qian was recognized as most outstanding in the classics category. The following year, having made the B list in the examinations administered by the Ministry of Rites, he was selected to be a middle-level official in a ministry. All this was accomplished behind the scenes by Mistress Liu.

One day Qian visited the prince's residence on official business. The prince ordered the various other officials to withdraw and summoned

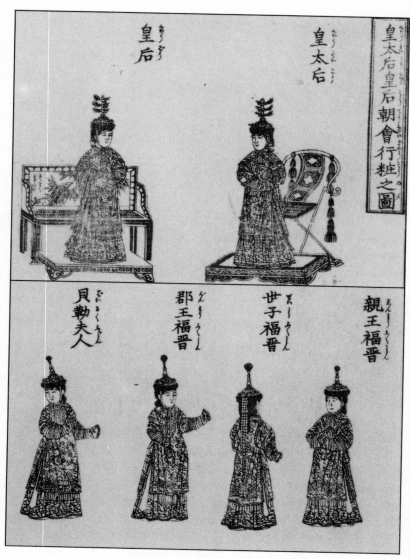

Figure 12. Qing imperial women in formal attire, with the empress dowager and the empress above. If the story of Liu Sanxiu is true, she probably dressed like those pictured in the lower section.

Qian to come forward and meet him. He then asked Qian if he would like to meet yet another person and led him to the inner quarters, where he had Mistress Liu come out. She had taken to wearing Manchu-style clothes—that day a golden brocade gown with an ermine jacket and a headband of red sable. Pearls and jade ornaments covered her head and shone resplendently like bright stars in her glossy hair. She had changed from shoes to boots—tiny, narrow ones in which she took small steps like a goddess walking on waves.

When she saw Qian Shenkun, she flushed with happiness and said, "I've been thinking of Zhen for a long time. Recently I've acquired a house. I want you to take some time off to go home and move your wife and child to Beijing to live. Also, Second Brother* is suffering from diabetes, and I'm afraid the prognosis isn't certain. You could accompany him back to his home in the countryside." So Qian set out homeward with Second Brother, but the latter died on the way. Qian took charge of his funeral and burial in Changshu before bringing Zhen to the capital.

When Mistress Liu and Zhen met, they embraced each other and cried, but before long they were as happy as before. When my mistress would occasionally go over to Zhen's place—wearing Chinese-style clothes—she rode in a lady's carriage accompanied by over a hundred female attendants and shielded within a corridor of curtains all along her route. But after arriving, she took care of household affairs for Zhen as though nothing had changed.

At over forty years of age, Mistress Liu still had a youthful face. Any flower or article of clothing that she wore took on added interest or doubled in charm. She became pregnant again and bore the prince a second son.

---

*He had taken advantage of his sister's high status to gain a lucrative clerical position in the prince's banner administration. First Brother had been bitterly disappointed at his sister's abandonment of widow chastity and eschewed contact with her.

7

"Better to Die at Sea":
Requesting Aid
From Japan

AS NANJING AND THE LOWER Yangzi region fell under Qing control, the next line of resistance for Ming loyalists became Hangzhou Bay and the Qiantang River to the east of Hangzhou. In central Zhejiang Province south of the bay and east of the river, a region traditionally called Eastern Zhe, the heritage of loyalism was especially strong. There in the late summer of 1645 social and political leaders persuaded the Ming Prince of Lu, named Zhu Yihai (1618–62),[1] to head an imperial regency centered in Shaoxing Prefecture. This resistance movement, though ardent, did not interrupt for long the southward march of the Qing armies. In July 1646, Qing cavalry advanced into Eastern Zhe, resistance was crushed in one locale after another, and Regent Lu, along with many of his supporters, was forced into a life of coastal island-hopping from which he never was extricated.[2]

Followers of the court of Regent Lu consequently made up a large percentage of the landlubber scholar-officials whose Ming loyalism cast them into physically and socially uncomfortable cooperation with Chinese maritime freebooters. The latter operated as sea traders, pirates, or legitimized naval personnel as opportunities arose, and the retreat of Ming-loyalist regimes to the southern coastal strip of China allowed them to combine the dispositions of their way of life with the interests of revanchist political leaders. Often such men were familiar with the seafaring elements in southern Japan, the northwest Pacific nexus of what was becoming not just an East Asian but a world maritime trade network. Not surprisingly, the seaborne anti-Qing resistance made several attempts to obtain aid from Japan—especially in the form of the renowned fighting men of that country.[3]

The Japanese shogunal government (*bakufu*) had been disturbed at the rise of Manchu power on the mainland ever since the brief Manchu invasion of Korea in 1627, and many advisers to the third Tokugawa shogun, Iemitsu (r. 1623–51), were not averse to taking military action to thwart the Qing progress in subjugating China.[4] However, by 1649 they had become aware that things were not going well for the Ming-loyalist courts. Other considerations as well disposed them to eschew directly assisting the Ming cause.

First, official relations between China and Japan had not been smooth during most of the Ming period, and tribute missions from the Japanese shogun to the Chinese emperor had ceased in 1549.[5] Thereafter, the considerable trade that had accompanied the official exchanges of tribute and gifts had continued as illicit smuggling and piracy, necessitated and enabled by the Ming government's long-standing but rather porous interdiction of private overseas trade. Raids along the coast from Guang-dong to Shandong by "Japanese pirates" (who were mostly Chinese) had become a major issue in Chinese politics in the latter half of the sixteenth century. Because of the inability of the Japanese to do anything about that activity from their side—by that time they were politically fragmented by civil war—China completely severed relations in 1557.[6] The atmosphere was hardly improved in 1592, when the Japanese hegemonic lord Toyotomi Hideyoshi (1536?–98) had the hubris to embark on a conquest of China by invading Korea, a loyal vassal-state to the Ming. The cost of military aid to the Koreans in repulsing that invasion seriously depleted the Chinese government's treasury reserves.[7] The only state to benefit from this situation was Portugal, which ran a lucrative indirect China-Japan trading business from its colony Macao.[8]

Although the domestic political scene in Japan had stabilized considerably since the restoration of shogunal rule at the beginning of the seventeenth century,[9] there was concern that overseas military adventures, which would involve the mobilization of forces under powerful lords in outlying regions, would destabilize things again—besides contravening prohibitions on Japanese voyages beyond Okinawa or Korea, instituted in the 1630s. These prohibitions were part of a series of measures adopted since the 1620s to restrict and control Japanese intercourse with the outside world; not least among them were bans on proselytizing or subscribing to the Christian religion. Catholicism in particular had become regarded as subversive by the Japanese authorities. Thus, the persistent, close relation between militant Catholicism and the Iberian sea powers had eventually led to the permanent denial of trading rights to the Portuguese, beginning in 1639, and to draconian persecutions of Catholic missionaries and believers in Japan.[10] Of the Europeans, only the Dutch were subsequently allowed to visit the designated foreign-trade entrepôt of Nagasaki, which was directly administered by officials from the shogunal capital, Edo (present-day Tokyo). The Japanese had become extremely sensitive about relations with the continent and with other foreign elements when a mission from the regime of Regent Lu, then based on Zhoushan Island, arrived seeking aid toward the end of 1649.

The circumstances sketched above had never dampened the Japanese desire for Chinese goods, which were still imported indirectly,[11] or Japanese interest in Chinese high culture, the main importers of which had traditionally been Buddhist monks.[12] Indeed, Chinese abbots of Buddhist monasteries in Japan frequently functioned as intermediaries between the Japanese and Chinese governments, and Buddhist writings were always high on the lists of books requested from China by the Japanese. So the idea—advanced by a Chinese monk returned from Japan—of using a set of the Tripitaka as a gift to ingratiate the Lu regime with the Japanese was not so strange as it might seem. Nevertheless, the head of the resulting ineffectual mission from Zhoushan to Nagasaki, the apparent author of the *Fengshi Riben jilue* (Brief Account of an Ambassadorial Mission to Japan),[13] makes his misgivings about the gambit clear, perhaps in retrospective apology for its failure.

In the winter of 1649 a [Chinese] monk named Zhanwei came from Japan and frequented the camp of the Barbarian-Quelling Earl, Ruan Jin.[14] Jin questioned him about conditions in southern Japan and about why previous requests for Japanese soldiers had not been granted. Zhanwei stated that the Japanese would place no value on anything that might be sent as an inducement other than the Buddhist Tripitaka.[15] He said, "If the general could request such from the court and depute an ambassador to present it with an imperial decree, soldiers would arrive immediately."

Jin was pleased and soon advocated asking for the fine copy of the Tripitaka that had been donated by the Xianmu empress, Empress

Dowager Li,[16] to Zhenhai Monastery on Putuo Island [fig. 13] to use as a gift in seeking soldiers from Japan. The Marquis of Dingxi, Zhang Mingzhen, seconded him in writing a joint memorial making this idea known [to the regent], the Prince [of Lu], who said, "It has truly been a prized possession of my imperial ancestors. If by chance the scriptures go but the soldiers don't come, the Tripitaka will have been endangered and resources wasted, amounting to a great loss." But Jin strenuously argued otherwise, so the regent submitted to court deliberation the selection of a talented, capable high minister to be the official ambassador. And he designated Jin's younger brother, Wave-Quelling General Ruan Mei, to second the minister. Everyone said that Minister of Rites Wu Zhongluan was the right man, but Sir Wu declined, citing his advanced age. Next they sought someone among the lesser ministers and together recommended me. That very day I was promoted to the second rank and granted the appropriate robe and sash.

The prince personally gave a banquet to comfort the delegation, and I made inquiries among people who'd been to that outlying country [Japan]. Everyone stuck out his tongue in shock and said, "No one has ever taken the Tripitaka across the seas. How could one allow such a weighty treasure to be lightly imperiled in a trip across ten thousand li of great ocean?" But I was thinking to myself, "If we're unable to make the crossing, it will be a matter of fate. Anyway, it would be better to die at sea than be killed by [Tartar] bandits like others before us. If there's a chance we'll get across and that soldiers will come, then even if it is more dangerous, how could I refuse?"

So on the 1st day of the 11th month [December 4], we departed [from Zhoushan] for Putuo.* Four days later we got under way on a small boat as light as a seagull. A vast expanse lay in all directions. The blue sky and black waters merged, showing no edge to the world. On the morning of the 10th [December 13] an experienced hand told me that he saw in the distance the shape of an island emerging from the clouds and fog, and I felt glad. In the early evening he spoke to me again, saying, "Although the island is close, we don't know which one it is. We know there are some islands in the sea about one day's sail from Nagasaki. Reaching those islands is like having Japan as close as eyebrows and eyelashes."

*Putuo Island, part of the Zhoushan Archipelago off the northeastern coast of Zhejiang Province, is due east of the largest island, called Zhoushan (Boat Island).

Figure 13. The beach at the monastery on Putuo Island.

By that time the weather had turned murkily dark, so even Huo-chang, the head of the recruited crewmen, was confused and couldn't identify the island. All we could do was continue sailing eastward through the night.

Just before three in the morning a strong wind blew up, and by daybreak the island was out of sight. Gigantic waves seemed to come from the sky. Our boat was either lifted and tossed halfway into the air or plunged to the base of a wave. Everyone holed up, unable to move. I saw only three helmsmen doing anything. They had lashed the rudder with a rope and were standing there, making great efforts to keep it wedged between them securely. Toward noon the wind grew even worse; dense clouds and dark rain combined to make morning and evening indistinguishable.

The officer in charge of the ship, Ruan Jin,* invited me out of the cabin to see two red fish darting in and out of the black waves. Surrounding them were large numbers of black and white creatures, fishlike in shape,† now floating up, now submerged in the obscuring clouds and fog. At that time my spirit was disoriented and my eyesight was so dazed that I couldn't scrutinize them. When all those scales and fins appeared, the assembled crewmen bowed and prayed to the fish, anxious to extricate themselves from the border between the [human and watery] realms. They burned two decrees of the Dragon King and hung up two previously prepared gold plaques excusing the fish from paying him court.[7] In just a short while the wind abated and dusk came. The crewmen congratulated each other, saying that if the stormy situation hadn't passed, we would have lost our lives because the boat wouldn't have been able to ride the waves in the cloudy darkness.

Toward morning another island appeared. Huochang looked at it discriminatingly and, much alarmed, said, "This is not the Nagasaki island."‡ Considering that we'd been blown by heavy winds for a day and a night, there's no telling how many thousands of li we were off course. It might even have been the coast of Korea! We made haste to turn the sails and head southward, but all along the way we saw islands that looked pretty much the same. Not until dusk did the crew recognize the passage to the Nagasaki island, and they let the sails fill to enter it.

*The character for the personal name is different from that of the Barbarian-Quelling Earl, mentioned above. The two men were probably related, however.

†Probably orcas.

‡The port of Nagasaki is on a peninsula on the west side of Kyushu.

On the 13th [December 16] we moored [in Nagasaki harbor], and Ruan Mei's boat soon arrived. I asked how dangerous the winds and waves had been for him, and he said, "Not too bad." Then I knew [that the awful storm had hit] my boat because we had the Tripitaka on board.*

According to the regulations of that country, whenever a merchant vessel moored there, a small "on-duty" boat was sent to inquire about nationality, personnel, and cargo. Then another was sent to tie up tightly to the stern of the visiting ship—for "supervision and protection," they said. Soon I ordered our translator to board the Japanese boat and inform them of our purpose, and they responded positively. But later when we mentioned the monk named Zhanwei who was guarding the scriptures, they were flabbergasted and said, "How could that monk have come back? Now that he's come, it's a speedy death for him!" I asked why, and they told me all about Zhanwei's earlier activities.[18] They went on to say it was fortunate that I was an envoy from another country, so I wouldn't be harmed. Otherwise, calamity would befall everyone on the same boat with the monk. I knew the affair was queered, so I just showed them Regent Lu's decree, as I'd intended, and left.

The lord of Nagasaki[19] deliberated on the matter and wanted to keep the scriptures without accepting the decree [that soldiers be sent?].[20] He wished to have me come on shore but was not willing to observe ritual distinctions,† so any meeting was difficult to arrange. And throughout, they resented the presence of Zhanwei. Over the course of three or four days things could not be resolved.

The seven translators tried to negotiate our leaving the scriptures in return for several tens of thousands of taels. But I thought, "How inappropriate to sell the court's imperial possession like a peddler." Moreover, having been unable to fulfill my charge to obtain soldiers, the least I could do was report back with the whole precious set of texts intact. To change my mission from an official one to a mercantile one would have undermined the greater imperial order. So on the 20th

---

*The author apparently regards the storm as cosmic punishment for wrongly moving the Tripitaka. It is possible, however, that he thinks the Dragon King generated the storm in an attempt to seize the Tripitaka for himself.

†This probably means the distinctions between an official representative of the purportedly superior imperial regent of the Central Florescence (China) and the representative of the military overseer (shogun) of an inferior peripheral country (Japan).

[December 23], I decided to return [south]westward with the scriptures. On the 28th [December 31] we were again propelled by strong winds, now to Nantian,* where we were received into Ruan Jin's camp. After I reported on the mission [to the regent, on Zhoushan Island], the scriptures were returned to Putuo.†

In sum, the round-trip took one month, entailing a sea route of over seventeen hundred li. I braved dangers and trod in peril, virtually heedless of intimidation. That the matter ended unsuccessfully was heaven's will.

---

*Nantian, on an island off the Zhejiang coast south of the Zhoushan Archipelago, was a favorite location for freebooters, such as the Ruans, who were supporting Regent Lu's regime.

†The author adds in a postscript that he prevented Ruan from killing Zhanwei, who departed for some remote islands, never to be heard of again.

8

"THIS FOUNDERING OLD HORSE":
A RIGHTEOUS MINISTER'S
LAST CRUSADE

IN THE CONFUSION following the collapse of the Hongguang court in Nanjing, another court—in addition to the rump court of Regent Lu (see Chap. 7)—was established by the Prince of Tang (with the reign title Longwu) at another temporary capital, Fuzhou in Fujian Province. The most prestigious official to participate in the formation of the Longwu regime was the Fujian native Huang Daozhou (1585–1646), who was quickly given the most important civil-bureaucratic positions.[1]

Huang was widely respected as a prolific classicist and magnetic teacher, but his political fame derived from the leadership he had exercised in the Eastern Grove (Donglin) political reform movement; and after that "party" was destroyed in the late 1620s, he had become the special hero of a younger generation of reformers who identified with the Restoration Society (Fushe).[2] The hallmark of the Donglin and Fushe activists was a moral stridency, a determination to "throw the rascals out" and attain good government by securing appointments for good men. Conflicts with individual officials and factions outside the reformers' ranks were often sharp, sometimes deadly. And the late-Ming emperors all found exasperating the constant criticisms by the "righteous elements." Huang himself had been ignored, demoted, imprisoned, and banished for his pertinacity. Especially virulent had been his attacks on factional enemies in charge of the Chongzhen emperor's military programs for dealing with the roving rebels and the Manchus in the late 1630s. Although he had been summoned to high position in the Hongguang court at Nanjing, Huang had found equally repugnant there the alliance between unsavory bureaucrats and self-serving militarists, and he had taken leave of that situation in March 1645.

The Longwu regime presented a combination of elements that were certain to stir the ardor and indignation of Huang Daozhou, then a vigorous gray eminence in his sixtieth year: the Ming dynasty in imminent danger of extinction, the expectations of his fellow provincials, a ruler with whom he felt deep rapport, and actual power in the hands of militarists whose legitimacy and motivations were questionable. The Prince of Tang (1602–46), who ascended the imperial throne in Fuzhou and declared the beginning of the Longwu reign on August 18, 1645, was, like Huang Daozhou, a devoted scholar and veteran crusader. His proposals and actions to change the debilitating conditions of the Ming imperial princes had earned him disapproval and imprisonment during the Chongzhen reign.[3] Now he saw his chance to play a crucial role, and he looked to Huang Daozhou for supportive leadership.

Both the emperor and Huang were hampered, however, by the fact that the preponderant naval and land-based military power in Fujian lay in the hands of the powerful Zheng family, headed at that time by Zheng Zhilong (1604–61) and his younger brother, Zheng Hongkui (d. 1657).[4] To a certain extent, the Zhengs welcomed the establishment of the Longwu court in their home territory as a means of augmenting their power. Zheng Zhilong, his relatives, and his associates were immediately elevated in positions, ranks, and official prerogatives—which naturally expanded their unofficial prerogatives. But when it came to sacrificing the resources of the Zheng organization to carry the restorationist cause of the Longwu court out of Fujian and back into the political heartland of China, the Zhengs demurred, sometimes citing unfavorable conditions but also making excuses for inaction.

Huang Daozhou shared the eagerness of the Longwu emperor to reestablish the court in a less remote location than Fuzhou. Immediately upon his arrival in Fuzhou, Huang and the emperor began planning to launch a campaign back "out the passes." Cognizant of the need to open the way for such a campaign and of the foot-dragging already evident in the military establishment, Huang set out on his own advance campaign within two and a half weeks of his arrival in Fuzhou (map 5). With almost no funds, supplies, or men and with absolutely no experience in such undertakings, Huang relied idealistically on the

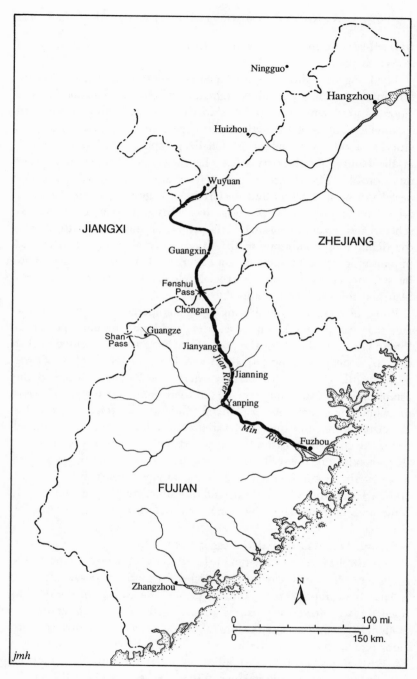

Map 5. Huang Daozhou's Last Crusade

presumed spontaneous response of the people to his righteous promotion of a sincere cause.

Translated below is a series of memorials that Huang submitted to the throne in connection with this campaign. They constitute a diary of the struggle to maintain the optimism and faith in human nature that were characteristic of Confucian scholars, like Huang, in the face of hard realities and perfidies of the sort dealt with regularly by military men.[5] Although Huang is quick to concede his lack of generalship, his experiences do not lead him to greater respect for men whose business is the application of brute force—much less to an admission that the military leaders in Fuzhou (that is, the Zhengs) are justified in their caution. His disparagement of militarists, typical of civil officials since the middle Ming period, and his preferred reliance on the force of human will and spirit in the face of peril, typical of Confucian reformers in any period, remain unchanged.

Distinguishing a man of Huang Daozhou's high scholar-official status from even moderately well-educated ordinary people is his vividly historical worldview. Unlike others who, when faced with an emergency, think first about the safety and well-being of family members and friends,* men like Huang immediately surround themselves mentally with figures from analogous situations in China's past and draw lessons and inspiration from them. The classics and histories provide meaning even to defeat.

FIRST MEMORIAL MAKING A PERSONAL REQUEST TO PROCEED TO THE BORDER

7th month [early September, at Fuzhou]

This servant respectfully submits that heaven's punishment [of the Qing] cannot long be deferred and that the policy of closed passes will prove interminable. He begs to personally proceed ahead to the border

*Note the contrast between Shi Kefa's concern for his portrait in history and Wang Xiuchu's concern for his family members, in Chapter 2. In this respect Huang Daozhou's attitude can be compared to that of Yao Wenxi in Chapter 4 or to that of the old man in Chapter 5.

[of Fujian and Jiangxi] to project the greater righteousness and rouse the spirits of the masses.

This servant has observed that since primordial times no state-founding ruler or minister has been content to stay within [a secure base area]. Our Great Founder [of the Ming] was groomed by wind and rain for seventeen years.[6] The Guangwu emperor [founder of the Later Han], relied on the merits of his ancestors in the previous [Han] era to gather clouds of supporters with a single rallying cry. But he still had to rush about for four years, too occupied to take a respite.[7] [His follower] Deng Yu, though a solitary student, spent morning and night mapping strategy in a tent, and he further asked that twenty thousand men be separately placed under his command so he could represent his leader in entering [Tong] Pass.[8] He campaigned westward into Hedong,* surrounded the city of Anyi, and carried on in the field for another full year. How could less-than-mediocre people like this servant shirk such duty? Today all under heaven is our territory, and both sides of the Great [Yangzi] River are of the imperial house.[†] It is regrettable that people there have followed one another in fearful avoidance of harm and offered themselves up obeisantly to the enemy. Han Huaiyin once said, "People's hearts become set over time and are hard to move."[9] This servant, however, fears that if moved after a long time, they will be hard to settle again. . . .

Although this servant has grown old and has no special qualities, his minor reputation does have some currency on people's lips. On both sides of the Great River, they have considerable trust in his words. He laments being unable to cooperate with Deng Zhi, who went downriver to the lower Yangzi region to gather great heroes.[10] If this servant were to make a great deal of his own prowess in evincing eagerness to depart, then in death he surely would be laughed at by Ma Yuan.[11]

Now the imperially sealed order has been issued, but the campaign has not proceeded more than a hundred *li*.[‡] No one near or far

*The southern part of present-day Shanxi Province.

†Literally, to the "left" and "right" of the Great River, referring to the territories of present-day Jiangsu and Jiangxi provinces, respectively.

‡On September 1, three days after he formally assumed the throne as the Longwu emperor, Zhu Yujian left to lead a campaign back across the passes out of Fujian. He had proceeded only to a transport station on the Min River near Fuzhou, however, before

knows what the court is doing. This servant, too, remains securely behind his screens and blinds, with none so accomplished as those at Kunyang to herald his advance nor any so meritorious as those in Hebei to look after the rear.[12] If we sojourn here for months, the world will sneer at us, saying that ruler and ministers are fecklessly content in the South, on a par with Langya or Yizhou.[13] This will add to doubt and confusion on both sides of the Great River.

The court has just been established, and neither organization nor plans are complete, so perhaps our great troops cannot go forth immediately. But the region of Guangze, Chongan, Pucheng, and Zhenghe has four passes and several dozen routes that twist and turn for several thousand li. This servant cannot but traverse them day by day to note strategic points and to obtain the goodwill of the local people. As for the length, depth, or narrowness of those passages, we have never paced out any of them. Moreover, the people's hearts have been disrupted, the imperial design is not yet pervasive, and the militarists cannot be depended on for a strong defense.

Of old, Deng Yu was talented at rallying comrades but lacked control; he was good at laying plans but poor in responding to changes. Still, he would step down from his carriage wherever he went so that old and young could take pleasure in meeting him. Hence, the men of whole counties and commanderies looked to him as toward the wind and came with their families in hand. What need is there for people to harbor the sincerity of Cen Peng when he cast off his sword in submission[14] or to receive collective reports of such ardor as that of the commander who excised his intestines?[15]

MEMORIAL DISSUADING THE EMPEROR FROM
PERSONALLY LEADING A CAMPAIGN

8th month [September–October]

Imperially commanded to summon the loyal and attack the invaders in the provinces and in directly administered regions, with plenipo-

---

he was blocked by local leaders who begged him not to act hastily. Only ten days before, he had proclaimed that he would lead such a campaign beginning in the middle of the eighth month (October 5–7).

tentiary authority to coordinate the restoration of Nanjing and places north of the Yangzi River, Junior Guardian and Grand Preceptor of the Heir Apparent, Minister of Personnel and War, and Grand Secretary of the Wuying Hall, Huang Daozhou respectfully submits that since people's hearts are easily disturbed but hard to quiet and the nation's government should have weight for stability, it is greatly hoped that the Imperial Carriage* remain in a secure and definite place [Fuzhou] to calm people's hearts and solidify heaven's command. . . .

The Throne is godlike in perspicacity, with vision that reaches as far as ten thousand li. The Emperor's strategic plans to shake the realm truly are not this benighted person's to know. However, from this servant's vantage, the outlying areas are exhausted, and any sense of collectivity is gone. The people regard their ruler lightly, and subordinates reject their superiors. Things look half gone, without any vital cohesion. This servant embarked on a military mission with no supplies twenty days ago. He has asked in every locale but has not received a single arrowhead, piece of armor, knife, or soldier. Donations from gentry families do not suffice to supply a thousand men for one month. The weakness of our momentum can roughly be known from these manifest conditions. The Throne, being kind and warmhearted [toward taxpayers], is restrained in spending. Even assuming frugality, however, it is very difficult to contemplate providing the necessary attendants, bridges, boats, carriages, and lodgings or raising donations for meals and escorts along the Imperial Steeds' itinerary.

In times past, Emperor Wen of the Han dynasty [r. 180–157 B.C.] wanted to go to Bazhou [in Shaanxi to deal with the Xiongnu], and Emperor Guangwu wanted to lead campaigns against [the Qiang tribes] in western Shaanxi and Sichuan. But their close advisers risked impertinence [to oppose those moves], and everyone thought to "cut the carriage couplings." Now the danger is greater and the situation more dire than in those times or places. Among the group of high and mighty ministers at court, how is it that none has acted to halt the Emperor's departure?

.   .   .

*This, as well as "Dragon Carriage," is an indirect, respectful way to refer to the emperor and his immediate party.

This servant has now been on the Jian River at Yanping for ten days, bogged down in heavy rains and unable to proceed through Shan Pass. But it is probable that all the gentry families and better commoners of the two counties surrounding Shan Pass have already scattered in fright. Moreover, the two bandits Wang [Deren] and Jin [Shenghuan] have occupied northeastern Jiangxi.* Were this servant to throw his solitary self into their midst, it would be impossible to call up patriots or punish invaders, even if he could "grapple bare-handed with tigers and cross rivers with no boat."[16]

.   .   .

Rather, this servant has decided to go out the middle route to join others in Huizhou,† though such would never be attempted even by those who *do* brave tigers and rivers. This servant is small and lowly. How dare he compare himself with men of the past or even with chief ministers of recent times? The latter have put forth larger armies of over 200,000 and smaller ones of 30,000–50,000; the former advanced larger armies of 30,000 and smaller ones of 7,000–8,000. Now, this servant has with him only three or five minor-degree holders who wish to go out on the trail of ravenous beasts with just the insignia and the 2,600 or more taels that were granted to this servant by the Throne. With more than 200 housemen brought by my sons and nephews and 800–900 men recruited in Yanping and Jianning, one morning's provisions used up that money as if it were spit in the hands. This servant truly has not received one iota of supplies from the Ministry of Revenues, nor has the Ministry of War provided one lone soldier, nor has the armory helped with one item of weaponry or one grain of gunpowder. When this servant's project goes well, it is hindered by forces inside and outside the court; when it does not go well, those same forces mock it. Hindrance and mockery are the same in effect.

But this servant carries on. He cannot allow the universe of exalted emperors to be defiled by [the stinking barbarians].‡ The

---

*See *SM*, pp. 125–26. Huang refers to these former Ming generals as bandits because they have turned coat and are serving the Qing.

†The prefecture at the far southern tip of South Zhili. The former prefectural seat is present-day Xi County in the southernmost part of Anhui Province. See map 5.

‡Numerous written characters in the text, presumably pejorative references to the

830-year span of the Great Ming has not yet ended.* It is just that this extremely ignorant and benighted person has become mired in circumstances from which he cannot honorably escape.[17] It is said that no one knows officials as well as their ruler does. Now the caliber of the other ministers cannot be hidden from the Throne. The Throne is more courageous and wise than Shang Tang or King Wu,[†] but men as talented as [their respective councillors] Yi Yin and Lü Shang have not appeared again through the ages.

In his own estimation this servant is as far as possible below mediocrity—both pen and tongue are frayed. Unsuccessful at escaping his fate in mountain caves, he later fled into the ranks of the military. If unsuccessful in the latter, he should go back to the former. He wishes only that the Throne take every care, be calm for reinforcement, and be generously tolerant in affairs. Suspend the imperial procession out of the capital [Fuzhou] to nurture auspiciousness for the Palace Occupant. This servant, holding firm to his duty, pushes onward. Whenever there is a slight positive development, he will report it promptly. . . .

MEMORIAL REPORTING ACCURATELY ON THE IMMINENT ADVANCEMENT OF TROOPS

9th month [October–November]

. . . In the latter part of the 8th month, when this servant intended to go out [Shan] Pass, his troops barely numbered two thousand, and we also encountered a foul seasonal ether. Diseases from overexposure to both cold and heat have spread, so six or seven men in every platoon are incapacitated at any given time. This servant has prayed to the gods with a chaste heart and provided doctors

---

Manchus or the Qing dynasty, have been blackened out. Such censorship is very common in writings from the late Ming period and the conquest period that were published under Qing rule. In this translation, guesses as to the original terms are bracketed.

*Liu Ji (Liu Chi, 1311–75), the most respected adviser to the Ming founder, Zhu Yuanzhang, and a noted prognosticator, was thought to have predicted for Zhu that the Ming dynasty would last 830 years. On Liu, see *DMB*, I:932–38.

†Founders of the idealized Shang (circa 1700–1045 B.C.) and Zhou (circa 1045–256 B.C.) dynasties.

and medicines, but the pestilence remains uncured. Moreover, it is worst among the crack troops under my nephew, Ziyuan, and my grandnephew, Bao. For this reason we have hesitated and, for the time being, have camped on the Jian River to await additional troops being brought by various disciples. . . .

On the 6th day of the 8th month [September 25], when this servant was able to see the Sage Edict, he sighed with emotion while respectfully reading its contents, knowing the Throne's deep concern for him, strong sympathy for subordinates, judiciousness in deliberating affairs, and care in planning for the nation. During the past forty days just looking upon that edict has been, for this servant, like breaking through clouds and smoke to gaze at the blue sky. But this servant is most doltishly ineffectual and unversed in military affairs. He strives in this manner to requite one who understands him above and to rouse strangers on the road below, epitomizing what is called the [naive but sincere] "scholar who cannot forget his country."

.   .   .

In the past month, morning and night, reclining or standing, this servant has wanted to advance his troops to join others at Huizhou. But rice in Huizhou Prefecture has become three times more expensive than before, and Lin Zhen and the other officials there have been suasively pleading for aid from us. How can this servant ask for the dying efforts of multitudes of poorly armed soldiers? The Northwest is good territory for carriages, the Southeast for boats. On flat plains they use horses; only on marshy shores do they go on foot. This servant alone has to make his troops walk all the way from his home in Zhangzhou to Xin'an [Huizhou]—perhaps three thousand li—up high ravines and across steep ranges, their bloody heels visible the while. This servant truly cannot use soldiers weakened by illness to drive out formidable wielders of spears and swords. We must force ourselves to hold back for a short time and plan for complete victory. . . .

At present the troops under this servant's command number 3,600 and are divided into ten battalions of 360 men each. In addition, there are 24 [ten-man] patrols—altogether 3,840 troops.

Those recruited by this servant constitute one-third; the other two-thirds are men brought by his sons, brothers, and maternal relatives. Surely they have not come merely in response to the leadership and rallying cries [of their family members and superiors]. Beyond that is their determination not to discard honor toward their Ruler-Father, not to let the demarcation between [barbarians and Chinese] vanish. Each man, holding his bedroll, has risen up for the Throne.

.   .   .

As this servant was drafting the present memorial, a messenger arrived from Huizhou saying that Jing County has been penetrated [by the Qing] and that the whereabouts of Yin Minxing of the Bureau of Operations, Ministry of War, is not known. In consoling the messenger this official found himself shedding tears [fig. 14]. . . . He had always considered Huizhou and Ningguo prefectures to be the keys to restoration. Now that things have taken this turn, our routes are almost closed. There's only Yuhang to Lin'an [Hangzhou] to Guangde to Lishui to [Nanjing]. . . .

MEMORIAL RESPECTFULLY REPORTING
THE DATE OF EXIT THROUGH [FENSHUI] PASS
AND BRIEFLY STATING THE ACTUAL
CONDITION OF THE ARMY

9th month [November]

. . . It has been thirty-six days since this servant took leave of the court; thinking of the Imperial Gate makes him anxious at heart. Of the thirteen letters that were sent to gentry figures in Western and Eastern Zhejiang, the nine sent to Jiangxi, and the eight sent to Huizhou via thirteen or fourteen deputies, none has been answered. We do not know why the routes of communication have become blocked like this. Since the 7th month this servant has sent out seventy-six letters broadcasting the sound of imperial virtue to make contact with men of worth and means. But all the letters have vanished and have elicited no replies, giving this ser-

Figure 14. "Hearing of the Alarm at Jining," a patriotic poem in the original calligraphy of Huang Daozhou. It probably was written in 1640 to express Huang's outrage at the ineffectuality of his factional enemies in protecting Shandong Province from raids by Manchu and roving rebel armies. Not to be found in any Qing-period collections of Huang's writings, this expression of ardent Ming loyalism perhaps survived only through early removal to Japan.

vant much cause for trepidation. Words uttered in distress are not believed; calls by inferior people have little effect. Consequently this servant, concerned from a distance about the Imperial Carriage, has been reluctant to get under way.

.   .   .

This servant sits counting desperately on his fingers. Thanks to the magistrate of Jianyang, Shi Ju, who raised 2,193 taels from the iron levy, land tax, and delivery fees in response to our sudden arrival, we are not worried about empty coffers. It was all due to the overspreading example of the Sage Virtue, which Longwu officials, high and low, have emulated—not, as some might say, due to any opportune appearance of good fortune from heaven.

Besides that, the mustering of righteous troops by local leaders has been endless. They have come not to our call but spontaneously, nor would they go away if so directed. One can assess their resources by observing that, for every soldier whom [they got to] leave his home to join up, the leaders were able to spend only three or four taels to settle his dependents and buy clothing and armor. Paying six hundred to seven hundred taels to recruit two hundred men exhausted their will and strength completely. Beyond that, for monthly grain rations we must burden the Ministry of Revenue. The monthly ration for one soldier costs 1.5 taels. This does not include special provisions for the generals or expenses for corvée laborers, bearers, or runners. This servant's 3,600 men cost 4,500 taels per month, apart from expenses in settling their dependents and buying clothes and armor.

In his sixty years of life this servant has never stooped to calculating expenses, and he has sworn not to allow this sort of thing to trouble the Emperor's thoughts late into the night. But if this servant were not forthright about this reality, then he would deserve to be reported to the Founder of Agriculture for slipshod cultivation of the fields.[18] This servant owns not one plot of land nor a single building. Fortunately this [lack of concern for material possessions] has earned the sympathy of his ruler and the confidence of his relatives and friends. But he cannot expect it to earn him pardon from dogs, pigs, and wolfish beasts [that is, the Qing].

.   .   .

Until the 26th day [November 13, when Huang's advance guard proceeded across the pass], the sweltering heat did not abate; foul waters flowed down from all directions as this servant and his troops were passing from Yanping through Jianning. Being thirsty, the troops were allowed to drink, whereupon an average of eight or nine men in each platoon became ill. One day this servant's nephew, Ziyuan, went to lead drills and found that half the men in his ten platoons could not get up. Subsequently we lost our robust general Chen Boyu to the illness. To think that his heroic strategies, nine-of-ten-hits marksmanship, and thousand-pound strength were done in by a basin of water! Looking around at the corpses, how could one not have been grief-stricken?

Now that things have returned somewhat to normal, the men are forcing themselves to look more spirited in this servant's presence and are urging him to lead the full army out the pass. Surely our Sage Ruler must see the Ming imperial tombs,* the Central Plain must be recovered, the [Manchu barbarians] must never be served, and loyal obedience must never be forsaken. . . .

MEMORIAL ON FOUR MATTERS CAUSING RELUCTANCE

. . . On the 1st day of the 10th month [November 18] this servant reached Guangxin, which is not more than seven days from Huizhou. Estimating the time it would take the army to travel the distance if they moved in a continuous, orderly fashion at the very slowest pace, I calculate that it would be less than twenty days before we could join forces with Jin Sheng and Lin Zhen. Thereafter, we could plan with them for further advances. . . . But in the Huizhou-Ningguo region rice is dear, and it would be difficult to transport it from Raozhou [to the west] or Zhejiang [to the east]. The troops under certain other ministers all eat rice costing .06 to .10 tael per day, but those under this servant's command eat at most .04 tael's worth per day. They see this discrepancy, and altercations become a problem. Moreover, there are those at court who resist this servant's efforts more strongly than they resist the enemy and who hinder him more thoroughly than they thwart the bandits.

This servant was about to proceed to Xincheng when a distur-

*Located about twenty-six miles north of Beijing. See Ann Paludan, *The Ming Imperial Tombs* (New Haven: Yale University Press, 1981).

bance occurred in Xincheng; he was about to proceed to Guixi when a disturbance occurred there.* For every individual who reports a success, one hundred households remain silent. Just as this servant was setting out for Huizhou, reports that Huizhou had succumbed began to arrive four or five times a day. If those officials at court really are obstructing this servant in order to love and protect him, then how can their love be so deep but their statesmanship so careless?

This servant rates his own talent as meager—short on knowledge but long on plans, of a small strength incommensurate with a heavy task—and he truly fears that one day he will incompetently over-turn the cauldrons of state and become an embarrassment to every-one. But the virtuous Throne, acting in concert with the various leaders of the country, and with the wisdom of Shen Nong or Yu[19] and the force of Shang Tang or King Wu, delegated the exercise of a generalship to this servant. He is like a blade with no force of its own, only that of whoever wields it.

Before this servant arrived in Guangxin, the people, young and old, had run away, alarmed by every sound of the wind or the cranes. Although Governor Xu Shiyin had done what he could to summon them back, it was like calling out in the middle of a swamp. Only after we arrived did the many shops reopen and the peddlers gather again. But reports from Huizhou arrived, leading this servant to sigh that numbers of soldiers cannot compensate for poor tactics and that physical strength is worth little without virtue. With its wealth and its strategic advantages of mountains and streams, Huizhou held out for three months, the enemy not daring to approach. But [the resistance leaders] had demanded supplies too harshly, so the gentry's loyalty became doubtful, and the [Manchu barbarians] plucked the prefecture clean with just a few horsemen. How much more would it be the case with someone as destitute and alien to the people as this servant?

Although this servant's whip is long, it cannot reach across three thousand li to hold Huizhou.† Still, rather than try to save Wuhui [Suzhou] with an empty bowstring, it would be better to rescue

---

*Locales in northeastern Jiangxi, outside the Shan and Yunji passes, respectively.

†An allusion to a phrase in the *Tso Commentary* to the *Spring and Autumn Annals (Chunqiu)* that means "something beyond one's powers." See James Legge, trans., *The Chinese Classics*, vol. 5 (rpt., Taipei: Jinxue shuju, 1969), p. 327.

Huizhou with a weak one. If Huizhou can be preserved, then the root and stem of Jiangnan and Fujian will not wither. If Huizhou is lost, then the spirit linking the Yangzi delta with Fujian will not stay. . . . If the messages from Huizhou are true, then the efforts that this servant has made to coordinate resistance in the past sixty days will all have been in vain. . . .

MEMORIAL AGAIN EXPLAINING CONDITIONS OUTSIDE THE PASSES THAT BEAR ON TACTICAL DECISIONS

[Late in the 10th month, from Guangxin]

. . . This servant has thought to himself about the soldiers and officers barely making do from day to night. He has only monthly rations and official certificates of rank with which to rouse and encourage them. The monthly rations that he can offer run from 1 to 1.3 taels' worth at maximum; the official certificates are only for deputy station guard or at most a major's adjutant. The troops are ill and medicines are in short supply, so many end up dying.

When local heroes from Huizhou come to see this servant and find that he can give them positions only as captains' aides, they look at each other in dismay, throw the certificates on the ground, and leave, saying, "We'll go see an enlightened ruler and get titles as high nobles. Even appointments as vice regional commanders would be temporary." This servant can only self-deprecatingly acknowledge their words. According to precedent, when grand secretaries and board ministers function as field commanders [as Huang was doing at that time], their adjutants or pennant leaders carry the rank of full vice regional commander. The unwillingness of this servant, poor and miserly, to make men lieutenant-colonels is really a reluctance to see noble titles given for no merit, as though [conferring official positions on simpletons who present] squashes and fruits.[20] If that means being disparaged by the aristocratic heroes [at court], then fine—sincerely so.

As for military action, sizing up both the enemy and ourselves, it will be absolutely necessary to have 36,000 men. . . . With only 4,000 sickly soldiers and half a month's grain supply, this servant would not dare to make directly for the outskirts of Nanjing. But neither could he bear to act like the muddle-headed, do-nothing, obstructionist, self-protective high officials and military nobles [at court]. . . .

MEMORIAL ON CONDITIONS FOR RESTORING WUYUAN

. . . The considerable casualties that we inflicted in a successful battle on the route from Badu to Cow's Head Mountain on the 14th day of this [10th] month [December 1] have already been reported. . . . This has somewhat strengthened our position. The various generals following up on that victory have proceeded directly to Wuyuan and deployed their troops near the [Wu] River. . . .

This servant again has sternly announced the words of the Sage Edict against killing civilians caught in hostilities. But such civilians are contrarily used by the enemy to deceive our troops and lure them into ambushes. . . . When our troops are beaten, it is because they covet the enemy's horses; instead of hacking at the horses to bring the riders down, they hack at the [mounted barbarians], who shoot them with short arrows that are deadly within thirty paces. All the soldiers from Zhangzhou are able to fend off such arrows with their thick sleeping quilts and therefore often win. But the troops from Yanping and Jianning, relying on their firearms, have nothing with which to cover themselves, so they are defeated. . . . Now, this servant, being a general himself, is remiss for deputing troops two hundred li away and not personally treading among them to brave the arrows and stones. Moreover, he has no means to administer either handsome rewards or strict punishments and can only make cold, deprived soldiers face the enemy. . . .

In this servant's mind, Wuyuan is the shoulders and back of Guangxin, having high walls, deep moats, and a self-sufficiency of grains. Huizhou, however, lacks grain and must rely on Wuyuan for its security in this respect . . . . So this servant will again depute generals to show our flag in Wuyuan. If it can be subdued, then we will subdue it. If not, rather than enter into a standoff across firm walls, it would be better for our forces to leave and make for Huizhou. . . .

MEMORIAL FURTHER REPORTING ON CONDITIONS

[11th month, from Guangxin]

... If the enemy is bent on coming, it surely will be along the indirect route they used before—from Cow's Head Mountain to Badu and straight onto the back of Guangxin Prefecture, [at a point] less than sixty li from [here], Guangxin [the prefectural seat]. Both the newer and older troops trained by Governor Xu Shiyin cannot number more than one thousand; combined with this servant's, we have somewhat more than two thousand men. . . . But no aid comes from any direction as we vainly prepare to strike this [barbarian horde] with bare bowstrings. Although a few forces under various other ministers now are on their way, by rough estimate they are thirty days behind us. If this servant kept his isolated army exposed for thirty days, then every form of behavior would appear. The troops would just become disrupted by others, give up the cause, and head back.

The story goes that a bumpkin of infirm health impatiently abandoned his lame horse and went on foot. But he was beset by illness and fatigue after going less than ten li, whereupon the lame horse raised its head to the sky and laughed. Today this servant is the butt of lame-horse laughter. Nevertheless, he still wishes with naive bravado[21] to make greater righteousness known between heaven and earth.

Both of this servant's columns of troops, small in numbers and on separate routes, reported casualties on the 6th day [December 23]—another hundred men lost. This servant thinks that with one tael per month for food, they will not disturb one rice plant or piece of armament among the people. But should they on foot encounter several hundred ironclad horsemen, they would be overrun and completely destroyed. That would be this servant's fault for sitting in a room inside city walls and not braving arrows or stones at the front. This servant requests to take the blame for his generals and soldiers and to be stripped of office while confined on a coarse mat, awaiting the ax.

Guangxin being in peril, standing alone and lacking succor, would that the Emperor take thought for this foundering old horse and, with vast magnanimity, give recompense for his long service by letting him go back to the mountains for retirement. Then he and his parents in the netherworld would be moved to tears without end.

[Huang proceeded to his troops' forward position and was captured by a Qing unit about ten li from Wuyuan on February 9, 1646. He was executed in Nanjing on April 20 after refusing solid food the whole time since his capture.][22]

9

BLIND, SICK, AND GRIEVED:

A QING VICEROY

"PLEADS FOR HEAVENLY MERCY"

THE OFFICIAL ON THE QING side who was responsible for carrying out the decision to execute Huang Daozhou was the viceroy of Jiangnan, Hong Chengchou (1593–1665), a man whose name has become virtually synonymous with *turncoat* in China.¹ For a portrait, see figure 15. In 1642, while serving as the Ming viceroy in charge of repulsing Manchu expansion into the strategically crucial area west of the Liao River, Hong was captured after a long siege at Songshan. The Ming court at first thought that Hong had been killed, and ordered that sacrifices be held at specially constructed memorial shrines to extol his service and self-sacrifice. But later it was learned that he was alive and cooperating with the Manchus. One of the most enduring bits of conquest-period apocrypha is that when Hong addressed Huang Daozhou, hoping to persuade him to accept Qing authority, Huang derisively refused to acknowledge the identity of his captor, saying that the only Hong Chengchou he knew had died patriotically at Songshan. Juxtaposing Hong as the "black-hat" arch traitor with Huang as the "white-hat" arch loyalist obscures more interesting grounds for comparison between the two men.

Both came from respected scholarly families in southern Fujian. Broadly and classically educated, they both advanced steadily up the hierarchy of Ming civil service examinations. Hong Chengchou, however, evinced a strong interest in civil and military administration from an early stage in his learning. He consistently avoided entanglement in the factional type of warfare—with its abstractly moralistic, rhetorical ammunition—that so troubled the late Ming government. Unlike

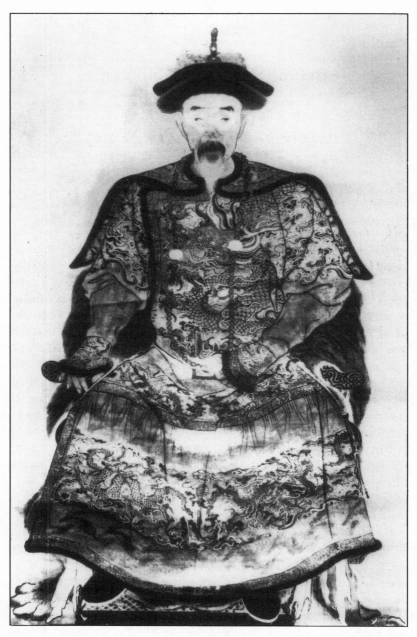

Figure 15. A gaunt and unseeing Hong Chengchou in formal viceroy's dress.

Huang Daozhou, whose more idealistic bent led him into scholarly and educational posts and into repeated dismissals and demotions for his censoriousness, Hong made his career in directing the suppression of large-scale rebellions, particularly in the harsh environment of Shaanxi Province.[2] Hong's comprehensive view of the social, economic, and military aspects of pacification, his learned yet realistic approach, his extraordinary diligence, attention to detail, and completely candid reporting, his reputation for objectivity and incorruptibility, and his successes in the field despite chronic shortages of funds, supplies, and trained personnel had earned him the emperor's respect and regular promotions. Although both Hong and Huang regretted the appointment of Yang Sichang (1588–1641) as minister of war in 1637,[3] Hong worked quietly from within to mitigate the effects of Yang's unrealistic policies, whereas Huang, a prominent adherent of the Donglin reform faction, reviled Yang from outside the government. Both men saw themselves as conscientious servants of their country, but in different ways.

The precise reasons why a man of Hong's probity decided to serve the enemy of the Ming remain shrouded, perhaps permanently, in the past.[4] As a specialist in military affairs seasoned by much field experience, Hong was probably frustrated with the unwise, ill-informed, factionally motivated orders that often came down from the Ming court, nullifying the hard-won progress made by dedicated men at the front. In fact, yet another demand for immediate offensive action and quick successes, heedless of supply problems or more subtle strategies, had resulted in Hong's predicament at Songshan.

In any case, Hong found ample room for the exercise of his talents under the Manchus. His intimate knowledge of both the roving rebel and the Ming armies, his experience in coordinating complex campaigns within China, and his keen judgment in assessing and employing other men—these were great assets on the military side of the "great enterprise" of conquest. His familiarity with government structures that were efficient and suitable for China and with the sorts of propaganda that would play well to Chinese ears, together with his ability to persuade both generals and scholar-officials (except Huang Daozhou) to join the Qing side, all were extremely important in helping a small coalition of mounted warriors from the northeastern frontier to establish a lasting order over the whole East Asian subcontinent.

The Qing leadership relied heavily on Hong Chengchou, especially in the complex and delicate task of subjugating the South, and rewarded him generously for his services while on duty. But Hong could not have been unaware of his secondary status in relation to the Manchu nobility, or of the precarious situation of a surrendered servitor who had held another allegiance before and who had many acquaintances among Ming loyalists. The likelihood that he would be rudely dispensed with should his usefulness to the Qing be reduced by errors in performance, physical incapacity, or suspicion that his devotion to duty was not pure surely bore on his mind when he wrote the memorials translated below.[5] His obsequious tone in addressing the Qing emperor and prince regent goes beyond the normal expectation in memorials from officials of his rank in the late imperial era and probably reflects the insecurity of his situation. Although Hong was eventually able to conclude his career successfully, neither he nor his family members were in any position to object to the slighting public recognition accorded to him by the Qing court at his retirement, at his death, or in later official historiography.

Viceroy of Military Operations and Supply Management, Imperially Assigned to Summon and Soothe in Various Areas of Jiangnan and Other Provinces; Palace Academician; Grand Guardian of the Heir Apparent; and Minister of War with Concurrent Appointment as Junior Vice Censor-in-Chief, Hong Chengchou respectfully reports that this insignificant servant's right eye is diseased,* so he is temporarily handling affairs in his personal office. He prudently wishes to set forth this subordinate's thoughts, and he looks upward, praying for the Sage [Emperor]'s supervisory opinion.

It has been one and a half years since this official was overspread by the Sage benevolence and specially ordered to summon [allegiance] and soothe [the submissive] in the South. His talent and intelligence being short and shallow, he has surely made many careless errors. He reflects often on the heavy responsibilities given by the Emperor and on the immense favor that he has received

*The loss of vision described below was probably due to senile cataracts, and it may have been exacerbated by retinal detachment in the right eye.

from the Imperial Uncle, the Prince Regent.* As though walking on ice, he does not dare let himself relax for a moment. But this official twice served as a viceroy during the previous dynasty. For over ten years he was continually fraught with the numerous exigencies of army operations, and his acumen was already exhausted. Now this official has received heavenly beneficence to an extraordinary degree, but his days of actual service have been few, and the sacrifice made by his brute body has not been sufficient recompense.

Nevertheless, it must be reported that this official—being already fifty-four years of age and gradually declining in vigor and disintegrating in spirit—at daybreak on the 29th day of the 11th month of this year [January 4, 1647], just as he was entering the government compound, suddenly felt that his right eye was obscured. When he arrived at his office to handle affairs, the pupil of his right eye had become hazy from within. If he covered his left eye, then he could not read with his right eye, nor could he recognize persons even closer than a few paces away. Only after opening his left eye could he read well enough to judge the contents of documents or see individuals.

Beginning on the 1st of the 12th month, he has been unable to enter the government compound. Each day since then he has stayed in his personal office to handle papers, thus reducing somewhat the stress of meeting with other officials. He intended to rest for no more than a few days, anticipating that the eye would clear up. Contrary to that expectation, today, twelve days later, the treatments by doctors who have been called in are still ineffective. The doctors say that the right eye is neither red nor swollen; there is just a blue film over the pupil. They further say that the loss of vision is caused by an internal injury and that I must set things aside and remain quiet for one or two months if I expect the internal cloudiness to abate and the right eye to clear.

It seems to this official that matters of military operations and revenues to supply the Manchu and Han-Chinese armies in Jiangnan, as well as the documents sent in from the various other

*The regent for the eight-year-old Shunzhi emperor was his uncle Dorgon, who wielded the actual power in the Qing court until his death in 1650. See Chap. 1, n. 18.

provinces, are most numerous. To stop and rest for even one day would not be easy. How could one venture to speak of remaining inactive for one or two months? From the 9th month of last year until the 11th month of this year, complexities of Manchu and Han-Chinese affairs have consumed the energies of this official every day. He has kept intimate company with his lamp until early evening and grasped the candle again hours before dawn in order to manage things. He has regarded this as daily routine and never dared to consider it taxing. Now his right eye is diseased so he cannot enter the lamplight early and late as before; and during the daylight hours he must concentrate carefully on handling business to avoid slight errors of inattention. Given the clouded state of the right eye, the left eye, after many days in a row of such strain, reads only with difficulty. This official now fears that if the internal film of the right eye proves hard to dispel and he must use solely the light of the left eye, both eyes might gradually become afflicted. Then the strength of this official's heart to repay the Sage benevolence would be defeated by the progressive weakness in his eyesight.

This official is deeply worried and does not know what to do. He has not been able to enter the government compound for over ten days. Moreover, he does not know whether the eye disease will be cured slowly or quickly. He is filled with fear by these chilling thoughts and dares not but frankly, in obeisance, lay them before his Ruler-Father, humbly beseeching the Emperor's sympathetic condescension to undertake a review [of the present problem]. . . .

> *3rd year of the Shunzhi reign, 12th month, 13th day*
> *[January 18, 1647] (Received in Beijing in the 4th year*
> *of Shunzhi, 1st month, 9th day [February 13, 1647])*

[Reply] edict: We have perused and understood your memorial. The minister is to temporarily handle affairs in his personal office. When somewhat recovered, he is to again enter the government compound. The offices concerned are to be notified.[6]

. . . Hong Chengchou respectfully reports that this insignificant servant, beset by grief and fatigue, his right eye having lost its sight and the left eye also [growing weak],* is utterly unable to forgo another earnest appeal. Looking upward, he begs for the Sage's kindness and condescending pity.

This official, after the middle of the 2nd month, was upset to learn of his father's passing;† moreover, the malady in his right eye had worsened. So on the 25th day of the 2nd month [March 30, 1647], he worshipfully memorialized, pleading to be allowed to observe mourning—both to preserve the true way of a son and to avoid harm to the great plan for securing the outlying regions.

This official should calmly accept the Sage's decision.‡ How could he dare to rudely broach the matter again? It is just that from the time he learned of his father's death on the 21st day of the 2nd month until today, the 10th of the 4th month—a period of fifty days—this official has been beside himself with acute grief and pain. He humbly wonders how this mournful survivor can presume to continue managing the important military affairs of the state.

Once the Sage's edicts are sent out and respectfully received, they cannot be held up for a moment; once needs are encountered for supplies and troops to exterminate the recalcitrant and soothe the submissive in the various provinces, whether near or far, there must be no delay. When the other viceroys,§ the commander in chief of river control, and other imperial servants see this official's grief-stricken state and his eye disease, they all unfailingly sympathize and urge him to moderate his sorrow, reduce his workload,

*A few characters in the text, here and at two more points below, are indecipherable. Translator's guesses are in brackets.

†The Hong family home was in Quanzhou, southern Fujian Province. Hong's father died in 1643, but Hong did not learn of this until after Fujian was subjugated and Quanzhou was occupied by the Qing.

‡The throne had responded to Hong's request to retire for mourning with the following edict: "Having perused the minister's memorial, We are deeply sympathetic. At the present time the realm has just begun to settle down. It would be truly difficult to select another important official of the minister's talent and abilities to serve as a replacement. Moreover, if the minister could observe mourning within his office, forcing himself in the midst of grief to handle public affairs, would that not be the complete fulfillment of both loyalty and filiality? Remain as you are and await a later edict authorizing exemption from mourning. The offices concerned are to be notified" ("Hong Chengchou bingmu ben" [Document on Hong Chengchou's Eye Disease]), in *Biji xiaoshuo daguan*, 12th ser., vol. 12 [Taipei: Xinxing shuju, 1976], pp. 5605–6).

§As military commissioner (*jinglue*), Hong functioned on a higher, coordinating level than other viceroys (*zongdu*) in the Southeast, such as Ma Mingpei (Jiangnan, Jiangxi, and Henan provinces) and Zhang Cunren (Zhejiang and Fujian provinces).

and recuperate by getting more rest. But as soon as important matters arise, they all press this official to act on them quickly with undivided attention. Under such conditions how can this official convalesce? The other government servants, correspondingly, are at a loss.

Recently, after the 20th day of the 3rd month, this official's right eye became wholly sightless. When the left eye is covered, not one person can be seen nor one thing distinguished even less than a foot away; from where I sit not one character on my writing table can be read. Before, one had to look closely to see the internal film, but now from a considerable distance it can be seen that the pupil is completely white with some blue. After the 1st day of the 4th month the left eye grew increasingly clouded. Neither eye can see the paper well; the pen moves, but characters cannot be properly formed. In earlier days this official could write several lines in no time; but now, even taking much time and care, he cannot write even a few characters. The doctors say that the left eye already is 50 or 60 percent diseased, and if its vision is fully relied on without any rest, then before long both eyes surely will become totally useless.

Although this official lives in painful sorrow and bitter hardship, when imperial documents are respectfully received, how dare he stop using his hands and eyes? When imperial Manchu messengers arrive, how dare he delay in responding? When he meets with pressing matters in the South, how dare he put them off? As the fires of his heart and mind burn hotter, the disease in his eyes becomes more incurable. This truly is a time when men cry out in distress to heaven and parents!

How dare this official say any more today? He can only appeal to the Emperor's sage benevolence and to the Prince Regent's profound mercy for a special grant of commiseration, that this official might at least be able to somewhat acquit the filiality of a son and minimally keep a ray of remaining vision. . . .

4th year of Shunzhi, 4th month, 10th day [May 14, 1647]
(*Received in Beijing in the 4th year of Shunzhi, 5th month, 1st day*
[*June 3, 1647*])

[Hong was not permitted to return to the capital for recuperation until early 1648. Even then, his recall was due more to political complications than to concern for his mental or physical health. After six months of rest and medication, he was ordered to resume administrative duties in the capital.]

Viceroy of Military Operations and Supply Management, Imperially Assigned as Military Commissioner for the Region Comprising Huguang, Jiangxi, Guangxi, Yunnan, and Guizhou; Grand Mentor and Grand Preceptor of the Heir Apparent; Grand Academician of the Palace Hanlin and Historiographical Academies; Minister of War with Concurrent Appointment as Junior Vice Censor-in-Chief, Hong Chengchou respectfully reports that since the course of this insignificant servant's illness has turned worse and military matters can hardly be slowed for one moment, he is more worried than ever and prudently communicates this for the Emperor's information.

The circumstances of this humble official's affliction were fully explained in a memorial of the 21st day of the 6th month of this year [July 31, 1657], which by this time should have reached the Throne for consideration. After this official had obeisantly memorialized, he unexpectedly developed a severe fever on the 22nd and 23rd, which has added to his vexations.*

From early each morning, he sits upright on the bed mat, for as soon as he tries to recline, phlegm obstructs his throat so badly that only after drinking hot water one or two times can he pull through the ordeal. Before long, his throat and tongue become so parched that he cannot exhale, and he has to drink hot water again to survive the bout. It has been like this continually, from early morning to suppertime. He cannot swallow a single grain of rice during the course of a day, nor does he have any thought to eat. He can scarcely attend to anything. The affliction becomes especially heavy at night, between six in the evening and six the next morning. As soon as his eyes close, courier reports and documents about troops, horses, money, and grain supplies crowd into his breast, causing hallucinations and incoherent speech. Right away his throat and tongue become parched again, so that only by drinking hot water two or three times in a two-hour period can he endure it. After resting a short while, his throat and tongue again become dehydrated and his breathing is blocked. Again he must

*The description below strongly suggests a case of bronchial pneumonia.

drink hot water regularly until around three. Only after four or so does he get a brief respite. Then from the time he arises, the situation is the same as on the previous day; and the next night, too, is like the night before. It has been this way for almost ten days. Also, for ten days now this official has not wished to swallow any solid food, and he has been constipated, his chest being congested by an inner fire.

Imperial servants from the garrison towns and circuits have daily brought in doctors to deliberate about treatments, but none of their methods has been at all effective. Counting up, it has been nineteen days since this official began to feel ill. It seems that he has come to this because after sixty-five long years of declining stamina his vitality is spent. Here at the Changsha headquarters, the commanders, lieutenants, and other banner officers have seen this for themselves; the various civil and military officials in the city, high-ranking and low, all learn of this when they meet him.

Down to the present, this official has always thought it his fate to labor strenuously a whole lifetime. Having been overspread by the Emperor's extraordinary, vast benevolence, he should work all the more arduously, vowing to repay imperial favor. But the past four years in southern Huguang have been enough to add several more years [than that to this official's life]. The environment is very different, miasmas have conspired to encroach on his health, and this year the great drought and the brutal heat have been especially unbearable, causing this very serious illness to arise. His mind wants to handle urgent matters, but his strength is not up to it; his eyes want to see, but his spirit fails him. If he slows down for even a short while, then the documents and courier reports on troops, horses, revenues, and supplies in two or three provinces must go without his personal attention. The more this official's mind is pressed, the worse his illness becomes.

[It is well known] how crucial the middle and far South is right now and how important the responsibilities of the military commissioner are. But this illness being so grave, how can the urgent situation be ameliorated? This official's one body is not worth caring about, but the chance that his condition might bring detriment to the great plan for securing the outlying regions is not a small matter. . . . So this official dares not but again—personally, truthfully, beseechingly—lay the actual conditions of his critical illness before his Ruler-Father. He respectfully crouches at his pillow and kowtows in submitting this memorial, begging, prostrate, that the Emperor, from his astute perspective, will soon hand down a decision to be carried out. . . .

> *14th year of Shunzhi, 6th month, 30th day* [*July 20, 1657*]
> (*Received in Beijing in the 14th year of Shunzhi,*
> *7th month, 22nd day* [*August 29, 1657*])

. . . Hong Chengchou respectfully expresses his reverential gratitude for Heavenly benevolence and looks up prayerfully for the Throne's supervisory judgment.

In the mid-afternoon of the 24th day of the 12th month of the 14th year of the Shunzhi reign [January 27, 1658], this official allowed . . . the delivery of a lateral communication, sealed for secrecy, from the Ministry of War, the contents of which concerned an imperial edict of the 5th day [January 8]: "In an earlier edict the Military Commissioner and Assisting Servant Hong Chengchou was permitted to be released from his post and to return to the capital for recuperation. Recently it was learned that his illness has been cured. So he should remain at his original post as before. Moreover, as circumstances dictate, [he is to] personally lead his own officials and troops to advance from southern Huguang to take possession of Guizhou Province—along with the Generalissimo Who Pacifies the South and Quells the Bandits, Banner Commander and Imperial Clansman Loto and others.* Respect this imperial directive." When the above secret communication reached this official, he was overcome with both trepidation and gratitude. Thereupon he worshipfully established an incense altar in the government compound and kowtowed toward it, giving thanks for the imperial benevolence. . . .

This official, in humility, has been thinking that during his four years as military commissioner, not an inch of land has been restored [to Qing control]. Then, as the troops and horses were being readied for a campaign, he was afflicted with a critical illness. He was gratified to be overspread by the Emperor's mercy and to be allowed release from his post to return to the capital for recovery.

---

*Loto (1616–65) was a grandnephew of the founder of the Manchu nation, Nurhaci. See *ECCP*, II:694.

Even if he taxed himself to the utmost, he could never do enough to repay this kindness. He met with the other viceroy and the governor* at the provincial capital to discuss the disposition of officials and troops, and he was waiting for those discussions to reach precise conclusions before dispatching a memorial in response and then getting under way according to the Imperial command.

But then he received the Emperor's special edict from above, which announced the condescending thought that this official's illness having been cured, he should remain at his original post and manage affairs as before and should also accompany the generalissimo and others in advancing to take Guizhou.

In this official's estimation, his assignment to labor over affairs in a contested outlying region has been his just lot in life. His recovery from a serious illness surely has been due to the Emperor's enveloping kindness. Being elderly, this official could reasonably appeal for retirement after such an illness. But conscientious servants of the state must prodigiously guard against using advanced age as an excuse to avoid difficulties. Renewed receipt of the Emperor's command conferring this heavy responsibility is even more chastening in this respect. This official can only rouse his spirits and energetically prepare to struggle onward, attending as carefully to the end [of his public service] as to the beginning. With the generalissimo and other government servants, he will plan comprehensively to carry out the extermination [of enemies] and the pacification [of the citizenry], hoping at least not to betray the Emperor's great intent in this delegation of tasks. . . .

14th year of Shunzhi, 12th month, 26th day
[January 29, 1658]

. . . Grand Academician of the Wuying Hall . . . Hong Chengchou respectfully reports that this insignificant servant's right eye has long since lost its sight, and his entire left eye is now dim. He prudently and truthfully sets forth the situation and earnestly pleads for the Emperor's sympathetic supervisory opinion so he can avoid harming the great plan for securing the outlying regions.

*The newly appointed viceroy of Huguang was Li Yinzu, and the governor of the province was Zhang Changgeng.

In the 4th month of the 15th year [of the Shunzhi reign; that is, May 1658], this official followed the troops to Guizhou. It was extremely desolate and dangerous; troops and civilians alike were under duress. The demands of supplying the troops allowed no leisure day or night. As usual, this official kept intimate company with his lamp while he worked on memorials and other pressing matters and was unable to stop and rest. During the tenth month, when he met with the armies at Yang and Luo,* he felt that his left eye was gradually becoming clouded. But through the winter and the following spring, he could still wield a pen and write. In the 3rd month [of 1659] he was still able to mount a horse and ride into Yunnan; and in the intercalary 3rd month and in the 4th month he could still move quickly looking straight ahead.[†] Then, in the 5th and 6th months his left eye became even more clouded, and he was no longer able to read small characters. Important courier reports and other written communications had to be transcribed into large characters before he could discern the contents. His eyes were scarcely aware of persons or the path ahead. But he made every effort to write out instructions on critical matters.

From the 7th to the 8th month he could not recognize the face of anyone he met at a distance of even one foot. Aides would have to announce them loudly and point at them before this official could know who they were. He could not discern height or depth in any stretch of walkway and needed to be supported from both right and left in order to walk around. And when he went outdoors to mount and ride, he could slowly follow along only if a white horse was used as a forward guide. Now he cannot read even standard script, whether small or large. He must have a reliable official point from the side and read each character aloud, for he cannot make out even the number of lines. Although he feels that he must try to grasp the pen, he cannot complete a single handwritten char-

---

*Probably references to the Yangyi Native Chief's Office in Pingyue County in central Guizhou and to the Luoyan Crossing of the North Pan River in the southwestern part of the province. Qing forces were concentrated in both areas during this campaign.

[†]The lunar calendar required periodic adjustment to the solar cycle. This was done by inserting an extra, intercalary month once every few years.

acter. Recently the imperially dispatched high officials Itu, Nengtu, and Margi arrived in Yunnan.* As soon as they saw this official, all were startled at how old, weak, emaciated, and weary he had become. . . .

At present this official is afraid to report that the various memorials that he always read over carefully with his own eyes in the past must now be read aloud to him by a trusted official word by word. He does not permit any memorial to be sealed until his own ears have heard no discrepancy. But after all, he remains concerned that listening is not as true as seeing. Should a single character be written incorrectly as a result of this official's conscientiousness at one end and inattention at the other, the mistake would be irremediable. Most deeply disturbing to this official is that now—his left eye having gone bad during his heaviest responsibilities in coordinating the affairs of five provinces, the Yunnan region being in direst straits—he must have each incoming message read aloud to him several times before he can understand its purport from beginning to end. Each time he has a draft drawn up it must be altered several times, but still there are discontinuous meanings. One matter takes the effort of several; a whole day yields decidedly fewer results than should a half. . . .

The bandit situation is unpredictable, the native chieftains watch for their chance to rebel, and renegade soldiers lie in the underbrush. Neither defensive fighting nor pacification can tolerate any delay. Now this official's loss of eyesight has become extreme, and he can no longer manage things from morning into the night. Should it get to the point that he overlooks critical matters and hinders the securing of this border region, even though the Emperor might continue to understand and pity this official's condition, how could he absolve himself of great fault?

For many years now, this official has not dared to avoid difficulties or hard work, nor has he dared to mention his advanced age or illnesses. But now his state of decline is apparent to all the Manchu and Han-Chinese officials, the troops, and the common people. If

*Itu was the Manchu minister of war, Nengtu was the Manchu senior censor-in-chief, and Margi was on special assignment away from his post as viceroy of North Zhili, Henan, and Shandong.

this official, out of reluctance to leave, were to bear his disability in silence and not honestly set it before his Ruler-Father, he would betray the Emperor's benevolence with deception. No conscientious imperial servant would ever hazard that. . . .

This insignificant official can only beg sincerely that the Emperor in his Heavenly mercy stoop to pity this official as though he were a dog or horse, grown old and useless in devoted service but living on, and confer a release from duties, allowing this unworthy one to convalesce somewhat and not become a complete invalid. This official, then, with every one of his sons and grandsons, could but salute the Heavenly grace and pray that the Emperor might live myriads of years without end. . . .

16th year of Shunzhi, 8th month, 28th day [October 13,
1659] (Received in Beijing in the 16th year of
Shunzhi, 10th month, 16th day [November 29, 1659])

[Hong was finally granted permission to return to the capital on February 14, 1660. The Shunzhi emperor died of smallpox less than one year later at the age of only twenty-two. Hong lived to the age of seventy-one, dying in April 1665.]

10

"Fool's Escapes": A Merchant Survives Slaughter and Pestilence

THE REGION IN WHICH Hong Chengchou fell prey to severe illness in 1657—the central stretch of the Xiang River in present-day eastern Hunan—was hit hard by diseases and military actions at mid-century. In 1643 the region had the unenviable distinction of serving as the main base of the most cruel and erratic of the late-Ming roving rebel leaders, Zhang Zianzhong (d. 1647), before he moved westward to ravage Sichuan.[1] With the collapse of Li Zicheng's rebel regime in 1645, most of the remaining viable parts of his enormous army sought haven in the region, as did several divisions of the disintegrating army of the renegade Ming general Zuo Liangyu (1598–1645).[2] It became a prime zone of contention between often-bewildered and desperate Qing forces and the armies of variable provenance and discipline that supported the fugitive Ming Yongli emperor in Guangdong, Guangxi, Guizhou, and Yunnan.

In the middle of that region lies the city of Xiangtan, which, besides being a county seat, functioned as a marketing and transshipment center near the juncture of the northward-flowing Xiang River and its largest eastward-flowing tributary, the Lian River. Xiangtan lay on the main overland route between Jiangxi Province in the east and the passes to Sichuan in the west (see Chap. 11 and map 6). Sojourning there with his maternal kin was a young trader named Wang Hui, who hailed from Huizhou, a prefecture distinguished since the middle sixteenth century for the far-flung activities of its professional merchants.[3] In 1643, when Wang was thirteen years old, his father disappeared during the despoliation of Wuchang by Zhang Xianzhong's soldiers, which was why Wang and his mother had joined her family in Xiangtan, undergoing considerable peril on the way.

Wang Hui's full narrative, *Xiangshang chi tuonan zalu* (Miscellaneous Record of a Fool's Escapes on the Xiang River),[4] from which the translation below is taken, recounts eight acute dangers that he survived, from a bandit raid on Ningxiang in 1643 to a pestilence in Xiangtan in 1649. The last is one of many cases that made the 1580s and the 1640s the most epidemic-ridden decades in late imperial Chinese history.[5] Prior to learning of pathogenic microbes in the twentieth century, the Chinese attributed outbreaks of pestilence to the increase or influx of harmful *qi* (vapors), which tended to arise more frequently during times of disruption in the cosmic harmonies. Such miasmas were thought to pervade certain locations. Consequently, rather than avoiding persons who were afflicted with an epidemic disease, the unafflicted tried to avoid or escape miasmatic places.[6] This spread the contagion further, as Wang Hui may have done on the boat to Yongfeng. In that respect, he was more of a fool in his last escape than he could have known.

In the 1st month of the 6th year of the Shunzhi reign [February 1649], the [Qing] government troops arrived in force. [The renegade general] Ma Jinzhong[7] had been spending every day in a drunken stupor. So before noon on the 18th [February 28], when a hundred horsemen came on a reconnaisance patrol from behind the county seat to Gongji Gate, the bandit horde, without time to either put on their armor or saddle their horses, held up their arms to shield their heads and scurried away like mice. The Qing patrol gave pursuit, killing many of them at Jiangyu and Cloud Lake* and forcing others all the way into [the next county,] Xiangxiang. Two days later the troops came back and set up camp at Sandy Ridge, rampantly pillaging among the common people. We still didn't know that they were soldiers under a high official and [Manchu] prince of the blood.[8] We were bewildered and, not thinking to run for our lives, just hoped it would be like

*Located about fifteen and twenty miles, respectively, to the west of the Xiangtan county seat.

before, when the soldiers of the Three Princes[9] didn't disrupt the city at all.

Earlier, on the eve of the 17th, I felt ill at ease and restless. Half asleep, I saw a man wearing the long sleeves and cap of a Daoist priest. He said, "Go back, go back," and urged me out Peak Vista Gate.* Waking up, I thought to myself that Xiangtan city had all along been a dangerous place and that I shouldn't stay a minute longer. Alas, the roads had been blocked, and anyway, I'd been waiting for a companion who was supposed to go with me to South Peak on the 20th. But that dream was not auspicious, and the companion could no longer be waited for.

At dawn I went alone out Peak Vista Gate, crossed the river [that came from] Xiangxiang, and proceeded to Twin Planks Bridge. After resting a bit, I'd reached Old Dike Bridge when I heard from a lot of people that the main Qing force[10] had already arrived and that Ma's bandits had run away. So for the time being, I stopped at Mingjiang to listen for reliable news.

For several days all was quiet, and I heard nothing. Then, at the end of the month, I heard something about a massacre in Xiangtan, but I doubted that it was true. Absolutely no one was going to or coming from the city. At the beginning of the 2nd month the Qing troops moved their camp to King's Gate to pasture their horses in the countryside. After that, people who went toward the city to find out something definite saw many corpses lying about in the suburbs, and they all came back horrified.

In the middle of the second month I went with my companion to the Xiangtan market. Our feet grew feeble as we walked forward; even though we wanted to withdraw, we couldn't. Our souls left us, and our hearts chilled in fright. Traces of blood were still fresh, and the rank odor was oppressive. One could hardly remain standing, nor could one swallow any food. There was only the sight of corpses and heads strewn everywhere, too ghastly to talk about. That was the sixth trial that I personally went through.

After I'd stayed at the market for a couple of days, my mind and spirit steadied somewhat, but the stench remained hard to take. There were no more than twenty or thirty people left at the market, and inside

*Here, as elsewhere in this account, the author refers to himself as the fool. Such self-references have been rendered "I," "me," and so forth, in this translation.

the city walls there were fewer than a hundred. Several dozen people who'd been wounded but not killed said that the swords had come out on the 21st and that the slaughter had continued until the 26th, when they were sheathed again. It was the 29th before they stopped entirely. Some said that Sir He [Tengjiao] had been killed on the slope near Running Water Bridge, after which a monk in attendance had pushed over a dirt wall to cover the body.''

Over several days' time people gradually returned to their hearths in the city, and the dead bodies were either taken care of or cast away. Many were thrown into the river, and not a few were put in the scrublands outside the city. Some were cremated using firewood obtained by tearing down their houses, and others received burials paid for [by charitable survivors]. Some were "interred" in the bellies of dogs; only their bones remained. Other carcasses became nests for rats, the abdomens and chests being completely eaten out. Those who had been recognized by family members and taken in for proper burials were one or two in a hundred.

Then boats began stopping again, with merchants getting on and off. So [thinking it was probably safe], I entered the city to look for my relatives. The body of my cousin, Wang Yushang, couldn't be recovered. The body of Ding Yi, the senior relative on my mother's side, was the first to be burned.

One day some Manchu soldiers arrived and, as they went through, grabbed men to operate some boats. As soon as the people in the market heard of this, they tried to run away. But I was hauled onto a boat and made steersman. When we got to Three Gate Shoals, the river was swollen and the crew was inexperienced with high river waters, so the boat capsized in a strong wind. The soldiers took us to the official in charge of their unit for punishment, but a Colonel Zheng under the regional vice-commander came to our rescue and ordered us escorted out of the campsite. Only then could I return to Xiangtan. That was the seventh trial that I personally went through.

In Xiangtan County the populace had just recovered when a pestilence ensued. As it spread from one rural area to another, nine in ten people were stricken. There being neither medicines nor doctors, it got so bad that everyone in a household would succumb to the fever, leaving no one to take care of the bodies. Or, in some villages where it was less severe, the residents closed their doors and didn't go out. With few people on the roads and no signs of life around the houses, tigers

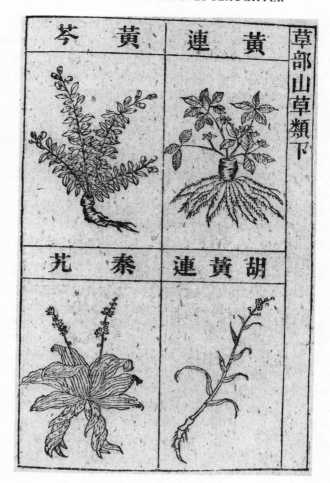

Figure 16. Examples of the sorts of herbs used in remedies mentioned by Wang Hui. In the upper left is coelestina (*Scutellaria baicalensis*).

and leopards became numerous, and hungry dogs roamed in packs. The massacre having been insufficient to punish people for their sins, the epidemic added more misery.

People in the city market would chat and laugh in the morning, break out in a fever after the noon hour, become delirious in the evening, and be partly eaten by rats when found dead at sunrise. About 20–30 percent died right away after falling ill; about 50–60 percent died three days after falling ill. After about three days some went mad, jumped into the river, and drowned. Those who survived the disease for as long as seven days relied on medicinal plants for cures. [Roots of] rhubarb, angelica, and coelestina were sold out [fig. 16];* black apricot cost a tael for two or three doses; snow pears cost two or three taels each. Two or three doses of the auxiliary medicines scallion and ginger or one of ginseng were going for fifteen or sixteen taels.[12] Ah, what an awful time! The bones from the massacre hadn't all been removed before the bodies of pestilence victims were strewn along the riverbank. We happened to have heavy rains in the 4th and 5th months, however, which floated away more than half of the piled-up corpses.

I set out for Shaoyang,† wanting to get away from that wretched place. No sooner had I boarded the boat than the disease spread through my body. Even though I was delirious as we went through Xiangxiang, fortunately I was able to keep my mind and spirit somewhat under control. I simply had the boatmen fill the small fishing dinghy with water so I could lie in it and cool off a bit. Then I could go back into the cabin and sleep soundly. After three days we arrived at Jiangkou. There I entered the Temple of the Five Manifestation Gods[13] and pressed my chest to the damp floor. Soon my four limbs were just pleasantly warm, and I felt like eating and drinking again. So I boiled some bean curd in water. After eating it my illness was reduced by half, and by the time we got to Ceshui, it was 70–80 percent cured. Although I'd originally planned to go to Shaoyang, I stopped at Yongfeng to recuperate because [I was so weak].‡ Besides congee, I ate only bean curd boiled in water as a remedy. Thus, I was able to return to Xiangtan, where I was pleased to find things different from before. That was the eighth [and last] great trial that I personally went through.

---

*"Angelica" here refers to *Angelica pubescens*, not the common *Angelica sinensis*. Coelestina is also known as Baikal skullcap, or *Scutellaria baicalensis*.

†The second county to the southwest of Xiangtan.

‡Slightly more than halfway from Xiangtan to Shaoyang.

11

"WHERE THERE'S

A WILL . . . ":

AN ARTIST'S FILIAL TREK

UNFORTUNATELY FOR WANG HUI and other residents of Xiangtan, Huguang Province remained the scene of almost continual troop movements and warfare for a decade after his escapes of 1649. This was largely because of complex developments in the bordering provinces to the south and west.

After the notorious rebel leader Zhang Xianzhong was killed in Sichuan early in 1647,* the four generals who commanded the armies of his "Great Western Kingdom" occupied Guizhou and Yunnan, wresting the latter from an aboriginal chieftain, Sha Dingzhou, who had overthrown the Ming authorities in eastern Yunnan in 1646. Subsequently, the two strongest leaders among Zhang Xianzhong's princelings, Li Dingguo and Sun Kewang,[1] in an amazing transmogrification of loyalties, became the main military supporters of the fugitive Ming Yongli emperor as his entourage fled into Guangxi, then Guizhou, then Yunnan. Having won Ming court recognition, Li and Sun turned back eastward from Yunnan to occupy Guizhou in force and from there to seriously challenge Qing positions in Huguang, Guangxi, and Guangdong, inflicting some stunning losses on the Qing side.[2]

One result was that the rugged mountains separating central Huguang from the higher elevations of Guizhou, which made communications difficult under the best conditions, became a tense militarized zone of conflict between the fiercest armies that could be fielded by either the Ming or the Qing, and power seesawed in that region for several years. Normal trade, travel, and postal services between the south-

*See Introduction, n. 7, and Chap. 10, n. 1.

western provinces and the rest of China were all but severed as western Huguang and contiguous westward areas became depopulated and dangerous.

Painfully affected by this state of affairs was a landscape artist of repute, Huang Xiangjian (1609–73), a resident of Suzhou whose father, Huang Kongzhao, had been appointed magistrate of Dayao County in Yunnan in 1643. The father had served scarcely two years in his new post before the revolt of Sha Dingzhou ensued, followed by the invāsion of the Great Western Kingdom armies. Since that time, Huang Xiangjian had heard nothing from his father—nor from his mother or cousin, who had accompanied his father to Dayao. He did not know exactly why he had not heard or whether they were dead or alive. The psychological burden that this situation would place on anyone's offspring was intensified by the Confucian value of filiality in Chinese literati culture. After years of wondering and worrying, in late 1651 Huang could not bear it any longer, so he embarked on what became one of the most celebrated treks in late imperial Chinese history—celebrated because of the filial attitude that prompted it, because of the album of paintings in which Huang later captured scenes from the trip,[3] and because of the vivid accounts that he wrote of his journey to Yunnan and back again, covering 2,800 miles as the crow flies, in 558 days (map 6).[4]

Huang Xiangjian's stark travel accounts and his evocative paintings of places he went through exemplify contiguous facets of seventeenth-century Chinese culture. The travelogue genre, which assumed a definite place in the literati repertoire during the Song period (960–1279), became one of the most widely practiced forms of literary expression in the Ming-Qing period.[5] Among the many figures who wrote in increasingly concrete terms about their travels was the intrepid geographer-explorer Xu Hongzu, better known as Xu Xiake (1586–1641), from a county adjacent to that of Huang's ancestral home.[6] In the visual medium, Huang's paintings have been compared with the realistic landscapes of his contemporary Zhang Hong (1577–1652 or later), also of Suzhou.[7] Whether wielding the brush to write or to paint, men like Huang Xiangjian were no longer satisfied with the imaginative vicarious "spirit journeys" of earlier figures. They sought to produce more objective, informative travel reports with a learned cachet.[8] The dynastic cataclysm forced Huang Xiangjian to acquire materials for these modes of expression in an arduous way.

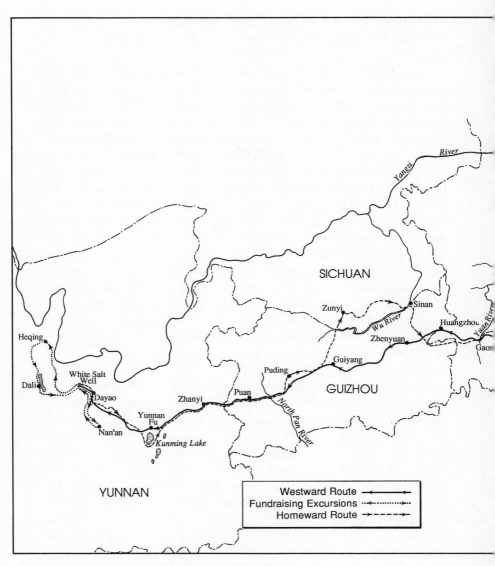

Map 6. Huang Xiangjian's Filial Round-Trip

JIANGNAN
(SOUTH ZHILI)

Jingkou

Jiangning
(Nanjing)

Suzhou

Grand Canal

Wuhu

Chizhou

Hangzhou

Han River

Wuchang

Qizhou

Yangzi River

Qiantang River

ZHEJIANG

Jiujiang

Yuezhou

Dongting
Lake

Poyang Lake

Lanqi

Xiangyin

Guangxin

Linjiang

Xiangtan

Fuzhou

Xiangyang

Liling

tian

JIANGXI

Baoqing

Gan River

Xiang River

HUGUANG

East China Sea

N

0   50   100 150   200 kilometers

0   100 miles

jmh

In 1643 my father was appointed magistrate of Dayao County in Yunnan, and he took my mother and my junior cousin with him to the post. After that, we encountered the change of dynasties. Mountain passes were blocked off, and travel routes were filled with armed conflict. Being unable even to speculate on the date of my parents' return made me uneasy morning and night, and the pain showed in my eyes. Moreover, through the depredations of outside offenders,* I came to have almost no family. I stayed in the fields by myself, enduring bitter hardships. My brushes and ink slabs were covered with dust, and I scarcely ventured to contemplate security or sufficiency. At times I would bow beside the tombs of my ancestors and indict myself for unfiliality—for leaving my parents in an isolated region and never visiting them. Could I still act as anyone's descendant? In deep melancholy and distress my every reflective thought was that although mountains and waters may stretch far, there is no absolute limit to the foot's itinerary. I feared only that the day would never come when I would, after all, muster the courage to step out my front gate. In time the calamities abated somewhat, and my spirit became agitated as though my parents were summoning me.

So I hurried my family members to put together some simple clothing for a long journey and check it over for me. Holding in their grief, they encouraged me, never uttering one word to hinder or delay my departure. . . . On the first day of the 12th month of the *xinmao* year of the Shunzhi reign [January 11, 1652],⁹ I took leave of the ancestral graves and my family. As the time to go drew near, I regarded my body as an empty husk, and I didn't allow the children to cry woefully or pull at my clothes. I couldn't bear to look back or give them a single parting instruction. Five or six older and younger close relatives accompanied me to the boat. . . .

In five days I reached Hangzhou and sought another boat at the mouth of the [Qiantang] River. Looking southward at the receding layers of cloudy hills and at the immensity of the river's flow, I sat down under the sail and shed hot tears uncontrollably. . . . Arriving at Deng Family Harbor, we found that it had been burned and pillaged by a gang of bandits. The smoke and flames had not yet died away, so the boatmen

*Probably a reference to the conflicts over Suzhou between Qing and Ming-loyalist forces in 1645–46.

didn't dare go ashore. Instead, they anchored in mid-channel and waited till the next morning before going on.

From that point I began entrusting my feet to grass sandals. Along the way there were many bandits and tigers, which turned the beautiful mountains and streams into abhorrent surroundings. On the road I often encountered rain and snow, and my heels and toes split open painfully, causing me to fall down over and over again. My body became like a big clod of mud and seemed to me worthy of pity. Frequently I had to lie down at the wayside. Learning that there were many branches in the road ahead, when I entered Shuinan and rested in a farm household, I made inquiries and found two men to be my traveling companions. Seeing that I was alone, feeble, and timid and that it was hard for me to walk, they both strongly urged me to go back home forthwith. They spoke for my benefit about how warfare had not yet ceased on the road ahead, how travel had long been cut off, making tigers and wolves worrisome along the byways, and how one had to be concerned about falling ill. But I was of no mind to retreat, nor did I show any fear, and I insisted on going with them.

On the night of the 19th [of the 1st month; February 27], we took advantage of the moonlight and set out, almost falling into a mountain stream on the way. In the morning we reached Camphor Tree Town and crossed the great [Gan] River. We asked directions in a most out-of-the-way place in a mountain valley. . . . [From there onward] all the village dwellings pressed close to either mountainsides or streams. Although they had only thatched roofs and dirt walls, they did afford secure resting places. The indirect mountain paths were rugged, however, with many bridges that were dilapidated or broken away from the bank, so that one's thighs trembled in approaching them. In some places no one lived at all, so we had to carry food with us. Stumbling and emaciated, I went on like that through thirteen stopovers.

On the 10th of the 2nd month [March 19] we were able to cross the Xiang River and lodge outside the Xiangtan city wall.* A blood blister on my left foot had become so red and swollen that the pain was unbearable. So I used a sliver of broken tile to lance it. Haggard and incoherent, I could scarcely eat or sleep. My traveling companions felt very sorry for me and again put forth words of doubt and caution,

---

*This is the same place that had suffered massacre and pestilence three years earlier, described by Wang Hui in Chap. 10.

hoping to dissuade me from going on. I acknowledged but declined their advice, saying, "When I went out my gate, I let go of all cares. Although it's difficult and dangerous, I must exert myself." Sealing a letter to my family with tears, I gave it to my companions to send back.

After nursing my foot for five days, I crossed the [Lian] River at Xiangxiang and headed westward to Baoqing Prefecture. Around me I saw desolate hills and fields that were mostly overgrown with weeds. Human skulls lay everywhere, and there were tiger tracks as deep as bowls. Another frightening thing was that when I saw groups of deer occupying the path and tried to drive them away, they would sometimes surround me belligerently. Each day at the place where I stayed, I asked the way through the next pass. As I ascended steep ranges, sweat soaked my back; as I forded deep streams, the cold stabbed into my bones. Fortunately the strength of my feet gradually improved, and I could walk and eat well. Only having to hold up my umbrella every day caused me some dull aching pain. But after a long while, I didn't think about it anymore.

After walking exactly fifteen days through on-again, off-again wind and rain, I reached Gaoshashi, sixty *li* from Wugang Subprefecture. Raising my head toward the sky to the south, I saw range upon range of mountains wrapped in clouds, stretching endlessly like the long ribbon of the Great Wall.* In that area, where aboriginal tribes live, is what people call Five Hill Stream. From there I took an indirect route over lofty mountains and doubled-back creeks. My feet may have moved forward vigorously by then, but my eyes were almost blind with despair. During the night, while I was resting in a tumbledown shack on a streamside embankment, rain came down in buckets, making me so uncomfortable that I couldn't sleep. So I sat under my propped-up umbrella and waited for dawn.

I was about to go out through Hong River Pass when I learned that the Northern [that is, Qing] troops were guarding that strategic point, so I hesitated to proceed. Moving on anyway, I found that no people lived in that area anymore. Whether through stands of bamboo in deep valleys, over the tops of ridges, or across the bottoms of mountain streams, the going was extraordinarily tough, affording one's body almost no secure place to pause. Early one morning I headed up toward Peach Crag. In that area were Miao and Liao tribespeople, who were

*See Introduction, n. 2.

known to harm others.[10] So the peasants in those mountains tilled in teams with spears and bows at hand. Entering the tight passage of Great Dragon Cliff, I got a one-plank boat and thereon crossed the big stream three times. The jagged bank jutted out over angry waves, and I shook in fear of both the heights and the depths. In the mountains there were thick groves of bamboo and virgin trees, so dark and close that they barred the sun. Everywhere it was a matter of finding a path where none existed. There were unusual flowers of intermingled red and purple, as well as strange birds, which sang mournfully all the time. Even a leaf would be fully one foot long, and fallen flower petals lay like the layers of a quilt. Catching a glimpse of a deserted grave mound and signs of sacrifices and sweeping, I had lonely thoughts of the grave site of my own lineage.

At the time I was still in the border region of Yuanzhou and Jingxian [in Huguang Province] and Guangxi Province. I requested a local guide to take me through the Willow Barrier of West Stream—in Miao territory. The Miao people tie their hair in mallet-shaped topknots and wear rings [around their necks]. They speak a shrikelike aboriginal tongue, though some understand Han-Chinese speech and also know to provide completely for guests. Their fermented liquor is like honey, and their pounded rice like snow. The dark depths of their ravines and caverns and the bizarre qualities of their springs and rocks are little seen by people of the outside world.

.   .   .

Proceeding again, I saw a stout enclosure of hewn wooden posts planted upright to form a wall-like palisade. In an empty niche hung a large bell. Soldiers standing near a story-high ladder questioned me in an intimidating tone, and as I continued forward, they kept spewing a lot of harsh words, regarding me as a spy. An order was transmitted to open the palisade and let me in. The general in charge put on an angry look, and the guards to his left and right would not have hesitated to use their spears. They asked my place of registration and my name, what I had come for, and where I was going. I told them, kneeling and sobbing, that I had come alone, braving perils, simply because my parents in Yunnan and for several years we had had no communication. I didn't even know if they were still alive, so I'd come on a special mission to inquire about them and had no other purpose. The general discerned that I was sincere. Looking at his guards, he said, "The road ahead is still long. Weak and timid as he is, how can he go that far?" They put me up in the barracks and at dawn sent me to Pingxi under the custody of a rider to see a Commander Gao. Again I told my whole story with sincerity, and Gao commiserated with me, saying, "If you really want to find your parents, we'll give you a pass and let you go on." . . .

[Four days later,] along a desolate riverbank, everything I saw alarmed me. Some relay soldiers shouted, "You shouldn't walk through there, or at least you should be careful of tigers in the mountains ahead." I was terrified and actually saw a profusion of tiger tracks as I went forward. Going over Cock's Crow Pass, with its staggered precipices, sheer cliffs, and narrow passages, I reached Zhenyuan Prefecture [in Guizhou Province].

.   .   .

In Pingyue Prefecture the mountain formations were majestic, and the roads were as tortuous as sheep's guts. On both sides [of the route] were the lairs of Miao aborigines, who in years past were always a hazard to officials and merchants traveling through. So patrol posts [had been established] on the most sharply protruding mountains in preparation for emergencies. Every ten li there was a relay station, but now the relay soldiers had been carried off by tigers. At the tops of ridges or the bottoms of slopes, skeletons lay one upon another, and absolutely no merchants or travelers set foot there.'' One only saw barrages of horsemen flying back and forth. I also saw people whose ears and noses had been cut off, as well as some whose arms were both gone but who were still able to bear heavy loads for long distances—terribly cruel. Although there were fascinating mountains and unusual streams, I didn't dare scan the scenery. I stopped at one mountain monastery and one relay station but only to cook some food and warm myself by the fire. I couldn't lie down to sleep. It must have taken over a month to travel from Gaoshashi [in Huguang] to Guiyang Prefecture [in central Guizhou]. . . .

Whenever I ran across the abode of a spirit along the way, I was sure to go in and offer ritual prayers. At one time I visited a deity's temple to divine news of my parents. Someone spying on me saw that my hair had not fully grown out and wanted to detain me.* But a man

*Huang had surely been forced to shave his head in the Manchu style in Suzhou. But during his trek, once he left territory that was well controlled by the Qing, he

named Cheng who happened to be there was dumbfounded and listened respectfully when I spoke of coming from afar to seek my parents. He looked at me and said, "I'm originally from Shin'an, and I used to reside in Luzhou.* When young, I was kidnapped and taken to Sichuan—it's been twenty years now. I don't even know where my parents live." His voice choked with sorrow for a long while before he said, "I'll go to the government office to look into your father's service history. Then you can know what's happened." That evening he brought back in his sleeve a small piece of paper on which had been copied the circumstances of my father's resignation—he'd been out of office since the winter of 1647.

I was deeply pleased. If we could rejoin one another, then the date of our return home would not be far off. But I didn't know where Father had secluded himself. So [Cheng] again spoke, telling me that I should send a petition to the chief commander of that area. Only with a pass from him could I go on with my search. In my quarters I wielded the brush and composed a brief account of my ten-thousand li quest for my parents. Near dawn I went out into the rain, the petition in my sleeve. But before I'd reached the [Guiyang] prefectural office, I ran into guardsmen standing in closed ranks and horses and elephants blocking the way. I got caught up among them, so my petition didn't get submitted. It was the 1st day of the 4th month [May 8]. The next morning, however, I did submit it, and that evening official approval came down, certifying that I was someone seeking his parents, not a vile enemy operative, and that I should receive a pass and be allowed to go. On the 3rd of the month my departure pass was issued, but only after they interrogated me several times over.

.   .

Not halfway up [the Guansuo Range], I became short of breath, my strength waned, and I collapsed on the mountainside. But an old monk gave me some tea to drink, and I revived. Taking short steps and using my umbrella as a staff, I climbed to the top of the range. There I saw military tents pitched everywhere in the mountainous terrain and herds

---

probably let it grow again. Having entered territory that still nominally at least was under Ming sovereignty, his recently grown head of hair would have raised suspicions that he was a Qing agent.

*Shin'an refers to the Huizhou area (present-day Xi County), and Luzhou is present-day Hefei. Both are in what is now Anhui Province.

of horses released to graze. Flags and pennants filled the air, and the sound of firearms was like thunder. After recuperating a bit, I headed down the other side of the range, but a horseman abruptly seized me and took me to the camp, where they questioned me and checked my pass. Then, hearing my story of hardships on the road, they commiserated with me and had a servant bring me some food. Not feeling well, I declined, so they gave me a large bowl of gruel. In the middle of the night they pulled up camp and left.*

I rested at a crude inn for two days before binding up my travel pouch and walking on. Again I saw masses of troops and horses winding down the range. Whether driving elephants or riding horses, the troops flew banners and pennons that dazzled the eye, and the mountain valleys rumbled. Toward sunset I dashed to find a place to stay and again saw a rear unit, now camped below the mountains, cooking dinner. A profusion of horsemen were galloping around, and things looked as martial as before. They checked my pass, and off I went again. Seeing that a lot of elephants were blocking the way, I stayed at White Mouth Slope.

After entering the passes [into Guizhou], every prefecture, county, and garrison I passed through had wide open roads along which relay stations had been established every ten li to serially check passes and make inspections. If one had no pass, then one was an enemy agent, so travelers stayed their feet. Next I stopped at the [North] Pan River. Over that roiling mass of waves in a steep gorge was a bridge of iron links, long renowned as a strategic point, so in crossing I was interrogated most severely. Also, it was a key entry point into Yunnan. . . .

As the brutal sun was roasting my body, all at once clouds gathered, the sheering wind of a thunderstorm dragged away my umbrella, and I had no cover from the drenching rain. From an old wall I ran toward a Miao stockade, but there I saw only one or two old Miao women, who bawled at me with open mouths amid a dirty bunch of cows and pigs. So I bore the rain and hurried on. As I went up a terracelike mountain, the rain gathered into streamlets, which soon became angry torrents of splashing waves that surged down fiercely. My legs buckled, and I almost went under. But the stronger the rain, the more robust I was, too, and eventually I found respite at Sea Horse Villa. Lacking

---

*Mobility and speed characterized the late Ming rebel armies, making them formidable even to the Manchus.

rice, I wasn't able to eat a full meal. I dried my clothes by the fire but didn't sleep until well into the night. Of all the severe frosts and freezing snowfalls, abrading winds and bitter rains that had soaked my head and obliterated my feet since leaving my home, none was as bad as that day's.

.   .   .

Resting at Pingyi Garrison, I met Master Qian Shisu from Eastern Zhejiang, who had formerly been the magistrate of Yangzong County in Yunnan. After losing his post, he procured an appointment as an education official. Because I paid my visit in straw sandals, he stared down at me, keeping his hands in his sleeves. I explained that I was a man from Suzhou who'd come in search of his father, [the former Magistrate] Huang of Dayao. He observed my face intently. Then he saluted me, shook my hands, and wept grievously. We sat down in a corner and Master Qian spoke in great detail as I asked what had happened to my father. He said that everyone suffered about equally while the soldiers killed and looted, but that none was like my father or me in the ability to enter and escape danger. Before long he asked about how things were looking in Shanyin,* and again he felt a combination of sorrow and joy. He boiled two eggs to go with a pot of wine, which he poured himself. We chatted until very late before calling it a night. That day I had learned that my father and mother were unharmed and that their precise place of residence was White Salt Well in Dayao County. The next morning I arose in good spirits for a vigorous hike. Although the mountain streams along my route were brimming, I lifted my trousers and still managed to walk twenty li without feeling the slightest stress. . . .

When I registered [with the authorities in Qujing Prefecture], the various officials were in the local temple praying for clear skies. The doorman received my pass and took it in for inspection. The men inside began speaking among themselves in surprised voices, and they ordered a functionary to bring me in to see them. In a short jacket and straw sandals, I kowtowed ceremoniously in their presence, tearful and not daring to look upward at their visages. Seeing that I looked poorly because of an eye ailment, they all exclaimed in amazement and concern

*Shaoxing Prefecture, south of Hangzhou Bay in Zhejiang Province.

and offered condolences. But I was so choked up with woe that I couldn't respond.

I went to my quarters, [but after one of the officials,] Circuit Intendant Gu Xin, returned to his office, he invited me to go there. Taking me to his couch, he told me everything about the tribulations that my father had been through. Now happily out of office, my father's heart had come to rest in the Buddhist canon, on peaceful waters, and he was regarded as a true immortal or true Buddha. Then Gu asked about conditions in the Central Plain.* I spoke discreetly, and he acknowledged silently. When he heard that I wanted to take my parents back home, he was silent for a long while before saying, "Not being an official and having no other attachments, he can go home." He went on to calculate how hard it was going to be to raise travel funds, and to contemplate the relative dangers of various passes and crossings, grasping throughout a small cup and speaking intensely with a knitted brow. In the early evening he sent me off with a donation. . . .

.   .   .

Going through Dingyuan County and over the Zhuge Range, I made Yaoan Prefecture by late afternoon. There was nothing but ruined walls and tumbledown houses—desolation as far as one could see. I happened to meet a functionary who had served under my father, Shi Qikun, who painfully recounted the cruelties committed by soldiers in the three counties of Yaoan and who said it was fortunate that my venerable father had resigned from office early on. I paid visits to the prefect, Ren Xi, and the subprefect, Yan Shilong. Both had been students together under my father's tutelage, and each presented me with travel gifts, which I acknowledged with bows. They gave a banquet for me at the Qinglian Monastery, where all they talked about was the chaotic disintegration during the past few years. They said how wonderfully lucky it was that my venerable father had been able to avoid catastrophe and stay in one piece. They went on and on about how good it was that after being separated by what seemed an infinite distance of ten thousand li, my father and I would now be reunited. And they had a servant accompany me onward for a long way.

I stayed at Manhai Yard and in the morning went up Liwu Slope,

*That is, in the strategically crucial north-central part of China.

passing by Waterdrop Cloister on the way. Pines and firs lined the lofty, rugged path. Eyes focused and feet stepping high, my whole body felt light and free. I was as happy as if I were returning to my home village. Going downhill on the other side, I passed Willow Dike, where a cluster of peaks almost touched one's face. When I saw houses with smoke emerging from one corner, I knew I'd arrived at White Salt Well. I anxiously inquired where my father lived of a man on the road, who looked me over carefully and asked where this guest came from. I replied, "From Suzhou. I've come seeking my father, [the former Magistrate] Huang of Dayao." Then everyone around exclaimed in surprise and pointed at me from a distance.

Tears welling forth, I ran feverishly . . . to my father's residence. Inside the gate all was quiet and still. I saw only a maidservant from earlier times sitting under an eave. Her fixed gaze turned to recognition, and she shouted loudly in astonishment, "The young gentleman of our home has come!" My mother, not believing her, said, "How could that be." But I'd already gotten to the main room, where I flung down my travel bag and hollered, "Father! Mother!" My dear old father had not yet awakened from his noontime nap. He gave a start and blurted out, "Who is it?" "Our son has come," replied my dear old mother. Then it was my father who didn't believe it. As I hurried into his sleeping room, Father spoke as though still asleep and rubbed his eyes, not knowing what to do. Suddenly we looked at each other, and I fell into a bow before his couch. Then we hugged each other and sobbed loudly until we were almost spent and couldn't rise. Eventually getting up, we still supported one another and cried heavily without stopping.

Soon I joined my two parents in doing obeisances to heaven and earth. Then we sat awhile, and I asked about their daily lives. Inquiring about the male servants they'd had in years past, I learned that all of them had scattered. My parents for their part commiserated with me over the hardships I'd undergone and asked how I'd come. Seeing that my appearance was not as before—disheveled hair sticking straight out,* gray in my beard, burnished face and swollen eyes, short jacket and grass footwear—they looked at one another in pity for me and sighed again and again.

Then my junior cousin came back with a load of firewood and stood outside the gate looking in inquisitively. My dear old father shouted

*See pp. 170–71n.

for him to come in, and we bowed to one another tearfully. Father's various students and the respected local elders offered congratulations, crowding around the steps to the main room, for they couldn't be seated in order. There wasn't a valuable item in the place, which was as bleak as a monk's cell. In the middle of one wall hung a large likeness of Guanyin, and on the desk were only such books as Fuxi's *Changes* and some Buddhist sutras.[12]

My mother prepared some wine and set out some fruit and dishes of food. I toasted my parents, wishing them long life. My father laughed and said to my mother, "Since becoming separated from our home, we've had no prospect of seeing our flesh and blood again. It's been enough to hope that a letter might get through. How could we ever have expected to see a day like this!" We then sat under a lamp and recounted the military conflicts in both places [Suzhou and Yaoan], which we all had been lucky to get through alive. Before long he asked about the rise or fall, survival or loss of the sons and daughters of our associates, in-laws, and maternal relatives in the home neighborhood— tales of extreme happiness and woe. I got around to explaining that because he had assumed a far-off post and not returned, his possessions had been registered and confiscated [by the Qing authorities]. That and other such things had brought on year after year of hardship, during which time we relied on the silent assistance of our senior relative, Shangzhi. Father sighed with deep regret. But when he heard that our grave sites had not been harmed and that in 1646 he had gained a grandson, he was overjoyed. We talked on and on through the night, and before we knew it the cock had crowed. That was the night of the 15th day of the 5th month [June 20].

From Suzhou to there, I estimated it was over ten thousand li by courier routes. But many obstructions along the way had caused me to make twists and turns. In all, I'd traveled half a year plus half a month to see my two parents. But having found them, I no longer thought at all about the exhaustion in my feet or the discouragements of the road. Wasn't it a case of "so far and yet so near"? I recalled that back when I was about to leave by the gate, my teacher, Chengying of Tiao River, had come up, and with him I'd discussed making such a long trip. He had instructed me, saying, "Where there's a will, there's a way." Today indeed verifies it.

[Huang Xiangjian then hiked around central Yunnan to solicit travel funds from his father's students, former colleagues, and friends, ex-

Figure 17. One leaf from the album *Ten Thousand Li [Journey] in Search of My Parents* by Huang Xiangjian, showing Huang himself, followed by his father and mother in palanquins and his cousin, approaching a guarded bridge on their trip home from Yunnan to Suzhou.

periencing a major earthquake on the way. On December 4, 1652, he led the way back home, with his father and mother behind in separate palanquins and his cousin bringing up the rear (fig. 17). From the middle of Guizhou to the middle of southern Huguang, the journey was especially hazardous because they happened to encounter an ambitious campaign by Sun Kewang against Qing positions in Huguang,[13] so they had to avoid the main travel routes (see map 6). Finding the border region between Huguang and Jiangxi impassable because of bandits, they proceeded from Xiangtan by boat the rest of the way, experiencing the perils of that mode of transportation in crossing Dongting Lake in particular. They arrived back in Suzhou on July 12, 1653.]

12

SOARING PHOENIX OR CAGED PANTHER?
FATHER AND SON
CHOOSE OPPOSITE SIDES

IN THE TURBULENCE of mid-century not all fathers and sons had such ideal relations as the Huangs (see Chap. 10). In any society tensions can arise between disciplinarian fathers and self-assertive sons in their late teens or early twenties, and those can be worsened by social and political ruptures. In Chinese culture especially, the strong emphasis on obedience to fatherlike rulers and to rulerlike fathers and on the reconciliation of any conflicts between family and state loyalties could cause dramatic dissension among leading figures in the social-political elite. One such case had far-reaching consequences for the history of the Ming-Qing dynastic struggle—that of the mogul of China's maritime trade zone, the pirate cum marquis Zheng Zhilong (1604–61), and his eldest son, a brilliant organizer and military strategist now famed in history, propaganda, drama, and folklore, Zheng Chenggong (1624–62; figs. 18 and 19).[1]

The father, himself physically strong and rebellious as a young man, left the home of his own father, a minor Ming official in Quanzhou Prefecture, in his late teens to learn the ropes of international maritime trade in Macao, where he worked in some capacity for the Portuguese. In 1621 he moved to Japan, where he became an aide to the Chinese merchant, smuggler, and pirate Li Dan, who dominated the flourishing Chinese shipping trade at the key ports of Hirado and Nagasaki.[2] Li's death in 1625, as well as the increased friction between Chinese authorities on the seaboard and the Dutch East India Company,* gave Zhilong momentous opportunities. He responded with an astute knowl-

*See Chaps. 4 and 13.

Figure 18. A Chinese portrait of Zheng Chenggong. It is probably a version
of the portrait described by Yan Xing as "the treasured holding of Zheng's
eighth-generation descendant, Yuchun" ("Zheng Chenggong yirong jinkao"
[A Present-Day Inquiry into Zheng Chenggong's Physical Appearance],
Tainan wenhua, 5.1 [February 1956]: 7). The long earlobes, which originally
signified wisdom in Buddhist iconography, came to be a conventional feature
in Chinese portraits of extraordinary figures.

edge of the highly competitive, often belligerent maritime commercial
scene along the East Asian coast; he knew the political interests on
various sides, the coastal weather and geography, and not least, the
social and economic conditions peculiar to the people of littoral Fujian.[3]

Within a few years of successfully commandeering Li Dan's organization, Zhilong eliminated his competitors in the Zhangzhou-

Figure 19. A European portrait of Zheng Chenggong. Although the conventions of illustration differ greatly, the soft, winsome features and civilian attire are ironic in both the Chinese and European portraits of a man who was famed as a stern disciplinarian and brilliant military strategist. (Because of the engraving techniques of European illustrators, their approximations of Chinese script often turned out backward when printed in Europe, as here.)

Quanzhou area, persuaded the Dutch to leave the Chinese coast and the Pescadores in return for undisturbed use of Taiwan as a trade depot, and bullied the Ming government into giving him an appointment as a naval commander in charge of keeping the peace on the southeastern seaboard—if by self-serving means, then so be it. Having added official sanction to his position, Zhilong even more confidently gave preferential treatment to his own ships, levied his own import and export taxes on others, collected protection fees from fishermen, merchant marines, and their agents, organized exclusive manufactories and commodity-delivery systems, and built on the tendency of that economically precarious region to generate large, tightly organized, combative lineages.[4] Zhilong garnered immense wealth, lived like a prince, and made the Zhengs of Anping a force to be reckoned with in both national and international politics.[5]

During his sojourn in Hirado, Zhilong mated with the daughter of a samurai family,* and she bore his first son, Zheng Sen (called Fukumatsu in his Japanese home)—the future Zheng Chenggong. Zhilong went back to China, apparently even before the birth, and he did not send for his son until six or seven years later. The mother was not brought to the Zheng home in Fujian until 1645; there she was secondary to Zhilong's formal wife, a Chinese woman surnamed Yan, by whom he sired five other sons. By that time Zhilong, now an aspiring pillar of the Ming establishment, had been grooming his firstborn for an influential political career by providing him with the classical education that Zhilong himself had shirked as a young man. When the Zheng organization became the main military support of the Longwu regime, centered at Fuzhou, the Longwu emperor, himself still childless, was so impressed with the twenty-one-year-old Zheng Sen that he bestowed on him the imperial surname, Zhu, and a new personal name, Chenggong, thereby symbolically adopting him.[†]

The next year, 1646, heavy blows came the way of our prodigy,

---

*The Tagawa, retainers to the Matsuura daimyo of Hyōgo Prefecture. The woman later bore a second son, named Shichizaemon, by a Japanese man. Zheng Chenggong remained in warm contact with his Japanese half brother for the rest of his life.

[†]From this circumstance arose the name by which Zheng Chenggong has been most commonly referred to in popular sources: Guoxingye (Lord of the State Surname)— Koxinga, or Cocksinja, in European writings, Kokusenya in Japanese. On the Longwu court and the Zhengs' role therein, see Chap. 8.

thereafter most often referred to in histories as Zheng Chenggong. The Longwu regime was crushed by the Manchus, and the emperor slain.[6] Zhilong, heedless of emotional dissuasions from his eldest son and others, responded to Qing inducements by surrendering to the enemy. Chenggong's mother, to whom he was deeply attached, committed suicide during the first of repeated Qing raids on the Zheng home base in Anping County. It is not difficult to see a strong psychological element—among the economic, political, and ideological ones—in Chenggong's subsequent implacability toward his father and toward the Qing.

During the next several years Chenggong worked hard to build his own following and to establish leadership over more senior figures in the Zheng clan organization. He reinforced his military command center, Zhongzuo Base, on Xiamen Island in Xiamen Bay, which controlled sea access to the Zheng home to the northeast and Haicheng to the southwest (see map 7). Haicheng had been the most important maritime entrepôt in Fujian since 1567, when it was designated by the Ming government as the only port for legitimate private overseas trade.[7] Chenggong's ability to thwart Qing efforts to secure the maritime Southeast grew steadily, and in 1653, after suffering a sharp blow from his amphibious forces, the Qing court decided that a major effort to summon Chenggong to allegiance was in order. They realized that to defeat him by force in his own domain—in a watery environment with which they were not at all familiar—would entail enormous expenditures and losses. Thus, a great deal was staked on their diplomatic offensive, in which Zheng Zhilong and his family members in Beijing were made uneasy intermediaries.

The extant Chinese historical writings on Zheng Chenggong were mostly secondary and prone to fabulation until 1927, when a dilapidated manuscript was discovered in the Zhengs' former home village, Shijing. It turned out to be a detailed primary record of Chenggong's affairs. However, because front and back parts of the manuscript had surrendered to time, it has not been possible to ascertain the original temporal span nor the original title.[8] The author's identity fortunately is clear: Yang Ying, who served for many years as one of Chenggong's revenue officers and who apparently had subsidiary duties as a chronicler. From his account we get an intimate view of a well-run seaboard regime, of the de facto autocrat of that regime, and of the strategies that made the regime and its head so formidable.

[1st month (February) of 1653]. Zhou Jiwu*—having been deputed by Grand Preceptor and Duke of Pingguo [Zheng Zhilong][†]—arrived at Xiamen from Beijing and transmitted a message from Zhilong informing the prince [Zheng Chenggong] that the Qing court wished to talk peace and ordering him to engage in such talks. The prince deputed Li De with a return letter to the grand preceptor, which said in part: "It has been several years since your son went southward,[‡] and he has already become a person beyond the pale. Zhang Xuesheng [the former Qing governor of Fujian] had no reason to start trouble arbitrarily [in the raids of 1651].[§] Your son could not but respond in kind. Now that he is riding a tiger, it's hard to get off; troops that have been gathered are hard to disperse."

.   .   .

[8th month (September–October)]. Li De, Zhou Jiwu, and others, having been deputed by the grand preceptor, the Duke of Pingguo, to present a letter in the duke's own hand to the prince, arrived and stated: "The Qing court wishes to confer land in exchange for peace. They wish to depute two high officials to present the seal of, and the documents bestowing the title of, Duke of Haicheng, authorizing the settlement of your followers in the lands of [Haicheng] Prefecture.[||] The mission would be guaranteed by [the current viceroy for Zhejiang and Fujian] Liu Qingtai. They have sent us in advance to ascertain your willingness. After we report back, they will order the court envoys to come and make the presentation." The prince said, "The Qing court wants to trick me, eh? One way or another we'll use the situation to extract plenty of supplies to feed the troops."

*Zhou Jiwu, Li De, Wang Yu, and others mentioned as go-betweens were personal aides and servants of Zheng Zhilong and Zheng Chenggong.
†The author consistently refers to Zhilong by the highest titles that he received under the Ming Longwu emperor. Out of respect for the father of his leader, the author observes the taboo against using Zhilong's personal name, even in transcribing edicts from the Qing court.
‡From fallen Fuzhou to the Zheng family stronghold in the Anping-Xiamen area.
§See below, in the next letter.
||Chenggong had recently inflicted a painful retaliatory defeat on Qing forces in Haicheng. See the following letter.

Then he wrote a return missive to the Duke of Pingguo and ordered Li De to gallop [day and] night to the [Qing] capital to report. The missive said: "For eight years now I have failed to serve at my father's knee. But then, since my father no longer regarded his son as such, I did not presume to consider myself a son. Consequently our inquiries after one another utterly ceased; not one word has gone between us. Circumstances have been so extraordinary as to alienate even flesh and blood.

"Since ancient times, the principle that the greater righteousness [in serving one's ruler and state] extinguishes one's duty to family[9] has been the instruction of men in sensible, not unstable, states of mind. When your son first learned to read, he straightaway respected this meaning of the *Spring and Autumn Annals*. I had been contemplating that principle for some time when, in the winter of 1646, Father's carriage entered the Qing capital and committed me to acting on it.

"Out of the blue I have received your stern directive that your son's capacity for loyalty be brought to reinforce filiality. As before, you transmit the oral edict of the Qing court, including talk about my having been an earl and a marquis [under the Ming, which would warrant] an expeditious elevation in rank. But if the Qing have lost credence with the father, how can the father's words bear credence with the son? When the Manchu prince [Bolo] entered the pass [to Fujian], my father had long since retreated home to avoid the situation. They then used ingratiating phrases and clever language delivered by envoys who came to woo you in entourages of horses and carriages that went back and forth no fewer than ten times. They went as far as to bait my father with a princely title and control over three provinces. At first they said that once you had come to the provincial capital, you could go home again; later they said that after you entered the national capital, you could assume command of the three provinces. Now it's been several years. Let's not speak of the princely title or the assumption of command*—now, even if you wanted to pass through your old neighborhood, you couldn't. How can their words be believed?

"When my father was in the Ming court, was he not the exalted Duke of Pingguo? Now that he's serving the Qing court, how is it that he's behind others? But it is that way even for those who went over to

---

*Zhilong was not even elevated to the status of a marquis until the plan to make Chenggong a duke was initiated.

the Qing first.* How much more so for the last to submit? Also laughable was that early on, your son sent Wang Yu to enter Beijing only because he had heard rumors about your circumstances and thought to have someone look into them. But Wang was abruptly put into prison and subjected to extremely cruel floggings. What could one Wang Yu have perpetrated? But seeing how they barked at shadows like that, the rest could be known.

"Nevertheless, in 1649 [I thought it safe] to sail into Guangdong Province to operate some colonies for a few years.[10] I never expected that they would take advantage of your son's being far away to recklessly initiate hostilities. They attacked and destroyed our base, Zhongzuo [fig. 20], devastated our lands, took spoils from our soldiers and people, captured and raped our womenfolk, and robbed us of over 900,000 gold taels, several hundred pounds of pearls and jewels, and many hundreds of thousands of bushels of grain. The valuables stolen from our soldiers and common people are incalculable. When they heard that your son was about to return, they begged for mercy from Fourth Junior Uncle [Zheng Hongkui].[†] Fortunately for them, he gave them some room to get away, so they were able to make it back alive. But having returned, they again treated us with suspicion and involved us in disputation.[11]

"All our generals and soldiers had such painful thoughts about the country's shame and our family's loss that their anger made their hair stand on end under their caps. That is why the military actions in Zhangzhou and Quanzhou prefectures ensued. The taking of [the former viceroy] Chen Jin's head and the repeated defeats of [Commander in Chief] Yang Minggao were assuredly in the natural course of getting back what one puts out. Not only that: troops from various neighboring foreign countries, such as Japan and Kampuchea,[12] should arrive any day now. They, too, wish to practice the greater righteousness of the *Spring and Autumn Annals.*

*That is, no matter how trusted the earlier, non-Manchu allies became, they never could attain the status of the Manchu leaders. Nor would those who surrendered in North China ever be trusted as much as those who submitted to the Manchus in Liaodong.

†See Chap. 8, n. 4. In truth, Chenggong was enraged with Hongkui for letting the Qing raiders go from Xiamen. Because Hongkui was his uncle, he couldn't have him executed, as he did the other generals and officials involved (including some relatives). But he did force Hongkui to relinquish military command, after which Chenggong, despite his youth, was nonpareil in the family organization.

Figure 20. The Zheng stronghold, Zhongzuo Base, on Xiamen Island.

"If I am to believe both my father's command and the Qing edict, then there is a contradiction: The edict that my father has transmitted says one thing, whereas the copy that I've obtained of the decree to be presented by Minister Liu Qingtai says another. There are thorny discrepancies between the former and the latter. We are already in full control of the seaboard. The resources of the eastern and western seas that we have propagated afford more than enough supplies for our offensive actions. Why should we be willing to revert from sitting and enjoying this surfeit to being constrained by others?

"Speaking in terms of Fujian, Guangdong, and Guangxi, the pros and cons [of the Qing effort to control these three provinces directly] are clear. Does no one at the Qing court understand this? The maritime provinces are several thousand li from the capital. The route is dauntingly long, exhausting for both men and horses. And their unfamiliarity with the environment once they arrive results in most of them dying off. Troop shortages are sure to make these regions hard for the Qing to hold. Increasing troop strength would necessitate recruitment from other regions. If that were done, it would surely prove difficult to sustain so many troops with provincial supplies. And if food for troops were not provided, then the regions certainly could not be held.

"To waste money and supplies trying to hold unholdable soil would bring harm but no advantage. Before, when my father had command over Fujian, Guangdong, and Guangxi, the lands and seas were as peaceful as could be, and the court did not have to expend so much as one arrow. Besides troop supplies, there was enough to send surpluses to the capital. The court enjoyed this service, and the people benefited. That brought advantage and no harm. If the Qing court is unable to learn from the astute calculation of my [Ming] dynasty, and instead sends its troops to labor in faraway ventures, year after year wasting unrenewable resources, how will they ever manage recovery later on?

"Perhaps they now intend to use an empty title to authority over three provinces—a title with which they previously baited the father—to turn around and bait the son. Your son truly does not categorically doubt his father's words, but under these particular circumstances, it is hard to believe them. If Liu Qingtai could actually take responsibility and truly confer control over the territory of three provinces on me, then the lands and seas could be free of the scourge of outlawry, and the Qing court would have no need to worry in looking southward—indeed, it would be their great good fortune. . . .

"Besides, at present we have several hundred thousand troops, and conditions would make them hard to disperse. If dispersed, they would form disruptive groups among themselves and cause unrest in the area. Keeping them together entails numerous expenditures—a big ten thousand taels each day. Without the territory and revenues of a province, it would be like the old scheme that they used to bait my father. The father having been deceived before, how can the son allow himself to be deceived again later?

"The Ming dynasty has conferred the imperial surname and a princely title on your son.* His official status already being the highest possible, how could the Qing add to it? Anyway, your son's concern for official titles has always been thin; much less is he interested in going through the hierarchy of conferrals again. I say this to someone who should know. Otherwise, if I were to display an empty, meaningless title while acquiescing in what actually was a disaster, then people's minds would tend to revolt against such falsity, and Jiangnan, too, would be hard to keep secure for long."

.   .   .

[1st month (February–March) of 1654]. The grand preceptor, Duke of Pingguo, again sent Li De to present a letter in his own hand and to state upon arrival: "The Qing court is deputing two envoys named Zheng and Jia to present the seal of the 'Duke of Haicheng,' as well as permission to lodge our troops in the four prefectures of Xinghua, Quanzhou, Zhangzhou, and Chaozhou.† They will reach the provincial capital [Fuzhou] at the end of this month." Our prince then appointed Chang Shouning, his deputy adjutant who kept the seal of the Army That Manifests Righteousness, as chief emissary and Zheng Qifeng of the Bureau of Processional Paraphernalia as his second. They were to proceed to the Fujian capital to receive the Qing envoys, [ostensibly] because of the grand preceptor's express wish that loyalty and filiality be fully reconciled. But the prince summoned Shouning and instructed him, saying, "On the matter of the peace negotiations, my will is already

---

*According to Yang Ying's record, Chenggong did not receive the title Prince of Yanping through an emissary of the Yongli emperor until the seventh lunar month of that year, 1654.

†The region comprising present-day Putian, Jinjiang, and Longxi in southeastern Fujian, and Chaoan in the extreme eastern part of Guangdong.

set, and you are not to discuss the matter. Your responses to the Qing emissaries should be just a show of decorum; you are not to detract from our dynasty's integrity. Resistance or compliance will be carried out according to times and circumstances. Avoid bringing shame on your mission, that's all."

.   .   .

The Shunzhi emperor's edict [of his intention to bestow the title] Duke of Haicheng:

Considering that military forces have become heavily concentrated in the remote Fujian maritime region, We feel that it is time to endow a noble lineage to bring peace to that border territory. You,* Zheng Chenggong, are the son of our dynasty's hereditary Marquis of Tongan, Zheng Zhilong. In the past when the Great Qing troops went down into Fujian, Zhilong led the way in coming to allegiance. Although this was recorded, at the time he was not rewarded commensurately with his merit. Prince Mergen,[13] being suspicious and listening too easily [to loose talk], was remiss in providing complete, benevolent nurture. This made you fearful and wary, and you hung back, preferring the outer sphere.

Reflecting on the greatness of the bond between fathers and sons and on the heavenly naturalness of their reciprocal kindness and filiality, We wonder how the son could wish to be inimical, now that the father has become a meritorious [Qing] official. But the road between you and the capital has been long and obstructed, and you have not been able to communicate your true feelings upward. When Li De and the others arrived with your family letter, I ordered the ministers of the Inner [Three] Departments to carefully interview the messenger and learn your truest feelings. We thought empathetically, How can any distinction be drawn between new subjects and old subjects if We are to treat all with heartfelt sincerity?

Even if the maritime sector is pacified, our defense commands will need talent. Rather than choosing someone else, would it not be better to employ you? Moreover, in making recommendations, your father, Zhilong, has not demurred in [pointing out exceptional ability among] his own relatives, and he has energetically vouched for you.[†] Thus, We [proclaim Our intent

*The word "you" is used only in the imperial edicts quoted here, which speak condescendingly from emperor to subject. Usually in formal or semiformal prose, terms of address were more politely indirect. This translation reflects some of that, but it also resorts to using "I," "you," "my," "your," and so forth, for readability in English and at many points where there are no such words in the text.

†This sentence and the paragraph above (there are no paragraph divisions in the

to] raise your noble title and bestow powers commensurate with those of others who have earned merit in establishing the Qing state. We especially congratulate you on continuing your family's hereditary status.

With the bestowal of the herewith mandated decree and seal, you shall be enfeoffed as the Duke of Haicheng, with command over Quanzhou and contiguous areas and emoluments according to precedent. All measures for defending against or eradicating sea pirates off the Fujian coast shall be at your discretion. All seagoing vessels shall be subject to your management, inspection, and collection of taxes. All current personnel shall remain under your control as before, until the time when their accomplishments can be recorded. The numbers of your people coming to allegiance should be reported in a memorial to facilitate their orderly placement.* Evaluations of local officials, civil affairs, litigations, and revenues shall, of course, be handled by the viceroys and governors.†

Receive this grand commendation responsibly, and strive to make recompense with all your heart's powers. The serenity of the seacoast shall be your accomplishment. . . . Do not disregard Our command! . . .'4

3rd month [April–May]. As the prince was setting out for [Anping (present-day Anhai), the place appointed for the] peace talks, he took advantage of the situation to dispatch his various chief and regional commanders to locales in the prefectures of Fuzhou, Xinghua, Quanzhou, and Zhangzhou to collect assessments and voluntary contributions.‡ Fearing that the Qing authorities would send troops to interfere, he wrote to Viceroy and Governor Liu Qingtai, saying: "My several hundred thousand soldiers are leaning on their armor waiting for peace. Although the talks may take a while, their stomachs absolutely cannot go empty. I presume that it is all right for some of them to go into various locales and do what they deem necessary to raise revenues and sustain troop supplies. . . . "

That month, having received [Liu Qingtai's uneasy] response, the prince personally led his great forces on an inspection tour to find out whether people complied with or resisted demands that they contribute supplies and to decide on corresponding measures of mollification or

---

Chinese text) respond to Chenggong's previous point that the Qing had reneged on their promises of rank and power to Zhilong and at the same time warns Chenggong that the father will be held hostage for the son's future actions.

*This is in response to Chenggong's claim that his large army could not be disbanded.

†This makes clear to Chenggong that his role will be solely naval and that he will act in coordination with the regular civil bureaucracy on land.

‡A euphemism for moneys and goods extorted from well-to-do local families.

chastisement. . . . [Then, before he returned to Xiamen in the 4th month, Chenggong led naval forces in punishing the populace in locales on and near Haitan Island, southeast of Fuzhou, for intercepting Zheng ships.]

5th month [June–July]. The prince, stationed at Zhongzuo Base, again sped a letter to Qingtai, [announcing that he would need to be offered] three provinces before he would move toward peace. Liu Qingtai sped a letter back, which said: "From afar I received your second missive, thinking that it would assuage this humble person's dismay, not that it would be further evidence of vacillating behavior. This humble person* hastened into Fujian and wrote to you extremely candidly, hoping to come to an early agreement about the seaboard, early fulfill the Sage [Emperor]'s charge, and early effect some outcome to the problem of loyalty and filiality between your respected father and his son. How could it be that Your Honor's reply is still a thousand li off the mark?

"All affairs under heaven consist of principles and circumstances— that is all. Your respected father has been elevated to noble status above the great ministers, and your grandmother is entering her frailest years.[†] Consider that the limited territory of Zhangzhou and Quanzhou, though not yet the final resting place of Your Honor's generation, is still the locus of your ancestors' tombs. That Your Honor's military actions in such a small area might bring injury to their surface deprives your respected father's spirit of as much as fifteen minutes' peace even in his dreams and your grandmother of as much as fifteen minutes' enjoyment in sleeping or eating.[‡] If Your Honor intends to carry on serenely among the billowing waves, can you credibly assert that this is calculated to earn you riches and high titles? That would be utterly devoid of feeling or reason.

"A further consideration is that the Manchu commanders have been ready to fight [literally, 'sleeping on their spears'] for some time. At present, Great Qing troops are stationed at the Zhangzhou border, and strong forces, knives drawn, are to the south of Quanzhou—some of

*Buning is a common term of polite self-reference. Here, like the corresponding term of polite address, "Your Honor" (zuxia), it is used almost sarcastically.

[†]This reminds Chenggong that not only his father but his paternal grandmother as well are in Beijing, subject to any action of the Qing court.

[‡]This reminds Chenggong that Qing forces have desecrated Zheng graves before, and they can do it again.

them unwilling to wait any longer. This humble person's official charge is to emphasize reconciliation, whereas the Manchu commanders' forte is attack. If Your Honor continues with this mindless braggadocio, how can this humble one impede their attack by continuing to insist on reconciliation? . . .

"Moreover, the things that Your Honor said in your family letter and in the missive to me have been sufficient to arouse condemnation in the official community and to provoke anger in the Sage Intelligence. This humble person hesitated to recopy those letters for formal submission. But because of your words he cannot but bare his feelings to you from a long-suffering heart: Saying that for a long time you were not conscious of having a father not only violated natural kindness but it also leaves cause for criticism from future generations. Your respected father was an important official of the late Ming. When his state was lost, he chose a new ruler. It was not a matter of betraying [Ming imperial] favor and serving its enemies. . . . Why does Your Honor extinguish a changeless familial bond to pursue an unnecessary righteousness? The old saying that loyal officials must be sought among filial sons would seem to have no basis.

"As for presenting you with three provinces, where did that preposterous talk come from? Now the center and periphery of all under heaven have been at peace for ten years. Your Honor's hegemonic sway in the watery realm could be ignored. Nevertheless, we wish to include you to expand the force of the Great Unity. Who would dare to lightly discuss the transfer of a submissive part of the national map with its wholly legitimate resources and revenues? There has never been such a policy nor such a border strategy.

"Also laughable, if one goes by what Your Honor says, is your statement that without three provinces you'll leave us and be loyal to another.* But if you were to get three provinces, would you necessarily cast off the other and be loyal to us? All such talk is false pretense, contrary to common sense, discernibly not Your Honor's true mind. . . . Whether in instructing your clan members or in planning with your experienced elders, Your Honor must be open and sincere and not conceal your head to change faces. There must be no more useless, unrepeatable claptrap about impossible things, which only foments

*Presumably the Ming Yongli emperor, who was a virtual prisoner of Sun Kewang at Anlong in far southwestern Guizhou at the time (see Chap. 15).

controversy. In the end you will lose this opportunity by failing to act properly.

"This humble person's words will stop here, his mind's energies exhausted. On another day, seeing your respected father in the ranks of officials at court, I can assure him that I have not been at fault. Whether to advance or not will be decided by the Manchu commanders and leaders. Success or failure will have to do with Your Honor, his father, and his brothers as a group. Although this humble one shoulders official responsibility in this matter, should he carry all the blame? Only Your Honor can judge that."

.   .   .

Draft imperial edict to Zheng Chenggong, Duke of Haicheng (imperial seal applied on the 28th day of the 6th month [August 10, 1654]):

Throughout history, brave and sterling figures who have understood their times and encountered rulers who treated men with sincerity have bared their innermost feelings and observed compliance, swearing to be loyal and to never take a second allegiance. Only then could they establish success in affairs and become exalted in both their persons and their reputations. None who have looked around in doubt or suspicion could be said to have understood their times or known heaven's command.

Having received aid and nurture from heaven, We now hold a realm that extends vastly in all directions. Could it be at all difficult to secure the maritime sector with just a partial deployment of troops? But the people of mountainous Fujian are my naked babes, whom We cannot bear to subject to military labors. Moreover, considering that your father, Zheng Zhilong, came early to Qing allegiance and has been commendably loyal and obedient, the benevolence and rewards given to him have been extended to you in the form of a ducal title verified with a decree and a seal. To enable you to station troops in the four prefectures of Quanzhou, Zhangzhou, Huizhou, and Chaozhou, supplies for your waterborne units have been allocated to support the officers and soldiers of your organization. Our treatment of you might well be called most conscientious. You naturally should shave your head, be wholly loyal, and desist from calculating [your own advantage].

But according to your memorial, even though you are willing to receive the decree and seal, you are not yet willing to shave your head.* You look forward to being delegated authority over all of Fujian, and on the pretext

*In the Manchu style, signifying allegiance to the Qing. See Chap. 1, n. 20.

of undertaking military actions, you also speak of colonizing Zhoushan Island and drawing supplementary revenues from nearby prefectures like Wenzhou, Taizhou, Ningbo, and Shaoxing.* These words are ridiculous; your demands are insatiable. You make yet another excuse, saying that Qing officials and troops have not yet withdrawn from the four prefectures. But you have not yet come to allegiance, so what sense would there be in our prior withdrawal?

If you, suspicious and hesitant, have never really intended to submit, then you should state that clearly and openly, differentiating the two poles of obedience and disobedience with one sentence. But if you honor Our original edict and act in accord with what it requires, that means you accept the decree and seal, shave your head, and come to submission— the matter is finished. Should you fail to submit, then think and plan very carefully to avoid future regrets.'5

7th month [August–September]. The prince received reports at Zhongzuo Base that the Qing court had sent reinforcements into Fujian, so again he deputed his chief and regional commanders to go into Zhangzhou, Quanzhou, Fuzhou, and Xinghua prefectures to collect taxes and contributions. Because the peace talks were not yet set, the caitiffs' troops did not dare hinder such activities. So the prince energetically sent even more [revenue agents].

[8th month,] 19th day [September 29]. Li De, Zhou Jiwu, and others arrived at Zhongzuo Base and stated: "[Your younger brother,] Master [Zheng] Du, who is accompanying two Qing high officials, has arrived in the provincial capital. They want you to . . . send some of your officers to invite them before they will come down farther." The prince knew that he would have to shave his head before he could receive the proclamation [of investiture as Duke of Haicheng], so he was not willing to send any officers. Instead, he ordered Zhou Jiwu to go back and invite them, carrying a letter, which said: "This lowly wanderer of the seaboard has planted his staff beyond the pale of normal society, and he has long had no thought of earning a meritorious name in human affairs. He never expected that after his family's tomb sites were desecrated, grand injunctions would arrive one upon another, reinforced with the silken missives of an emperor 'treating him with heartfelt sincerity.' By rights, how could I refuse? With humble gifts in hand, I wait expectantly for your vehicle. Some inner feelings have not yet been fully

*All are in Zhejiang Province, along the south side of Hangzhou Bay and the contiguous seacoast.

disclosed and require face-to-face discussions. My thoughts are in suspense as I await your early arrival. The cessation of hostilities in the Southeast virtually depends on one statement from the envoys. Men far and near will then hold the same loyalty, and subtle thoughts will gain expression across ten thousand li."*

24th day [October 4]. [The Qing emissaries] Ye Chengge and Ashan arrived in Quanzhou and ordered Zhou Jiwu to go [to Chenggong] and say: "If you do not shave your head, then you cannot receive the proclamation. If your head is not shaven, then we need not even meet." The prince scoffed at this and sent no reply but directed the envoys to wait in Quanzhou for something to report.

[9th month,] 4th day [October 13]. The prince sent Lü Tai, one of his rites functionaries, along with Li De to enter Quanzhou and present gifts to the Qing envoys. To dazzle them, Lü and Li emptied out the jewels that foreign countries had sent [Chenggong], but the two emissaries declined to accept any gifts, for the peace talks had not been joined. . . .

7th day [October 16]. The two emissaries ordered the inner imperial guardsman Master Du [Chenggong's first younger brother] and Master Yin [Chenggong's fourth younger brother] to visit the prince. When Master Du saw his elder brother, he knelt, tears streaming down his face, and declared, "Father has interceded for you again and again in the capital. If you don't go this time around, the security of the whole family will be hard to protect. Please force yourself to accept -the proclamation." But the prince replied: "You ordinary sons have never understood affairs of the world. Since ancient times, when dynasties have changed, those who have subordinated themselves to others have never come to a good end—the single exception being Emperor Guangwu of the Han.† Father having erred earlier, why should I enter the same trap later? For every day that I don't accept the proclamation, Father has one day of glory at court. Were I to feebly accept the proclamation and shave my head, then the fates of father and sons alike would be hard to predict. Don't say any more. Am I so inhuman as to forget our father? This sort of thing is not easy—not easy!"

---

*Chenggong is saying that he needs to dicker over some things in private before he can accept the deal that they are offering.

†Who accepted the Xin dynasty of Wang Mang but was later able to restore the Han dynasty. See Chap. 8, n. 7.

Each day he had them entertained with theatricals and wine to glad-
den their hearts and keep them from raising the peacemaking matter
again.

.   .   .

21st day [October 30]. The prince deputed an officer, Lin Hou, to
accompany Master Du back; they again carried a letter and gifts to the
emissaries. But the emissaries were even less willing to accept them
than before. The prince's letter read: "Splendid banners have come so
quickly across ten thousand li! That I was unable to respectfully greet
them fills my bosom with regret. Last month the messenger Li De came
and informed me that the Minister's pennon had reached the provincial
capital.* Just as I was about to depute a special officer to serve your
needs fully, the report came that your party had already arrived in
Quanzhou.

"Recently my second youngest brother came to see me. This awkward person† charged him with conveying my intentions, and I agreed
with him to set a date for our meeting. By that time the Minister had
personally brought his pennon to Anping once again. The nocturnal,
starlit travels of the Honored Minister were too abrupt; as for this
awkward one, I did not hasten to grease my cart axles and thus missed
meeting and receiving you. Hopefully, these lapses in protocol can be
excused. . . .

"This awkward person is planning to fully disclose his inferior
thoughts in a face-to-face talk—things that cannot be expressed in writing. An auspicious date for sweeping the marble guest couch has already
been divined. The poor gifts sent previously were not accepted. But
again I have prepared some offerings to somewhat fulfill the role of host,
still praying that you will assess and accept them. Pen in hand, I look
forward to your arrival."

The two emissaries wrote back, saying: " . . . On the 18th and 19th
Li De and Huang Zhengming‡ came [to Anping] and said that you

*The chief emissary, Ye Chengge, was a vice-minister of one of the Six Ministries.
He had previously been assigned to Jiangning, where he had vigorously prosecuted
persons suspected of having contact with seaborne Ming loyalists.
†Chenggong's conventionally polite term of self-reference throughout this letter.
‡Zhilong's nephew by marriage, thus, Chenggong's maternal cousin, whom the Qing
had also enlisted to help in the mediation.

would neither accept the proclamation nor shave your head. We, your juniors, thus returned to Quanzhou on the 20th. Now we have received another letter saying that an auspicious meeting date has been divined. We cannot tell whether the two messengers, Huang and Li, were wrong in what they said before or whether the Gentleman now has reconsidered shaving his head and accepting the proclamation. . . . If we meet, it will just be a matter of making the emperor's vastly generous and virtuous intentions broadly known, submitting the Gentleman's written expression of gratitude for favor after he has shaved his head, and discussing the disposition of your fine officer corps, as well as defense measures and troop levels for the four prefectures—nothing more. Why mention anything else? It seems that the Gentleman again has inappropriately gone into extraneous matters.

"We junior ones bear [the weight of] the court's command on our small persons. The Imperial stipulation is that we return to the capital within the 10th month. How dare we delay any longer and test the law with our bodies? We humbly implore you to make one decisive statement soon, so that we can gallop speedily to report on our mission. . . . "

On the night of the 24th [November 2], Masters Du and Yin, Zhou Jiwu, Huang Zhengming, and others came again and tearfully, beseechingly, said, "If the two emissaries are disappointed this time and go back, the greater plan will be hard to sustain. After we report the results of our mission, there will surely be little reason to keep us alive, and the Old Master, the grand preceptor will also be in difficulty." The prince replied, "No matter how much is said or how much things change, my mind is made up. Say no more!"

.   .   .

The Duke of Pingguo [Zhilong] wrote a letter to [his younger brother, Chenggong's uncle] the Duke of Dingguo [Zheng Hongkui], telling him to persuade the prince to accept the proclamation and informing Dingguo that the Qing court wished to give him a noble title, too. At this time Dingguo wrote a letter in return, which read: "After the winter of 1646, when I tearfully parted from Elder Brother's visage on Sea Tortoise River,* your younger brother lived quietly with the various

*Which debouches east of the family home at Shijing.

generals on our islands, willing that his eyes be pierced through by the sight of your return. After some rumors came from Suqian,* he did not expect that the route northward through Jianning would be obstructed and that news of you would fall into a long silence. . . .

"[After the incident of 1651, when Qing forces ravaged Xiamen,] your younger brother, because of a bad foot ailment, chose a place on White Beach [not far from the brothers' home at Shijing] and built a crude thatch cottage there. All his warships, large and small, were converted for fishing and trade. He has lived at peace in that place for three years now. . . .

"In the first month of the new year I successively received Elder Brother's instruction, a copy of an imperial edict, and a letter from a Minister Liu presenting a decree: I could remain where I was and not go to the capital; though already included among [the Qing] marquises and earls, I would be elevated further. Your younger brother has borne this foot ailment, which grows worse daily, for over ten years. It is not something he just began speaking of today. Whenever he moves a few short steps, two persons must support him between them. So any thoughts of gaining a meritorious name have long since turned to ash. Everyone in the world, especially Elder Brother, knows that in the summer of 1646, I turned in my seal, took the Buddhist tonsure, and resigned from office. Anyway, your younger brother received magnanimous treatment from his own [Ming] dynasty, under which he held high positions and titles. So he cannot rightly betray that former benevolence out of greed for new glories. In sum, I wish to stay quietly at White Beach nursing my ailment, satisfied with my allotment from heaven and at peace with my surroundings—that's all. . . .

"As for Eldest Nephew, your younger brother has been at White Beach and the nephew at Zhongzuo Base. Not only are the two places far apart but your younger brother's afflicted foot makes it hard for him to walk even a little, and the nephew's military movements are indefinite, so we've seen each other very seldom. But in this case, when Elder Brother's letter arrived, his younger brother, despite his affliction, went by boat and made every effort to persuade Eldest Nephew. Eldest Nephew just said, 'The greater righteousness lies in extinguishing concern for one's kin. Since early on, I've pursued this principle, and my

*A strategic city on the Grand Canal in far northern South Zhili (Jiangnan), through which Zhilong probably passed when being taken to Beijing.

plans to realize it are decided.' He never would listen to you, the elder brother. Why would he be willing to listen to me, the younger?

"I am sending an officer with this return missive posthaste, hoping you will convey [to the Qing leadership] your younger brother's sentiments. Should my retirement place at White Beach again be disturbed by the Qing, then your younger brother will have to sail off to a more distant place to avoid them. Even if it means incurring danger on the surging waves, I will do so gladly.

"The road is long, and my pen is short, so I haven't said all that I'd like to. Gratified by your luminous understanding, I look up to you in overwhelming admiration."

.   .   .

29th day [November 7]. With Master Du, Li De, Zhou Jiwu, Huang Zhengming, and [Zheng Zhilong's wife, Chenggong's formal but not actual mother] Madam Yan, the two Qing emissaries hastened back to the capital to report on their mission. The peace talks had not come about. . . .

.   .   .

The prince wrote a parting letter to Master Du, which read: "After being separated for several years, elder and younger brothers were able to be together only a few days before you were suddenly taken away again: this is a matter of heaven, a matter of fate. Younger Brother, his thorough persuasions reinforced with poignant sobs, can be said to have tried everything to the utmost. But your elder brother for his part held steadfastly to true virtue. Not only could considerations of profit or loss never move my heart, but it would not change my determination even if an ax or sword were applied to my neck. Why? The right course was decided long ago; I have already thought it through. Your elder brother's present feelings all were expressed in his return letter to our father. What Younger Brother has heard of that letter should enable you to understand.

"In general it was simply that if the Qing court trusted your elder brother's words, then he would become a man of the Qing; if they did not, then he would remain a servant of the Ming. What else was there to discuss? . . . The envoys used just one word throughout: *threaten*. If one uses threats, then it should be with weapons, not the way Ye Chengge and Ashan did. Besides, is your elder brother someone who can be threatened? . . .

"When panthers live in the deep mountains, every other animal fears them. Once they enter the barred trap, they wave their tails and beg for mercy, knowing they are powerless. But the phoenix soars eight thousand feet high, going anywhere it wishes in the vast reaches of the universe, above and free from the common world. Your brother's reputation has been known among the Chinese and the barbarians for some time now, and he is experienced in using troops. How could he relinquish being a free phoenix to become a caged panther?

"Younger Brother must now take good care of Father and Mother. In that, completely follow the filial path. But do not worry hereafter about your elder brother. Indeed, the Han had its Ziyu but also its Kongming; and Chu had its Wu Shang but also its Zixu.[16] Your elder brother may not be up to [following such historical examples], but Younger Brother must do his best.

"I bid you adieu now, not saying all that I would."

.   .   .

The prince's letter to the grand preceptor read: "In 1648 your son sent Wang Yu to the capital to inquire after Father's welfare and activities; as a result, Father was surrounded by guards, and Wang Yu was barred from contact with him. Since that time, I haven't dared communicate a single word. Not only were no messengers willing to go but we also feared causing trouble for you. At the end of 1652, Zhou Jiwu and the others suddenly arrived and presented Father's letter. Your son was both surprised and suspicious, . . . so he sent Li De to the capital to investigate whether you were there. To tell the truth, I'd heard that you were no longer alive. I composed a missive, explaining a bit how I've always felt. Actually, from the start, talking peace was never on my mind. Otherwise, if I had welcomed being summoned and reconciled, why would I have expressed myself like that? This could be known without my pointing it out.

"Unexpectedly there arrived the Qing court's command that I accept one prefecture and the title Duke of Haicheng. Your son could do little else but hold back his troops to show good faith. The command that I take four prefectures arrived after that. Again, your son could not but receive the edict to show good faith. As for requesting more territory, it arose from the need to settle my several hundred thousand troops and to make definite, thorough plans for relief after hostilities. How could it be said that my 'words were ridiculous' or that I 'arrogantly made insatiable demands'? Again unexpectedly, the territory in question was not increased; even the four prefectures eventually became just an enticing illusion [literally, "a picture of a cookie"]. That they wanted to repeat the same trick they had used to trap my father before was not outside my usual expectations of them. Then all at once the proclamation about shaving my head came down, and in my armies the men's hair stood on end! . . .

"The Qing court uses head shaving as a petty excuse. In the whole world where is there a man who would rush to declare himself the servant of a state before he had received lands? Where in the world is there a man who would shave his head with alacrity before declaring himself the servant of a state? Where in the world is there a case of one side not being concrete in its offers and the other side being concrete in its response? Where in the world can an unbelieving mind get anywhere by expecting to be believed? And where in the world are those who do not trust with the heart but expect to place trust in men's hair?! . . .

"Before I received the first edict, the Manchus were still quite courteous. Only after that did they begin to pressure and threaten me arbitrarily. The ambassadors being like that, the attitude of the court can be known. Could one not feel imperiled? Could one not be awakened? Besides, your son's name is well known among both the Chinese and the barbarians. If he were to handle things lamely, he would be disesteemed by the Qing court, and he would also become the laughingstock of the world. Generally speaking, the Qing court treats my father with superficial decorum, but they actually look on him as just a valuable commodity. This round of imperial decrees and the behavior of the emissaries show very clearly that the court wishes to use the father to intimidate the son. One threat leads to no end of threats. But your son is hardly someone who can be intimidated!

"Moreover, when my father went to see the Manchu princes, he had already made himself the target of their drawn bows. That he has survived to the present is but a great good fortune. The hopefully slight chance that my father will see misfortune at their hands is a matter of heaven and fate. If that should happen, your son could only take revenge

in mourning dress and bring closure to the matter of loyalty and filiality.
. . . At this time he can do no more than feed his horses and sharpen
his weapons, awaiting enemy attack. What else is there to say? What
else is there to say? . . . "

[The following year Zhilong fell prey to charges of colluding with
Chenggong and was stripped of his titles and imprisoned. In November
1661 he was executed, along with all the members of his family in
Beijing. Chenggong, who had found it prudent to move his base to
Taiwan,* learned in short succession of a case of disobedience in his
own son, of the capture and probable demise of the Yongli emperor in
the extreme southwest,† and of his father's execution. In a state of
delirium probably induced by acute distress and some pestilential disease, he died on June 23, 1662, at the age of thirty-seven.]

*See Chap. 13.
†See Chap. 15.

13

Under the "Blood-Flag": Dutch and Chinese Views of the Battle for Taiwan

AFTER THE COLLAPSE of peace talks between Zheng Chenggong and the Qing court in 1654, the conflict over control of the southeastern seaboard intensified. Zheng's mistakenly low estimation of Qing abilities eventually led him to carry out a spectacularly unsuccessful siege of Nanjing in 1659, after which he realized that he would always be on the defensive at his base in southern Fujian. The Qing for their part began the first stages of what soon became a draconian ban on all coastal activity—enforced by moving the whole population several miles inland—which caused catastrophic losses to the Chinese maritime economy for over two decades.

These developments were worrisome for the officers of the Dutch East India Company stationed at Tai Bay, on the island they called Formosa.* Since the mid-1620s, when the company had agreed to move to Taiwan as compensation for staying away from the Fujian coast and the Pescadores (some entrepôt in that region being necessary for carrying on its lucrative Japan trade), the company had maintained an uneasy truce with the Zhengs. The knowledge that Zheng Chenggong was building enormous armies and fleets to pursue his war with the Tartars naturally gave the Dutch reason to fear the day when he might need to leave Fujian for safer haven elsewhere. The disruptions of the coastal economy caused by that hostility made trading conditions unpredictable

---

*The Dutch referred separately to the main island, Formosa, and to the bay and its formative sand island where they had their colony—Taiwan (Terrace Bay) in Chinese and Tayouan or Tayowan as romanized in European accounts. In contemporaneous Chinese writings the name of the bay was extended to refer to the main island as well.

and swelled the numbers of poor Chinese commoners who emigrated from the Zhangzhou-Quanzhou region to settle around Tai Bay. Although the company was not averse to having more productive hands, thus more heads to tax, in their colony (the Chinese settlement of which was called Sakam—Chikan in Chinese), this immigrant population grew more restive as rumors from the mainland grew more ominous.[1]

Repeated warnings from the governor of the Dutch colony, Frederik Coyet (1620–89), to the headquarters of the governor-general of the Dutch East India Company in Batavia (present-day Jakarta) that the defenses of the Taiwan installation urgently needed reinforcement were ineffectual. In spite of the great importance of Taiwan to the fortunes of the company in the East Asian maritime trade network, a combination of jealousy, niggardliness, stupidity, cowardice, and other human perfidies kept responses to Coyet's appeals at a minimum. The resulting change of hands that Taiwan underwent in 1661 was momentous for the history of Dutch imperialism and even more so for the history of China.[2]

After the seizure of Tai Bay and expulsion of the Dutch by Zheng Chenggong, Governor Coyet was made the scapegoat for company failures. Upon his return to Batavia, Coyet was imprisoned and maltreated for three years. In June 1655 he was exiled to a desolate islet in the Malayan Archipelago for life. In 1674, however, his children and some friends gained his release and permission for him to return to Holland from the Prince of Orange.* Fortunately, Coyet was allowed to take all the local company records with him when he vacated Castle Zeelandia, his fortress at Tai Bay. In subsequent years he put those records to good use in writing an extensive, detailed vindication of his role in the Taiwan debacle. His account, 't Verwaerloosde Formosa (Neglected Formosa), published in Amsterdam by J. C. ten Hoorn in 1675, stands as a valuable history of a crucial event.[3]

Coyet's account gains even more interest when placed side by side with a chronicle written from the Zheng perspective—that of Chenggong's revenue officer, Yang Ying.[4] Governor Coyet, representing a civilization in which a man of status was often expected to be "a soldier and a gentleman," describes battles, armaments, fighting styles, and generalship exhaustively and with panache. Yang Ying, a literate man in a civilization that exalted letters, did not partake of a military identity,

*See n. 6, below.

even though he served as a cog in the machinery of a thoroughly military organization. He shows little interest in recording the details, or even the occurrence, of battles. Rather, partly because of his specific duties, he is absorbed in such civil service matters as logistics and gauging the temperament of troops and populace. Coyet sees the fate of Taiwan—and of Christianity there—as dependent on putting the gentleman-soldier's wisdom and honor into effect. Yang Ying, although he candidly records great difficulties on the Zheng side and even implies some criticism of Zheng Chenggong's judgment, is convinced of the cosmic destiny of his prince to succeed, at least in the bid to take Taiwan. In spite of these radical differences in perspective, however, we find each side well apprised of the capabilities and intentions of the other. To twist Confucius a bit: People differ widely in culture, but their eyes and ears are much the same.[5]

FREDERIK COYET   When, in the previous century, our beloved Fatherland had fallen into such extremity that it seemed no longer possible to resist the power of the Spaniards, and when the Church had to all appearance become their slave, that highly celebrated Prince,[6] the greatest politician of the time, whose memory is so dear to the Dutch nation, and on whose martyrdom the first foundations of our precious freedom were laid, forced the desperate Council to surrender their country to the mercy of the waters by breaking the dykes and dams; thus causing it to sink away as if in a precipice, and compelling the people, with their wives, children, and moveable property, to take refuge in their ships.[7] They would then have to depend absolutely on God's mercy, and go to sea in search of other countries, where they could found a new republic. . . .

In like manner Koxinga [Zheng Chenggong],* after many long years of wars with the Tartars, who pursued him very vigorously, was brought to a state of great extremity; so much so that he was forced to hide his wife and children and all their moveable goods in his junks, and to remove from one island to another.

Being sorely pressed by the Tartars, he was obliged to seek safety

*Koxinga is a corruption of the Minnanese pronunciation of Guoxingye, "Lord of the State Surname." See pp. 182n, 211n.

in some other country free from their power; for, through lack of vessels and ignorance of the laws of navigation, the Tartars were unable to cross the sea.

YANG YING   15th year [of the Ming Yongli reign,[8] 1661], 1st month [February]. The prince, at Si-Ming Subprefecture,* sent down a directive to prepare ships on a large scale and await orders to go out on campaign. He gathered his various generals for a secret conference and said to them:

> Heaven is not yet surfeited with disorder, and the illegitimate [Qing] regime still exists, having caused our advance on the Southern Capital to become a rout.[9] Last year, although we beat back one attack by the caitiff Dasu,† the false [Qing] court will not necessarily straightaway regret making war on us. So having to charge north and south on [defensive] campaigns will inevitably fatigue our families.
>
> The year before last, He Tingbin‡ portrayed Taiwan as having ten thousand hectares of fields and gardens, a thousand li of undeveloped fertile land, and revenues of several hundred thousand [taels per year]. Shipbuilding and arms manufacture could be done well if our skilled people were concentrated there. Lately it has been occupied by the red-haired foreigners [the Dutch], but within the walled fortress they don't have more than a thousand people. We could capture it without lifting a hand. I want to conquer Taiwan to use as a base. After settling you generals' families there, we could campaign to the east and chastise those to the west without worrying about the home front. What's more, it would help build resources and inculcate determination.

At the time none in the group dared oppose this idea, though all looked uncomfortable. Only Wu Hao of the Declare Resolve Rear Division, who had been to the place, said that its geomantic features were bad[10] and its waters and soils were full of pestilence. The prince

---

*Zheng's main military command center, formerly called Zhongzuo Base. He changed the name to Si-Ming (Think of the Ming) early in 1654.

†Chamberlain of the Imperial Bodyguard, of the Bordered Yellow Banner. As the General Who Pacifies the South, he had tried unsuccessfully to dislodge Zheng from Xiamen in September 1660.

‡He Tingbin was a former interpreter (called Pincqua) for the Dutch East India Company who was employed in communicating with Zheng Chenggong beginning in 1657. He was dismissed in February 1659 for running a confidence scheme involving excise taxes on shipping between Taiwan and Zheng's territories. Hoping to take revenge, he then went to Zheng Chenggong's camp and tried to persuade him to move against Taiwan.

resented Wu's words and said he was obstructing army operations. The vice-director of the military headquarters of the Five Armies,[11] Yang Chaodong, alone spoke in favor of going, and the prince commended him. Later, when the conquest was completed, he consequently made Yang governor of [the capital] prefecture,[12] and he executed Wu Hao.*

COYET   The island of Formosa appeared to suit him most, as he could there remain safe and free. Moreover, a splendid opportunity now offered itself, for van der Laan[†] had gone back to Batavia with his officers, and the ships of the succour-fleet had been separated and dispatched to different localities. Then, the force sent to render assistance consisted of not more than six hundred men; but these, even including the resident garrison, could not afford protection for the vast possessions of Formosa. Another most important factor was that the north monsoon had almost closed, so that it would be next to impossible for any vessel to reach Batavia in quest of renewed help if Formosa were to be attacked. Koxinga was, therefore, sure that no danger could come from Batavia, so long as he could prevent tidings of his attack reaching it, a thing which seemed certain owing to the lapse of the north winds.[13]

YANG   3rd month, 10th day [April 8]. The prince's ship reached Liaoluo Bay[‡] and awaited a favorable wind for embarkation. At the time many of the officers thought it was a hardship to cross the open sea and wanted to desert, so the captain of the glorious Soldier Guard, Chen Rui, was delegated to round them up and bring them in under arrest.

.   .   .

22nd day [April 20]. All officers and soldiers were urged to board ship. At noon on the 23rd, the sky became clear and still, and the fleet set out to sea. On the 24th the various ships arrived in close order at the Penghu Archipelago [the Pescadores],[§] and the crews camped on

*See 5th month, 2nd day, below.

[†]In the summer of 1660, the governor-general of the Dutch East India Company at Batavia sent a fleet of twelve ships and six hundred soldiers under Jan van der Lann ostensibly to reinforce the Tai Bay colony. But both the governor-general and van der Laan were more sanguine about attacking the Portuguese at Macao, so when no invasion by Zheng Chenggong materialized in 1660, van der Laan soon departed, in September of that year.

[‡]On the southern side of Jinmen (Quemoy) Island.

[§]A distance of seventy-nine nautical miles.

separate islands in the group. The prince's ship anchored at Shinei Peninsula* and again waited for a favorable wind to go on [map 7].

27th day. Our great forces embarked but got only to the Ganji Islands† before they encountered bad winds and had to return to the Shinei Peninsula. Most of the soldiers had not brought travel supplies, for He Tingbin had said that Taiwan would be reached within a few days, and then grain would be plentiful. But now supplies were running low in the delay caused by the bad winds. So the prince ordered a revenue manager to accompany Major Hong in getting travel supplies from the thirty-six islands and atolls of the Penghu group. . . . Then the headmen of the various harbors were assembled and made to press their people for provisions. They tried to come up with what was demanded for two days but then returned and said, "Our islands really have no fields for planting grains extensively. There are only yams, barley, and millet, gathered and brought in by the pint and peck—altogether little over a hundred piculs—and not enough to provide one meal for your great army."

The prince was surprised at the lack of grain and also feared that the northern monsoon [which was to carry them southward to Tai Bay] would not last much longer. So he sent down an order to set out on the evening of the 30th. At the time the high winds reportedly had not ceased, and there were gusty rains and dark fog. Those in charge of the Center Army ships, such as Cai Yi and Chen Guang, knelt and petitioned to wait awhile, until the wind and rain subsided, before setting out. But the prince lectured them, saying, "Whether ice is hard enough to walk across depends on heaven's wish. If heaven wishes us to conquer Tai Bay, then after we embark tonight, the winds and waves will smooth out naturally. In any case, how can we bear to sit here, getting hungrier, stranded on these fragmented isles?" Early that evening the order came down to get under way. Although the wind and rain lessened somewhat, the terrifying waves did not abate. After one in the morning, however, the clouds went away, the rain dispersed, and the weather became crystal clear as we sailed along with a favorable wind.

4th month, 1st day [April 29].[14] At the crack of dawn the prince's

---

*On the southwest part of the main island, forming a bay.
†Now called the West Ji and East Ji islands—familiar signposts for mariners traveling between the Penghu Islands and Tai Bay.

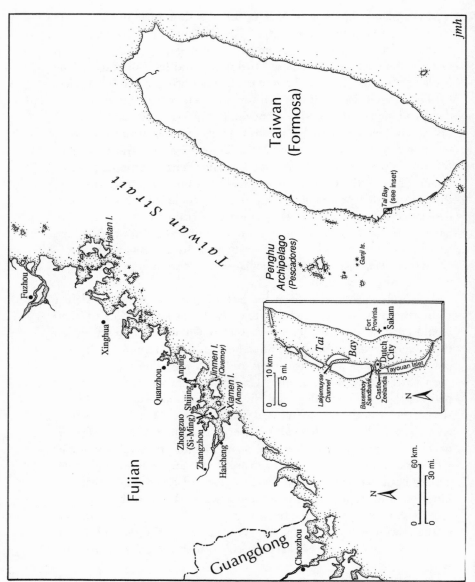

Map 7. Zheng Chenggong versus the Qing and the Dutch

Taiwan (Formosa)

Taiwan Strait

Fujian

Guangdong

Fuzhou

Haitan I.

Xinghua

Quanzhou

Anping
Zhongzuo (Si-Ming)
Shijing
Zhangzhou
Haicheng
Jinmen I. (Quemoy)
Xiamen I. (Amoy)

Chaozhou

Penghu Archipelago (Pescadores)

Ganji Is.

Tai Bay (see inset)

Tai Bay
Lakjemuyse Channel
Baxemboy Sandbank
Castle Zeelandia
Dutch City
Fort Provintia
Sakam
Tayouan Islet

N

10 km.
5 mi.
0

60 km.
30 mi.
0

N

jmh

fleet reached the sandspit outside Tai Bay,* and the ships linked together in an unbroken cordon. After seven, when it was completely light, we closed in on Deer's Ear Channel [Lakjemuyse Canal].† Our prince had a small patrol go ashore there first to reconnoiter for campsites. After the noon hour our big warships entered Deer's Ear Channel together. Before, this bay had been quite shallow and could not accommodate big ships. But on that day the water had risen several feet, so even our largest vessels had no difficulty—surely it was the silent aid of heaven's wish.‡ That evening all our boats having arrived, we moored at Heliao Inlet and went ashore to set up camp. . . . The Tiger Guard of the Declare Resolve Front Division was to position its men-of-war at Deer's Ear Channel to check any movement of the Dutch sailors or their wedge-hulled ships[15] and defend against any enemy approach via the Northline Tail [Baxemboy Sandbank; see inset, map 7].

COYET This monsoon having now lapsed, he risked the chance, and appeared with several hundreds of war vessels on 31 April 1661§ at daybreak, off the Formosan coast in sight of Castle Zeelandia. On board there were about twenty-five thousand soldiers, who had been all well trained in the Tartar wars.

His chief officer was Bepontok, a deserted Tartar,|| well acquainted with warfare. This officer headed the fleet with his Nankin junks, and suddenly sailed between the little North islands through the Lakjemuyse Canal [Channel], which is situated about one mile from Castle Zeelandia, and is so broad that some twenty could enter it abreast, if close to one another. Bepontok then scattered his vessels over the broad bay which separates Tayouan from Formosa, and landed his men. A few thousands of Chinese came to meet him, and assisted him with lorries and other appliances of landing. Thus, in less than two hours, a considerable part of the force had entered our bays, and a few thousand soldiers had landed on *terra firma*; while war-vessels were placed

*From Penghu, a distance of fifty-seven nautical miles.

†If pronounced in the Southern Min subdialect of Minnanese, Deer's Ear Channel (Luermen) becomes Lokdzimui—hence the Dutch approximation, Lakjemuyse. Similar correspondences can be found between other place-names in these two accounts.

‡The editor Chen Bisheng's note points out that Zheng had departed from Penghu in time to catch the especially high tide on the first day of the lunar month when he reached Tai Bay.

§See n. 14.

||This reference is puzzling. No major figure on the scene had such a name, and Zheng is not known to have had any Manchu officers.

in position between our two forts, Castle Zeelandia and the little Fort of Provintia.

The Governor and Council could only look on, without being able to prevent in the slightest this easy entrance and landing of the enemy. To devise means for this was extremely difficult, as they were completely non-plussed and unable to resist such a formidable enemy. They had been compelled by van der Laan and a few others to disperse the fleet, and send the ships to different places; keeping only two war-vessels, the *Hector* and the *'s Gravenlande*, the bark *Vink*, and the yacht *Maria*— small, flat-bottomed, and shallow-draught vessels, which were suited only for inland navigation.

Although principally intended for protection of the bay and the channel between, the two Castles, Zeelandia and Provintia, were found to be useless, owing to that faulty construction which had repeatedly been brought under notice of the [Dutch East India Company] Government.

Near Castle Zeelandia, there was but one single pilot-boat, which was of too deep draught to be taken close inshore, besides a few Chinese vessels which were totally unfitted for warfare. The number of people in the Castle was about one thousand one hundred, and [there were] fully forty armed men. The quantity of powder in the country was about thirty thousand pounds, besides a little on the ships; but practised war-officers, able constables, grenadiers, and engineers were few; while of all other kinds of ammunition and war material they had but a very limited supply. Still, although it was clear that they could not possibly prevent the hostile force from landing, owing to lack of men and ships, they courageously decided to make the best of it, and to retard and harm the enemy as much as possible.

They therefore ordered the two warships, with the *Vink* and the *Maria*, to advance and give battle to the Chinese junks. Captain Thomas Pedel offered and took upon himself to reconnoiter, skirmish, and, with two hundred and forty men, to dislodge the enemy, who had landed near the entrance of Lakjemuyse. . . . After the above ships sailed to the Lakjemuyse Canal, they were brought as near as possible to the shore. The men were in good spirits and anxious to attack the junks of the enemy, who also showed much activity.

YANG   That evening the head of the foreigners at the fortification in Chikan [that is, Fort Provintia in the Chinese settlement of Sakam],

Maonan Shiding [deputy governor Jacobus Valentyn], fired cannon on our encampment and burned the feed stored in the horse stables. On the streets of Chikan were the crude grass shelters of our [Chinese] residents. The prince feared that their grains would also be torched, so he sent me, Revenue Officer Yang Ying,* with a tagged arrow to authorize [two army units] to stand guard over the [grain stores], neither allowing our men to make off with the contents desultorily nor allowing the red-haired foreigners to burn them. The following day I took all the rice from those streets and distributed it to the various army divisions for supplies; the amounts were estimated to be sufficient for half a month.

COYET   About sixty of their largest junks, each provided with two guns, separated from the others to meet our men. And thus the naval battle was started by our ships under a terrible thunder of cannons. The *Hector*, being the largest and heaviest, took the lead, and gave promise of success; as on its first arrival with its large cannon, it bored so fortunately through many a junk which came too near, that very soon one or two could be seen sinking, while others kept at a respectable distance.

But the enemy, like brave soldiers, were not to be thus beaten back. Heated by the fight, five or six of the bravest junks attacked the *Hector* from all sides; whose warriors, in trying to save it, caused such a dense smoke by firing its cannon from below, above, front and behind, that neither the *Hector* nor the junks could be observed from the Castle, from which this battle could otherwise have been easily watched.

During the smoke, such a terrible explosion was heard that it caused the windows of the Castle to shake; and when the smoke had cleared away, neither the *Hector* nor the junks which had been nearest to it could be seen. Unfortunately the *Hector* had been blown up, and cargo and men were lost through an explosion of the powder on board [fig. 21]. . . .

The enemy's courage was whetted through this calamity, and they surrounded our other three ships as closely as ants; but, through the unfortunate and untimely loss of their companion, the latter had become more cautious, and kept clear of the shore by going out to open sea, so as to run no risk of stranding in case of stress from wind or weather. By these tactics, it was hoped that their hands would be more free,

*After this point Yang Ying's self-references are rendered in the first person.

Figure 21. The naval battle for Tai Bay. Castle Zeelandia is on the peninsula in the middle ground.

and that they would not be so easily surrounded. Thinking they had fled, the enemy started in pursuit, the one side being now more anxious than the other; but, getting into deep water, ours passed two or three times through the enemy's fleet and kept continually firing. Favoured by splendid weather and a soft breeze, they caused considerable damage amongst the invaders' ships and men; who, becoming somewhat alarmed, did not dare to come to close quarters, although they were far from giving up. With two large junks they boarded the *'s Gravenlande* and the *Vink* in the rear. The *Maria* not being fit for warfare, but simply a despatch-boat, and not having accommodation for men, had gone further out to sea, to prevent being seized and overpowered.

Behind these two they attached two others, and so on yet two more, so that they got five or six couples behind one another. Then the Captains with swords in hand drove the soldiers from the hindmost junks to the front, to fill up the places of those who had been shot. By continually pressing forwards to overpower those within our ships, they at length managed to set foot on the *'s Gravenlande*, notwithstanding the determined resistance. Some had already started to cut through the rigging, but our men made a final courageous attack, drove them back again and got their ship clear. At the same time, they fired from their guns in the forecastle and from the cabin (in which guns were placed), and threw hand grenades. In fact, they caused so great a loss among the attacking Chinese that, according to their own confession, more than a thousand were killed that day, not counting the wounded. Three or four times they had been attacked by Chinese junks which served as fire-boats; but these were all beaten off except one, which managed to attach itself by means of an iron chain to the *'s Gravenlande* bowsprit. Hereupon, she caught fire, but through the alacrity of our men this was soon extinguished, and the fire-boat became detached. At length the Chinese, who had spared no effort to conquer these two ships, departed and went with their junks close to the shore.

Meanwhile, if our men were busy at sea, those on land were not idle; but caused the Chinese as much trouble in all quarters as possible. Captain Pedel accompanied two hundred and forty brave picked men, who were embarked on the pilot-boat and on some Chinese vessels which had been left near the Castle. He went to Baxemboy, a sand plain of about a square mile in area.... Having arrived there, Pedel divided his troops into two companies, arranging them in position, and called upon them to be brave and to fear not the Chinese enemy, for he would certainly lead them to victory. Captain Pedel had himself a fixed and undoubted assurance of success, and his bright, hopeful attitude inspired the men, who were satisfied that the Chinese had no liking for the smell of powder, or the noise of muskets; and that after the first charge, in which only a few of them might be shot, they would immediately take flight and become completely disorganised.

... The Chinese in Formosa were regarded by the Hollanders as insignificant, and in warfare as cowardly and effeminate men. It was reckoned that twenty-five of them put together would barely equal one Dutch soldier, and the whole Chinese race was regarded in the same way, no distinction being made between Chinese peasants and soldiers; if he was but a native of China, then he was cowardly and had no stamina. This had come to be quite a fixed conclusion with our soldiers, and although they had often heard about Koxinga's brave exploits against the Tartars, proving his soldiers to be anything but cowardly, yet this did not seem to alter the general opinion. Their fighting had been against the poor, miserable Tartars, and no opportunity had yet been given them of showing their bravery against the Netherlanders, who would soon settle them, and make them laugh on the wrong sides of their faces.

Preoccupied with such thoughts, Captain Pedel, after a short prayer, marched with his men in good order straight towards the enemy. These had landed on the other side of Baxemboy, and mustering four thousand men in full fighting trim, they came to meet him. Noticing the small number of the Dutch troops, they detached from the main body seven or eight hundred soldiers, who marched round behind the hill to attack this little Dutch force in the rear.

The latter courageously marched in rows of twelve men towards the enemy, and when they came near enough, they charged by firing three volleys uniformly. The enemy, not less brave, discharged so great a storm of arrows that they seemed to darken the sky. From both sides some few fell *hors de combat*, but still the Chinese were not going to run away, as was imagined. The Dutch troops now noticed the separated Chinese squadron which came to surprise them from the rear; and seeing that those in front stubbornly held their ground, it now became a case of *sero sapiunt Phryges* [seeing the Phrygians—the enemy—too late]. They now discovered that they had been too confident of the weakness of the enemy, and had not anticipated such resistance. If they were courageous before the battle (seeking to emulate the actions

Figure 22. The land battle for Tai Bay.

of Gideon), fear now took the place of their courage, and many of them threw down their rifles without even discharging them at the enemy. Indeed, they took to their heels, with shameful haste, leaving their brave comrades and valiant Captain in the lurch. Pedel, judging that it would be the veriest folly to withstand such overwhelming numbers, wished to close together and retreat in good order, but his soldiers would not listen to him. Fear had the upper-hand, and life was dear to them; each therefore sought to save himself. The Chinese saw the disorder and attacked still more vigorously, cutting down all before them. They gave no quarter, but went on until the Captain with one hundred and eighteen of his army were slain on the field of battle, as a penalty for making light of the enemy [fig. 22]. . . .

.   .   .

The enemy's soldiers used various kinds of weapons. Some were armed with bows and arrows hanging down their backs; others had nothing save a shield on the left arm, and a good sword in the right hand; while many wielded with both hands a formidable battle-sword fixed to a stick half the length of a man. Every one was protected over the upper part of the body with a coat of iron scales, fitting below one another like the slates of a roof, the arms and legs being left bare. This afforded complete protection from rifle bullets and yet left ample freedom to move, as those coats only reached down to the knees, and were very flexible at the joints.

The archers formed Koxinga's best troops, and much depended on them, for even at a distance they contrived to handle their weapons with so great skill, that they very nearly eclipsed the riflemen.

The shield-bearers were used instead of cavalry. Every tenth man of them is a leader, who takes charge of and presses his men on to force themselves into the ranks of the enemy. With bent heads and their bodies hidden behind the shields, they try to break through the opposing ranks with such fury and dauntless courage, as if each one had still a spare body left at home. They continually press onwards, notwithstanding many are shot down; not stopping to consider, but ever rushing forward like mad dogs, not even looking round to see whether they are followed by their comrades or not.

Those with the swordsticks—called soap-knives by the Hollanders—render the same service as lancers, in preventing all breaking through of the enemy, and in this way establishing perfect order in the ranks; but when the enemy has been thrown into disorder, the sword-bearers follow this up with fearful massacre amongst the fugitives.

YANG [4th month,] 3rd day [May 1].* The Forward Division of the Declare Resolve Army sent officers and soldiers to camp on the Northline Tail. The foreigners' leader, Kuiyi [Coyet], seeing from atop the [Castle Zeelandia] wall that our men there were not yet prepared, deputed a general, Baguizi [Captain Pedel], to advance with several hundred riflemen in a lethal charge. But they met with the counteraction of our division commander and were annihilated on the first drumroll. . . .

COYET Meeting with no resistance, those invaders could land everywhere at their leisure, and dominate to their heart's content. They cut off all power of communication on sea as well as land, and besieged Fort Provintia, thereby separating it from Castle Zeelandia, and iso-

*Yang Ying's date differs by two days from that given by Coyet. Inexplicably, the two texts go on to differ by one to seven days in their chronology of events. See n. 14.

lating the one from the other. They were also complete masters in the country, and interdicted the Formosans from communicating with the beseiged, thus preventing any assistance being rendered by the former to the attacked party. Receiving help from the twenty-five thousand armed men of the Chinese colony, all this was accomplished within the space of three or four hours. Even the astonished and desperate Formosans were forced to submit themselves to the enemy, and were, with all the Chinese residents, made use of to do us harm.

This wonderful progress was brought about more through the stupidity and mismanagement of the Batavian officials than by the enemy's audacity, of which they had previously received sufficient warning. Koxinga, thus far successful in everything, haughtily demanded the surrender of both castles; and threatened that, if met with refusal, he would give orders to slay all within their walls.

The [Formosa] Council thereupon met, with the principal military and other officers, to take their bearings in the face of such a humiliating defeat. They saw that Fort Provintia was in imminent danger owing to its small garrison. They admitted too the Company's inability, through lack of men and vessels, to land there, or to stop the enemy's progress, and drive them back so as to save Provintia from their hands; further, that Castle Zeelandia was through its situation no longer defensible, the city Zeelandia* being also totally at the mercy of the enemy, who were surrounding it completely.

Having earnestly deliberated on these matters, and on how the Company's interest could best be secured, they at last decided to choose the least of two evils—*ex duobus malis minimum*: better lose one finger than the whole hand—by coming to some kind of terms with those formidable enemies, whom they could not resist for any length of time, and who had already gained such a foothold on the island that they would insist on retaining the greater portion of it for themselves.

The Hollanders therefore agreed that they would be willing to pay an indemnity if Koxinga would leave Formosa alone, abandon the conquests, and permit an undisturbed navigation; but in the event of his refusing to consent to this proposal and insisting on his demands, then they would surrender that which was already lost—namely the *terra firma* of Formosa, provided our people were granted liberty to come to Tayouan [Islet]. . . .

*A Dutch settlement outside the castle walls to the east. See inset, map 7.

It was thought probable that Koxinga would accept one of the alternatives, and keep on a friendly footing with the Company, rather than make for himself an irreconcilable enemy who could cause him much trouble at sea. They further decided to defend the Castle to the last drop of their blood, no matter what would be the result of these proposals.

·   ·   ·

Our people then also received word from two assistants of the commandant of Provintia, Jan van Valcken and Adriaen Pieck, to the effect that the refugees there were in want of water, as the well of the Fort had either collapsed or been closed up by the enemy. This difficulty was all the more serious seeing that the men, women, children, and slaves around Provintia had taken shelter within the walls on the approach of the enemy; who now surrounded them so closely that the garrison soldiers were fatigued through continual watching, and unable to hold out much longer, or stand more than one attack, especially as no assistance seemed to be forthcoming. . . .

The members [of the Council] unanimously agreed that there was no possibility of saving Fort Provintia from the enemy's grasp. It was therefore thought advisable that they should try to save the people and thereby strengthen Zeelandia, by pressing for a settlement on the grounds already stated.

For this purpose, the merchant Thomas van Iperen and the fiscal Mr. Leonards, two Councillors, were authorised verbally to inquire as to the purport of Koxinga's letter; to get to the object of his hostile attitude. . . . In the event of Koxinga refusing to relax any of his demands and insisting upon the full surrender of both Castles, then the two envoys were to return without making any further proposals. Before leaving, however, they were to confidently inform him that they were amply provided with men and resources for protection against the assailants; and that the Company would spare no effort to be revenged for this unprovoked invasion.

·   ·   ·

Having thus obtained their instructions, [the envoys] set out with a train of attendants on the morning of 3rd of May to Sakam, where

Koxinga with his whole army were encamped on the open field round about Fort Provintia.

He had constructed no trenches nor erected any batteries, although he was well acquainted with the modes of warfare, and amply provided with heavy guns, as was proved during a later stage of the war. He evidently thought the Fort could be captured without any such trouble.

.   .   .

On their arrival at Koxinga's quarters, the envoys were admitted by an officer and taken into a large tent, where they had to remain until Koxinga would be pleased to give them an audience. . . .

.   .   .

After [some] palaver, the envoys were at last granted an audience. Koxinga was sitting in an armchair at a square table, inside a blue tent, open from all sides. He was surrounded by the grandees of his people, who were dressed in long robes, like deacons. Neither they nor he himself carried rifles, and they stood there beside him like statues, very respectful and modest. [See fig. 19.] Our councillors passed right through the midst of those attendants, and went up close to the table. Having gone through the usual salutations, they stood there with uncovered heads, and handed over their credentials. One of them then made the following statement in the Dutch language, which was translated into Chinese by the son of Captain Pedel, who was well acquainted with the Chinese language.

> Serene and renowned Prince: Frederik Coyet, appointed Governor of Formosa by the Lord-general and Council of India at Batavia, in name of the Directors of the Netherlands East India Company, has ordered us to convey to Your Highness his friendly greetings, to inquire after your health and condition, and wish all prosperity to your intentions, so far as these do not tend to harm or damage the masters whom he is serving.
>
> The Lord-governor had heartily desired that he would have been able to greet Your Highness elsewhere, on another occasion, under different conditions, and from other motives; but since Your Highness has been pleased to appear on our shores so suddenly with all your forces, has landed your troops, has attacked the Company malignantly, commanding them to leave Formosa and surrender the Castles to Your Highness; therefore, the Lord-governor and his Council have thought fit to depute we two

members of [the] Council to express great astonishment, that without any previous denunciation or declaration of war, and without any reasonable complaint—at least so far as the Governor and Council are aware—Your Highness has been pleased to attack the Company here, and to demand the Castles and the entire country.

This action has been the more unexpected by the Governor, inasmuch as His Excellency looked for nothing save neighborly friendship from Your Highness, out of respect to the memory of Your Highness's highly esteemed Father,* who often showed his gratitude for the Honourable Company's numerous acts of kindness, for which he was much indebted to the Lord-governor personally, who always manifested good feeling and acted in a friendly way.

His Excellency the Governor, counting on Your Highness's friendship with the Company—in which he had much confidence—has always been convinced that, in case of disagreement with the Company, Your Highness would not enter into hostilities until notice had been sent, giving the reasons of discontent and stating what was demanded as satisfaction. In this case, however, Your Highness has not done so, but has suddenly taken up a hostile attitude towards the Honourable Company. Therefore our Lord-governor, after careful consideration, and being at a loss to discover any cause of displeasure incurred by him, has thought it his duty to ask Your Highness, through us, to kindly give a clear explanation of the letter which was sent to him yesterday.

. . .

Further, we are to request that Your Highness will be good enough to make known the reasons and motives of your displeasure against the Company, and the satisfaction demanded; so that, after investigation, such terms may be arranged, that the old friendship between the Company and Your Highness may again be speedily restored. . . .

To these requests Koxinga, without concerning himself much about the envoys' credentials, immediately replied that the friendship which the Company held towards him was of the same nature as that held towards . . . Indian Potentates and Princes: namely, that from their [Dutch] side, it lasted just so long as there was any advantage to be gained by it; for if they saw it [not] to be to their advantage, no such friendship was observed, but they would not scruple in the least to throw a net over any one's head when it suited them to do so.

*Zheng Zhilong. See Chap. 12.

He added that he was not at all obliged to give an account of his actions, but saw no need for concealing from them the fact that, in order [for] a successful prosecution of his war against the Tartars, he had thought it advisable to take possession of Formosa.

Hitherto this island had always belonged to China, and the Dutch had doubtless been permitted to live there, seeing that the Chinese did not require it for themselves; but requiring it now, it was only fair that Dutch strangers, who came from far regions, should give way to the masters of the island.

He came not with a view to wage war against the Company (although his men had on several occasions been very unkindly treated by them), but only to take possession of his belongings; and, to prove that he had no intention to enrich himself with the Company's means, he would allow them to embark [with] their goods and effects in his own junks, and to break down the Castles and remove the cannon with other materials to Batavia; provided all this were done immediately. In that case, the friendship between him and the Company would remain undisturbed, though they had already given great offense by attacking his junks and soldiers at sea and on land with their ships and men.

Surely he had been quite right in defending himself against them; but, inclined to be friendly with the Company, he would overlook these hostile actions if they would clear out in the way indicated from Formosa; which in reality belonged to him, and not to the Company. However, if they ignored his magnanimity, declined to restore to him his own property, and wished to keep that still longer from him, he would be compelled to urge his claims to the utmost with such resources as he possessed, and the Company would then have to defray the entire expense. He added further:

> You Hollanders are conceited and senseless people; you will make yourselves unworthy of the mercy which I now offer; you will subject yourselves to the highest punishment by proudly opposing the great force I have brought with the mere handful of men which I am told you have in your Castle; you will obstinately persevere in this. Do you not wish to be wiser? Let your losses at least teach you, that your power here cannot be compared to a thousandth part of mine.
>
> You have by this time surely seen with your own eyes what your iron ships, with which you think you can accomplish wonders and on which you boast so much, can do against my junks; how one of them has been

burned by one of my junks and disappeared in smoke; how the others would have met with the same doom had they not taken to flight and gone out to sea.

On land you saw how the pride of Captain Pedel was so much humbled that he with his men, who were as foolish as himself, could not even bear the look of my men; and how, on the mere sight of my warriors, they threw down their arms and willingly awaited their well-deserved punishment with outstretched necks. Are these not sufficient proofs of your incompetency and inability to resist my forces?

I will give you more and stronger ones. But if you still persist in refusing to listen to reason and decline to do my bidding, and if you wish deliberately to rush to your ruin, then I will shortly, in your presence, order your Castle to be stormed. . . . My smart boys will attack it, conquer it, and demolish it in such a way, that not one stone will remain standing. If I wish to set my forces to work, then I am able to move Heaven and Earth; wherever I go, I am destined to win. Therefore take warning, and think the matter well over.

The envoys then remonstrated that Formosa did not belong to China, but to the Company; for by a formal contract drawn up with the grandees of China, they had left the Pescadores and taken possession of Formosa;[16] therefore Koxinga could have no right or pretense of claim to it. They further protested very strongly against the improper manner of his invasion; insisted that he should specify any grounds of complaint he had against the Company; and expressed the desire to come to a mutual arrangement that might prove satisfactory to both parties. But after much discussion, Koxinga pretended not to understand; and declared his fixed intention to be that we should abandon the whole island, thus rendering it quite needless to carry on further negotiations.

He gave them until eight o'clock next morning to consider whether they would promptly leave the entire island and gratefully accept his mercy, or prefer to go to war and resist him. If we decided to leave Formosa, the Prince's flag should be hoisted; but, if the contrary, we had simply to unfurl the blood-flag,* without troubling him with further deliberations, which he would refuse to enter upon.

Hereupon the conference ended, and the envoys were permitted to leave; but, according to instructions, they strongly protested at this

*The flag of William III, Prince of Orange, signified amity; a red flag signified hostility.

stage, and said that the Company would use every means to protect itself against so great an injustice. Because, seeing that Koxinga would be satisfied with nothing else than the whole island, the envoys were pretty sure that . . . tomorrow no Prince's flag, but the blood-flag, would float from Castle Zeelandia. In fact, this prolonged discussion was quite unnecessary, for they were well aware that the Governor would await any attack like a soldier.

YANG   6th day [May 4]. Kuiyi deputed foreign leaders [and others] with Shiding [Valentyn].* . . . The prince gave them a banquet and treated them very cordially before having He Tingbin ask [them], "When will Kuiyi come out in surrender?" They replied, "He does not propose to surrender. If the prince's main forces would withdraw [immediately?], then every year on a regular basis we would remit a million taels in revenues and any local products . . . you wish. [Our] naval vessels that come here would pay a small [fee before] leaving. Our officers and soldiers are willing to send one hundred thousand taels of silver in compensation to your troops. Anything else we dare not discuss." The prince refused all their proposals and ordered that they go back to Tai Bay Fortress.†

COYET   In the afternoon of that same day, the envoys arrived back again in Castle Zeelandia, and related their experiences to the full meeting of officials. . . . As was to be expected, those present were completely at a loss [as to] what course to adopt; more particularly those who, like van der Laan, had maintained that the enemy would never attack Formosa, that too many useless fortifications had been made, and that it would be time enough to act on the defensive when the enemy had actually arrived. But now that the enemy had arrived, they were at their wits' end. What could they do? What means could they adopt to afford protection? There they sat, innocent, and with their hands through their hair. Communication between the two forts had stopped. Provintia was lost. Those shut up in it [Castle Zeelandia?] were cut off . . ., and could therefore expect neither food-supplies nor war-material.

Accordingly, our people at Tayouan could only look on and allow

*Coyet seems to have studiously avoided mentioning Valentyn's activities because he regarded his peremptory surrender of Fort Provintia as dishonorable.

†The text in the section above contains a number of illegible characters. Interpolations, guesses, and imponderables are indicated with brackets and ellipses.

the enemy to take complete possession. The place itself was but a barren sand-plain, where no grass would grow; and, surrounded on all sides by the sea, it was impossible to get away from it. Nor had they sufficient men or means to injure the enemy; so their only hope was to defend Castle Zeelandia, until they might obtain powerful aid from Batavia, only on the understanding, however, that they could meanwhile resist the enemy, and arrest his advance with the help of the Formosa natives. This seemed the only way to serve the Company.

.   .   .

YANG   The chiefs of the various nearby native villages—such as Xinshan and Kaigan—all came to welcome us and show their dependence.[17] The prince ordered a rich banquet for them and bestowed on them the formal gowns, caps, boots, and sashes of head and deputy-head native officials. As a result, the heads of the native villages to the north and south sniffed the wind and came, one on the heels of another, to proffer allegiance....

12th day [May 10]. The prince personally went to Mosquito Inlet [on the north side of Tai Bay] to assess the lay of the land. At the same time he took cognizance of the men and women of the four villages there, who welcomed him with special foods and came in such numbers that they clogged the road. The prince reassured and sympathized with them, bestowing wine and victuals. So they were happy and grateful.

Tai Bay Fortress had not been attacked because our army lacked supplies.

22nd day [May 20]. [Vice-Director] of the Military Headquarters Yang [Chaodong] and I accompanied the intermediary He Tingbin to inspect the various rural villages and report back on any rice, sugar, barley, or other foodstuffs that might have been accumulated by the red-haired foreigners for distribution as army supplies. We found an estimated six thousand piculs of grain and over three thousand piculs of sugar.

COYET   ...Daybreak had hardly commenced on the 26th of May when, from the east, a perfect thunder and lightning storm, caused by the multitude of bullets from the enemy's guns, struck the walls of Castle Zeelandia; whereupon our soldiers ran to the bulwarks with the object of responding in true Dutch fashion to this Chinese morning salute.

The Governor [Coyet], whose many duties occupied him throughout that night, had just laid himself down to rest when this terrific noise awoke him; and he too ran to the bulwarks to take a general survey. His practised eye at once observed the weak position of the enemy's cannon, which were entirely unprotected, and in great danger if attacked. The Governor could also see that the enemy—who appeared jubilant over the success of their firing, and very hopeful that a breach would be made in the walls—had wandered in great numbers outside their barricades, and were thus recklessly exposing themselves. He therefore restrained the anxiety of our men, and commanded that not a single shot should be fired in the meantime. All the pieces were then arranged in such a position that their respective shots would cross one another, and were charged with powder, musket-bullets, and large iron nails. The musketeers took up their places along the outskirts of the balustrades; and when at length a suitable opportunity arose, the word of command was given to fire on the unprotected Chinese from above, below, and all sides, simultaneously. This order was so well executed that, with the first charge, nearly the whole field was strewn with dead and wounded; the enemy being thus taught the lesson not to expose themselves so readily.

In spite of this, however, their commander, who seemed very obstinate, was said to have promised Koxinga, on the forfeit of his head, that he would storm the Castle in this first attack. Whether the rumour is correct or not, I will not at present discuss; still on two occasions he did act in a very rash way by bringing forward relays of men to replace those who had been slain, and doing so under the most furious cannonading from the Castle. It was bad generalship, for the occupants of the Castle, seizing their opportunity, sent such a volley of musket and cannon balls amongst those senseless people, that, if the current reports of prisoners and deserters are to be accepted, fully a thousand were killed and a great number wounded. Our bold assaulters were thus obliged to retire in confusion to the streets and lanes of the [evacuated Dutch] city. There they were protected from the muskets and cannon balls of the Castle; but they retired in such disorder, that their own cannons were abandoned, with the charges left inside. A few of them had been rendered useless by the Castle's fire.

.   .   .

. . . Scared by the failure of their former attack, the enemy seemed at this time to have abandoned all further thought of storming the

Castle. They were assured that by mere blockade the besieged were bound to fall into their hands. Therefore on 1 June, all the streets leading to the Castle were barricaded; and a fairly wide ditch was dug, into which was placed the storming apparatus with some light guns, the largest being a six-pounder. From that day until the succour-fleet arrived, nothing remarkable happened on either side, as the enemy was in no hurry, seeing that those inside were closely surrounded, so helpless that they could scarcely have broken a straw; whereas the enemy possessed beautiful and fertile grounds, in which the soldiers, who had roamed about the sea so long, might now rest in a leisurely manner; and, as a matter of fact, they took their full swing of comfort.

YANG   24th day [May 22]. Because Tai Bay Fortress was isolated, because it had no prospect of aid, and because attacking it would necessitate injury and loss of life, the prince concluded that he would place a blockade around it and wait for the besieged to surrender. So he assigned various divisions to occupy different areas and begin opening up land for fall planting.

5th month, 2nd day [May 29]. The prince, stationed on [the east side of] Tai Bay, assembled his civil and military officials to judge crimes involving the seizure of silver from the local people and the robbery and hording of their grain. Wu Hao of the Declare Resolve Rear Division was found guilty and executed. . . .

18th day [June 14]. Our prince issued an edict, which read:

This [new] establishment of the dynasty at the Ming Eastern Capital could become an unshakable foundation for future ages. Your prince has already put his hand to opening up grassy and little-known lands so that the families of civil and military officials and of the higher- and lower-ranking army officers could come and select places to dwell. A corpus of regulations must be promulgated regarding fields, houses, and such, to pass down to our sons and grandsons. But this "one exertion that will bring eternal ease" should be managed with your own strength. You are not permitted to disturb the native people or encroach on the farms or enterprises of the common [Han-Chinese] people. Herewith are listed regulatory clauses, which all are to be followed respectfully. Violations definitely shall be prosecuted. . . .

[26th?] day. Commanders Wan Yi of the Declare Resolve Left Division and Wan Lu of the Right Assault Division, garrisoned at Tongshan,* revolted and went over to the [Qing] barbarians. . . . The prince had previously ordered Wan Yi, Wan Lu, and their units to come in two contingents to the [Ming Eastern] Capital, but for the time being, they camped at Tongshan, and in spite of urgent demands, they never came. . . .

7th month [July–August]. . . . The rice transport ships of the Revenue Bureau not having arrived, the army was short on supplies, and in every village the price of a peck of rice had risen to at least four or five tenths of a tael. So anything like yams or potatoes was requisitioned from the people and rationed to the army.

COYET . . . (On 12 August) the succour-fleet under command of [Jacob] Caeuw arrived in the bay of Tayouan. Great satisfaction and rejoicing were shown on the arrival of this fleet. The sick lying in their cribs, the men from behind the walls, and every one else, looked upon it as succour from heaven, far in excess of the expectations.† They began already to think of unloading, and for that purpose at once despatched the pilot boat which lay close to the Castle; but although the wind had calmed a little, yet the Canal was still in too disturbed a condition to make commencement.

Next day, the water in the channel was still very rough, but with great risk they managed to land two thousand two hundred pounds of gunpowder and quantities of certain other much needed materials, also many soldiers; after which, the fleet was forced to move south and then put out to sea.

.   .   .

. . . The fleet remained away [because of bad weather] for twenty-eight days. It was a time of much anxiety to the besieged, during which they had much sinking of heart, and were made to feel that, after all, they had no great reason for rejoicing. They learned that this fleet brought reinforcements of seven hundred men, an addition which would have placed them in no better a position than they were at the beginning of the war. They would therefore have still to remain on the defensive, and be incapacitated from taking any forward movement against the enemy.

*On Dongshan Island near the Fujian-Guangdong border.
†The dispatch boat *Maria*, in a remarkable feat of navigation, had managed to reach Batavia in spite of the southern monsoon by sailing via the Philippines.

Meanwhile, the Koxingians made the best of their opportunity; for, on the same evening that the fleet anchored, they despatched one hundred and fifty vessels close inshore, all manned with armed soldiers. No doubt they were very much surprised (as was told us by deserters and prisoners) that a succour-fleet had so soon and unexpectedly been sent to assist the besieged. . . . Naturally, too, they concluded that, although the fleet consisted of but ten ships, these would carry at least two thousand soldiers.

But they were soon undeceived; for, on the same night that the fleet was driven back by the storm, the little craft *Urk* stranded on Formosa and was dashed to pieces. All her men fell into the hands of the enemy. Having been tortured and killed, after full information as to the strength of the fleet was extorted from them, Koxinga breathed more freely. . . .

In any case, the besieged could not now expect more assistance during this year, while it was clearly Koxinga's policy to reduce Castle Zeelandia before further aid could arrive. After the storm abated, the ships of the succour-fleet returned again to Tayouan bay on the 8th, 9th, and 10th of September; whereupon the remaining soldiers and materials were brought ashore, and five of the vessels entered the Canal and anchored before the Castle.

.   .   .

Just about this time, our people were informed by several deserters from the enemy that Koxinga's affairs in Formosa were faring as badly as they had done in China; that during this siege he had lost more than eight thousand of his ablest soldiers; that his junks and vessels cleared away whenever a suitable opportunity offered; that the loyalty of his soldiers and other Chinese in Formosa had somewhat diminished through this long continuing siege; and that food-supplies were no longer imported in such abundance as formerly.

YANG   Officers and troops of the Rear Reinforcement Division and of the Rear Assault Division instigated an uprising among the aborigines at Datu [Village], who then attacked and killed men in the camp of the Left Vanguard Division. Yang Zu, [commander of the Marvelous Troops Division,] engaged the natives in battle but was beaten, and returned to the capital [Sakam], where he died of a resulting illness. . . .

COYET   Tuesday, 16 August. This morning at daybreak, a soldier named Hendrick Robbertz came swimming to the Pine-apples, and afterwards to the redoubt. Having been carried into this place, he gave us the following account. Last month the interpreter Druyvendal and a young schoolmaster had each been fastened to a cross, nails having been driven through their hands, the calves of their legs, and into their backs. In this sad condition they were exhibited to public view before the house of the Governor,* our own people guarding these victims with naked swords. At the end of three or four days they expired, after meat and drink had been forbidden them all that time. The reason for their execution was said to be that they had incited the inhabitants against the Chinese. They, however, denied to their last breath that they had ever done so.

YANG   Eighth month [September–October]. . . . The Revenue Bureau rice boats had not yet come, so the officers and soldiers resorted to eating tree bark to allay their hunger, and daily we worried about mutiny. The prince was piqued by this and wrote in big characters outside his chamber, "The first to be punished will be Revenue Minister [Zheng Tai]." He then sent Prefect Yang [Chaodong] and me out to Deer's Ear Channel to wait for any grain boats. We were to buy up the cargo of any official or private boats that came with rice, for issuance to our soldiers.

22nd day [October 14]. I was deputed to go to the camps at Erlin and Nanshe with a rice boat under my charge to give out some grain to the troops. With Li Yin [office manager of the Board of War], I was also to inquire about the troops' state of mind and report on that. At the time grain supplies could not meet our needs, and the officers and soldiers were eating only two meals per day. Many of them had succumbed to illnesses, and the men felt like crying out in hunger.

28th day. The prince ordered me to take ten gold ingots and, with Yang Rong, speed to the four villages [of Mosquito Inlet] and purchase grain to meet army supply needs. We reported back that in our estimation the available grain would feed the troops for ten days. After that, I came down with a disease that was going around. No longer being informed about army affairs, I did not venture to record anything more.

*Valentyn, whom Coyet again impugns for cooperating with the invaders to an unnecessary degree.

[Subsequently a plan to join forces with the Qing leadership in Fujian fell through because of Jacob Cauew's betrayal of his mission and his abandonment of the Zeelanders. Then a Dutch deserter, Hans Jurgen Radis, informed Koxinga of the defenders' condition and of how best to attack the castle—that is, at a weak redoubt named the Utrecht. Thus, early in 1662 Koxinga reactivated the siege.]

COYET The enemy accomplished their task in the face of every difficulty, and in spite of the besieged; for, early in the morning of 25 January, they commenced to bombard the Ronduyt Uytrecht with their guns from the east and south sides; and after a couple of hours' firing, attempted twice in succession to storm the breach which was made at the south side. But again and again our brave defenders compelled a retreat with much loss in killed and wounded; so that, not wishing to sacrifice more men, the enemy resumed their bombardment, causing such havoc of the whole Ronduyt that, at night, scarcely one stone remained on another, and it was left a total ruin.

Hence, as their lives were in imminent danger, our people had no other resource than to seek shelter in the Castle; but before doing so, they first silenced all the guns which remained without damage. They also set fuses to four barrels of gunpowder left in the cellar; and soon after, the Ronduyt was blown up with several of the enemy, who had already posted themselves on the hill for the purpose of strengthening their position.

.   .   .

Of course, by reason of their success in the capture of Ronduyt Uytrecht, the Koxingians were roused to greater activity, and made hopeful in a continuance of their good luck; because that very night they entrenched themselves on the hill, and proceeded to construct a large battery. They also formed various trenches with their numerous gabions pointing from the hill downwards, towards the point called Gelderlandt, and the Network of the Castle.

The besieged attempted to stop proceedings by firing their cannon, mortars, muskets, and hand-grenades throughout the night, causing so much smoke and flames that it seemed as if the Castle had been set on fire. Moreover, as the thin parapets of the Gelderlandt projection were not higher than half the stature of an ordinary man, they were strengthened by the slaves and soldiers who could be spared for this work.

And because the wings which connected this projection with the upper Castle were not more than three and a half bricks in thickness, instructions were given that the roofs of the houses standing alongside of these wings should be taken off, for the purpose of filling the houses with sand and thereby strengthening the wings. Many other schemes were set on foot in order to set up greater resistance against the enemy, who were expected to renew their attack at any moment. Indeed, so much progress had been made during the night with these operations of defence that, at daybreak, it was thought the position was sufficiently strong to warrant them in acting on the offensive.

Meanwhile, the Council once more met in solemn conclave and were assisted by all the merchants and colour-sergeants. After consulting on the strong position of the enemy and their own extreme danger, it was clearly seen that they must either make a courageous united charge, await the coming storm, or surrender the Castle on as advantageous conditions as possible. These three points were then carefully examined, each person being urged to express his opinions with perfect frankness, as this was a matter on which their honour, their lives, and the very existence of the Company in Formosa, depended.

.   .   .

[Governor Coyet at length] consented to the all but unanimous opinion which [the Council] had come to, and it was decided that they should forthwith enter into negotiations with Koxinga regarding the capitulation of the Castle under fair conditions. Hence a message was sent immediately, a mutual truce was entered upon, and after five or six days of deliberation, [an eighteen-article] agreement with Koxinga was drawn up.

.   .   .

Thus, through neglect of all warnings from various sources regarding Koxinga's intention to surprise Formosa, through failure of the Batavia Council to make preparation for the enemy's attack, through refusal to sanction the construction of a few fortifications, by means of which the whole island might have been saved, through many disheartening words, causing the Formosan Council to lose courage . . . , through the despatch from Batavia of insufficient help, notwithstanding the courageous resolution of the Formosan Council to resist Koxinga to the last, through the villainous flight of Commander Caeuw, causing the besieged to become utterly desperate after a siege of nine full months, and through other experiences already referred to, the important Castle of Zeelandia, yea, the whole island of Formosa, fell a prey to that heathen idolater and devil-worshipper, Koxinga.

One result was that the East India Company were thereby prevented from accomplishing their chief purpose, namely, that of linking together the Chinese and Japanese trades by forming a basis in Formosa.[18]

But a more serious loss has also to be considered; for, as the swine wrought havoc by getting into the vineyard and harvest of the Lord (according to the prophet), in like manner, that Christianity [Calvinism] which had been established, nursed, and extended with so much pain and bloodshed by the clergy and schoolmasters, was in one fell swoop destroyed through the loss of Formosa, whose inhabitants were compelled to return again to their primitive idolatry.

14

"MY COMPLETE DEVOTION":

AN EMPRESS

APPEALS TO THE POPE

AS QING ARMIES were pushing Zheng Chenggong out to Taiwan, thereby marginalizing Ming resistance in the southeastern maritime zone, they were likewise pushing the court of the Yongli emperor out of Guangxi into ever more remote areas westward. Under such trying circumstances, it is not surprising that members of the court looked for solace—and possibly for practical aid—to a new, universal religion. The imperial women, especially Grand Empress Dowager Wang, were the most sanguine.

Madam Wang was the wife of the Prince of Gui, and she resided on his estate in Hengzhou, in southern Huguang Province (present-day Hunan), before it was taken over by a roving rebel army in 1643. Being the prince's wife, she was formally regarded as the mother of all his concubine's children, including Zhu Youlang, whose birth mother was a concubine surnamed Ma. At the crucial moment when Ming patriots in the far south needed a scion of the Ming imperial family around whom to rally support, Zhu Youlang was the eldest surviving male in the Gui princely line and next in succession to the Ming emperorship. An inexperienced young man of twenty-three, he was prevailed upon to accept enthronement with the reign title Yongli in December 1646. Madam Wang, who continued to dominate the affairs of her filial but weak-willed son, became the grand empress dowager, the emperor's actual mother became the empress dowager, and his wife, also surnamed Wang, became the empress (see Chap. 15). Shortly after the enthronement in Zhaoqing, Guangdong Province, the first Qing invasion of Guangdong forced the court to embark on a long, trying odyssey in

Guangxi and southern Huguang, during which time more than one son was born to the emperor's wife and concubines.[1]

Among the most important figures who established the Yongli court were several Christians—particularly Guangxi Provincial Governor Qu Shisi, his close compatriot, Regional Commander Jiao Lian, and the head eunuch, Director of Ceremonial Pang Tianshou. With the assistance of Qu and Jiao, the Jesuit priest Andreas Xavier Koffler was able to enter Guangxi from Annam (present-day Vietnam) in 1645, and he became closely associated with the Yongli court from its inception. In 1648, Koffler—surely introduced by the eunuch Pang—was able to convert Grand Empress Dowager Wang (who was given the Christian name Helena) and then Empress Dowager Ma (Maria) and Empress Wang (Anna), as well as to baptize (as Constantine) the infant son who was designated heir apparent. Although this conversion caused a great stir when news of it reached Europe in the early 1650s, no mention of it appears in any Chinese account of Yongli court affairs.

Because of a dramatic restoration of Ming fortunes in 1648, the Yongli court was able to return to Zhaoqing. But the second Qing campaign on Guangdong, led by Shang Kexi and Geng Jimao,[2] forced the court to flee westward again. Grand Empress Dowager Helena was probably in Wuzhou, Guangxi, anxiously awaiting word about the Qing siege of Canton (Guangzhou), when she and Pang Tianshou each wrote two letters—to the pope and to the general of the Society of Jesus in Rome. Those letters were given to Koffler's Jesuit assistant, Michael Boym, for transmittal.[3] In spite of opposition from many who were placing Catholic hopes on the Qing side or who feared Qing reprisals, Koffler, Boym, and others expected that the sensational news of their conversion of members of the Ming imperial family would dampen criticism of the Jesuits by other Catholic missionary orders and that the Church would encourage European states to aid the Ming cause.

After Boym finally arrived in Italy in 1652, however, for complex reasons he was not able to gain an audience with either Pope Innocent X, who died in 1655, or his successor, Pope Alexander VII. Boym departed on a hazardous return trip to China with a comforting but tepid missive from Pope Alexander in 1656. Unfortunately by the time he arrived in the Tonkin Gulf region in 1658, Andreas Koffler, the grand empress dowager, Pang Tianshou, Qu Shisi, and Jiao Lian all had died or been killed. And Boym was blocked by the Qing authorities from traveling through Guangdong or Guangxi to reach the Yongli court, then in desperate straits in far western Yunnan Province. Exhausted, discouraged, and heartsick, Boym died and was buried by a faithful Chinese companion in the border region between Annam and Guangxi in August 1659.[4]

———————

Helena, the Serenely Wise and Lovingly Respectful Grand Empress Dowager of the Great Ming, sends this missive before the throne of Pope Innocent, Vicar of God and Jesus on Earth, Exalted Ruler of the Catholic Church.

I, Helena, humbly reflect that being a daughter of China unworthily living in the imperial palace, I knew only the etiquette of the ladies' apartments and never understood even dimly the teachings of your faraway land. But owing to the proclamation of your holy religion by the Jesuit [Andreas] Xavier Koffler, I learned of it from outside. Thus, I came to believe, and received holy baptism three years ago. Consequently Empress Dowager Maria and Empress Anna [with] Crown Prince Constantine also requested to enter the faith and received baptism.

Although I have poured out my heart's blood most earnestly, it has not been with the slightest thought of personal gain. I have often thought to pay my respects before your throne and to receive your sage instruction personally. But your country is far away and hard to reach, and affairs here appear pressing. So I beg you, Holy Father, to take pity on us sinners in God's presence and, when we die, to bestow a special absolution.

Further, I hope that you, in concert with the Holy One Catholic Church, will on our behalf request of God protection and assistance in restoring peace in my country. Thereby, the eighteenth ruler of Our Great Ming [the Yongli emperor], the twelfth-generation descendant of the Great Founder, as well as his ministers, would all know to venerate the true Lord, Jesus. Also, I wish you to send more Jesuits to China to broadly disseminate the holy teachings.

Please consider all these matters with utmost compassion. Words cannot adequately express my complete devotion.

At present the Jesuit Michael Boym is familiar with circumstances in my country. So I am charging him to return to his

country [that is, to Europe] and speak for us in your presence,
Holy Father. He can explain my humble meaning in detail. When
peace returns, ambassadors will be dispatched to perform proper
ceremonies at the altars of Saints Peter and Paul.

Trusting that Your Holiness will receive [this missive] chari-
tably, in simple sincerity I specially command [its transmittal].

4th year of Yongli, 10th month, 11th day
[November 4, 1650]

15

"THERE WAS ONLY ME":
A BOY EUNUCH
SEES THE BITTER END

THE CIRCUMSTANCES UNDER which Grand Empress Dowager Wang felt moved to appeal for help all the way to Europe were dire indeed (see Chap. 14). She did not live long after the Yongli court's flight from Wuzhou to Nanning (in Guangxi Province), where she died in the fifth lunar month of 1651. At least she was spared the even worse experiences that the pitiful Yongli court underwent in the following decade. How did the imperial women who survived her—Empress Dowager Ma, Empress Wang, the one princess, and two concubines—manage to stay alive through extreme climatic conditions, threats from various armed elements, and virtual imprisonment under deplorable conditions as they fled through rugged terrain—from Guangxi, to Guizhou, across Yunnan, into Myanmar (Miandian in Chinese), and back again? Their perseverance and fortitude must have been extraordinary. Perhaps such qualities reinforced the courage and resourcefulness of at least one of their personal attendants, a boy eunuch who served them devotedly even after their deaths.

The Chinese state is unique in world history for the length and extent of its employment of eunuchs in government. From the Han dynasty through the Qing—for two thousand years—eunuchs were found indispensable to the operations of at least the imperial palace, and their duties sometimes extended far into the affairs of the military and the civil service. The influence of eunuchs in terms of the numbers employed and the sorts of powers wielded reached an almost disastrous peak in the late Ming period.[1] Scholars in many fields—history, political science, sociology, religion, and psychology—continue to debate the reasons why the Chinese government relied so heavily on eunuchs.[2] Suffice it to point out here that eunuchs were one of the most despised classes in China: their neutered condition made them unassimilable to normal society, their ranks were usually filled from the dregs of society, and they had access to high titles, political power, and state wealth and were known to abuse their privileges.

Historical portrayals have tended to focus on the more notorious eunuchs, like Wei Zhongxian (1568–1627), who, as head of the enormous eunuch subbureaucracy and extrajudicial secret service that evolved during the Ming period, came close to seizing the throne from the mentally deficient Tianqi emperor (r. 1620–27).[3] We know much less about the lives of the hundreds of thousands of ordinary eunuchs who served during the Ming period. It seems that most were forced or led to become eunuchs by the loss of family or livelihood or by reduction to servile status through capture in battle or conviction as criminals. Since castration was irrevocable, they looked on initiation into eunuch ranks as comparable to a Buddhist monk's departure from worldly affairs, and they became dependent on one another—as well as on those whom they served—for moral and practical support.

The story below is the memoir of a not very literate middle-aged or elderly eunuch looking back on his boyhood, when he was the personal servant of the Yongli emperor's wife, Empress Wang. In the introduction to his account, the *Yangjian biji* (Jottings of Eunuch Yang),[4] he explains that in 1640, when he was an infant, both of his parents were killed by roving rebels in Jingzhou Prefecture, in western Huguang, and that his wet nurse fell into rebel hands [fig. 23]. A rebel soldier surnamed Liu reared him as a foster son. Later, when Liu joined one of the armies supporting the Ming cause, the boy was upset to learn that Liu was not his real father but a member of the group who had killed him. Nevertheless, Liu seems to have cared about his little adoptee. We are told that in 1656, when the Yongli court was established in Yunnan Fu (present-day Kunming), an order was sent out that if more than seven years old (*sui*), sons of all higher military officers were to be sent to the court "to accompany the crown prince in his studies"— meaning that they would become eunuchs. Although Liu sacrificed a small fortune trying to get his foster son exempted, after about one month the boy and some twenty others entered service with "pure [asexual] bodies" in the forbidden quarters. The boy then chose a new surname, Yang, and was given a new personal name, Deze, by the emperor. He was proud that after three years he was mature enough

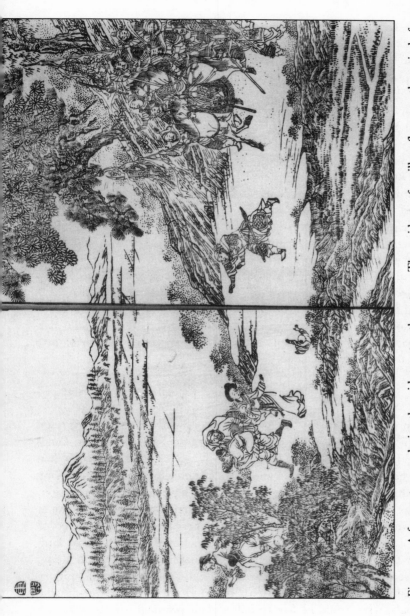

Figure 23. A frequent scene during the mid-seventeenth century: The residents of a village flee upon the arrival of a military unit. A soldier rushes to grab an infant who has fallen by the wayside as the mother struggles to escape with her other baby, and the father puts first priority on saving his parents. Soldiers often snatched up young children, especially boys, to rear as foster progeny, to keep as servants, or to sell as menials or adoptees.

to meet every delicate need of the inner apartments, to accompany the imperial party everywhere, and even to handle documents.

For her part the empress (Niangniang, as Yang affectionately calls her) provided all his food and clothing and "treated him like her own son." In fact, in Yang Deze's account we find more than one hint of siblinglike rivalry between himself and the crown prince, who was about his own age. It seems clear that Yang had found a surrogate family—especially a surrogate mother. Naturally his heroes were those who showed the greatest solicitude for that family—Li Dingguo and the Duke of Qianguo, Mu Tianbo.[5] This intensely pathetic personal circumstance apparently resulted in the Ming dynasty's being finally laid to rest by—what else?—a eunuch.

We join Yang Deze's long memoir about three-quarters of the way through. The Yongli imperial party has been chased out of eastern Yunnan during a Qing campaign headed by the turncoat general Wu Sangui.* On the Chinese side of what is now a much more clearly defined border between western Yunnan and Myanmar (compare map 8 and fig. 24), a Qing contingent is close on their heels, and some grave decisions must be made. Although the emperor has urged his followers to spare themselves by simply turning him over to their pursuers, they have declined this recourse.

On the 1st of the 3rd month of the 13th year of the Yongli reign [April 21, 1659], . . . the chief officials, with the Prince [of Jin, Li Dingguo], held the regular full court ritual in a place outside town. When they had finished, the prince and Duke Mu memorialized about moving the imperial party as follows: "We servants have come to a conclusion. Today we request that the Dragon Carriage temporarily enter Myanmar and sojourn there for one or two years, whereupon heaven's will could be reexamined. At present, Duke Mu is leading the Embroidered Uniform Guard; in addition, there is Regional Commander Pan Rong, whose troops number three thousand. High-ranking civil and military officials number over one hundred. This does not include lower-ranking officials, who would be free to follow their personal wishes."

*See Chap. 1, nn. 12 and 15.

The Prince of Jin also made a submission: "Your servant wants to follow the battalion and protect the Imperial Carriage; then, however, there would be no one to manage outside affairs. Your servant still must look outside the court for a turnabout in the shining of heaven's decree. Should a suitable location be obtained, your servant would then request that the Imperial Carriage move to another capital. The Sage Emperor's lofty thoughts can be released from worry. For fear of death, your servant would in no way scurrilously preserve his life and become a small-spirited man who greedily seeks wealth and high status [through surrender]."

When the Prince of Jin finished, the emperor embraced him tightly and wept painfully without stopping. Then the empress dowager, empress, crown prince, and princess came out and encircled Prince Li [Dingguo], all weeping heavily. The empress dowager said: "Prince Li, this mother and son have burdened you. Now we are about to part from you and enter a foreign land. We are confident that the Prince will be steadfast. Each day that this mother and son live will be a day of hope for the Prince, and we trust that he will not just leave us in a land of death. Even if this mother and son cannot recompense the Prince or the multitudes of civil and military officials, generals, and soldiers in our present lives, surely in future lives there will be recompense for all of you. We know that after the great disturbances in history, there have always been times of restoration. How could it be that our Zhu [Ming] dynasty will not have such a day? We fear only that the time set by heaven for [a Ming] restoration has not yet come. But we cannot know."

Then the empress dowager, speaking for the empress, crown prince, and princess, addressed Prince Li and the assembled ministers, saying: "Today we have nothing material with which to thank you.* We can only make this ceremonial gesture to you as a tiny expression of what is in the small heart of this old body of mine. Now, as this mother and son depart for a foreign land, our only hope is that you prince and ministers will remain loyal to the end and that you absolutely will not send us into an outer realm to be forgotten. I worry that later we will

*The empress dowager and the empress had already set an example for the other court ladies by donating all their jewelry and other valuables to support the military resistance effort.

not be able to get out and that you will have no way to deal with the situation. I cannot help but put this forth, praying that you will not take offense."

When the empress dowager finished speaking, the Prince of Jin and the other civil and military officials, having heard her heartrending words, bowed in unison, cried out [their unshakeable devotion,] and asked the empress dowager [and others] to return to the palace.*

The emperor then tore a piece of fabric from his own robe, bit open the tip of one finger, wrote a declaration in blood for the Prince of Jin, and said: "This document is for nothing other than to confirm what was promised orally to my minister that bygone day when you were in Guangdong,[6] when We originally granted an even half of the Ming world to you. It is only because armed conflict has not ceased, the date of restoration has not been set, and heaven's command has not been with us that We have delayed until the present day. It certainly is not that We have lost confidence in the Prince. Now let this lone man preserve and fulfill Our trust. The Prince is asked to accept this document and keep it on his person until a later time—when Our great undertaking either succeeds or not—as a concrete expression of the faith and righteousness between us, ruler and minister. We hope hereby to avoid ridicule in later ages."

... The Prince of Jin reluctantly submitted these words: "Under current circumstances your servant can only accept this declaration in blood, but he dares not acknowledge that the Emperor's magnanimity is justified.... It remains only for your servant to state his concerns: Myanmar is a place beyond the pale, where many things will be lacking. Your servant prays that the Emperor's sage heart will be indulgent, patient about everything, and protective of his own well-being. Moreover, we will be separated by a riverine passage, and your servant will be far away. So reports, alas, will take a while to reach the court. But for the past several years court governance has been conducted with superhuman, sage intelligence, so your servant is not worried about this. In departing now, your servant does not venture to posit a date of return to the court. But although he takes leave of the Dragon Visage today, your servant goes in order to restore some territory. That done, he will have someone report the victory, but he dares not lightly predict from what campsite [that report will come]. Now, each matter having

*That is, to where they were being housed in this small border locale.

been clearly explained, your servant abjectly begs his Sage Ruler to broaden the limits [on the time allowed for successful completion of his mission]." Thus, the Prince of Jin respectfully took his leave of the Imperial Carriage and, splashed with tears, also parted from the assembled civil and military officials.

When the emperor saw that the Prince of Jin had gone, his heart sank into true despair. Then he called the crown prince to him and chided the boy, saying: "This year you've turned thirteen and are no longer little. How is it that you know nothing of worldly affairs? Today when the Prince of Jin and I parted, even your mother, the empress, came out to pay respects to him. You are the crown prince of the whole dynasty and should have bowed to him and said a few words of farewell. It also is a matter of principle for a crown prince. How could you be so ignorant? Given an attitude like that, you shouldn't have come out at all!"

When the empress heard that the emperor had been moved to anger, she went over and gave the crown prince a severe scolding, too. Only when the empress dowager came and urged leniency did they stop. The emperor said: "If I had a good son, I could have him go along in [Prince Li's] party and accomplish some things. What can be done when I myself cannot endure much physical exertion,* and when I have no son with a good understanding of affairs? Really, what will the senior civil and military officials do [without a vigorous leader]? I can't help thinking of the great disruption during the reign of Emperor Ming of the Tang dynasty.[7] Fortunately he had a good son, so there was hope for the [Chinese] world. But now I've sired only this wormlike simpleton!"

Just as the emperor was venting his displeasure, Duke Mu and the other civil and military officials learned of it, and they came to dissuade him. Duke Mu said: "Would that the Emperor's Dragon Visage cease expressing anger. At present the crown prince is still young. Moreover, during these desperate and chaotic times, he is too frightened to look after himself. We ask that the Emperor take the protection and nurture of the Dragon Body as a most important matter."

[After an interval] Duke Mu requested that the Imperial Carriage be prepared to depart the following day, for that location was not suitable for a long stay. When the emperor heard this, he agreed to rely on the

---

*He suffered from asthma.

duke to arrange the next day's departure, when Regional Commander Pan Rong would lead his regular troops ahead in escort of the imperial entourage [see map 8].

Within a few days we arrived at the border of the Bhamo native chieftain's jurisdiction. We hardly expected that this scoundrel would be so full of villainous cunning. When the emperor arrived, the chieftain came to pay respects to the court, and when he saw the Imperial Carriage he bleated miserably: "This native jurisdiction is very small, and the native people all live in caves in the mountains. When they heard that the Heavenly Court of the Sage Ruler had entered the borders, they were frightened out of their wits, and now they dare not come out. No one has prepared men, horses, money, or grain for the court's use. There remain only these few natives who directly serve me, the chieftain. This native chief can only welcome the Imperial Carriage here and beg to be executed for malfeasance."

When the emperor heard the native chieftain's words, he asked Mu Tianbo and Pan Rong what they had to say about handling the situation, and they, with the high officials of the inner circle, submitted the following: "Wait until your servants have taken him out and questioned him thoroughly." [Shortly thereafter] Duke Mu asked the man: "Are you a real native chief or a false one? Speak up truthfully. Our Emperor of the Heavenly Court is just using your route temporarily for a brief trip; moreover, you and the others are recipients of imperial beneficence. Now we want nothing more than to take this one route of yours, and if you conscientiously escort us through this borderland, then on a later, peaceful day your merit naturally will be considered. If you employ traitorous schemes today, remember that our major forces are just outside. If you stubbornly refuse to bring forth grain and fodder, we won't be daunted by the perilousness of your convoluted and cave-pocked terrain. We'll send troops to destroy your place, and then you'll have no chance to regret your decision. Even today, since things have come to this, you'll be hard pressed to get away alive."

When the native chieftain heard this, he became a bit flustered and said: "How could I be unaware that the Emperor of the Heavenly Court is just passing through? But what can be done when the native people of this jurisdiction have all run away? How am I to manage things? Moreover, from here to Myanmar is still a long way, and there are two routes, by water and by land. One cannot get there in a day. How am I supposed to provide that much grain and fodder? With things at the point of impossibility, this native chieftain can only die and be done with it."

Duke Mu laughed loudly and said: "If you want to die, that's not hard. I'll oblige by simply ordering my subordinates to take you out and hack you up in a swordfest, just keeping your head to show the natives!"

The chieftain was scared witless when he heard this. He begged pitifully for mercy from the "Old Ancestral Master,"* whereupon Duke Mu had him released and let him go on speaking . . . : "This is a foreign land of cowardly, inferior people. Just now, seeing the generals and troops of the Heavenly Court carrying sharp knives and mechanical weapons, the native people were fearful and hid away. Would that the Old Ancestral Master would take my advice: Pardon their chieftain; in addition, send down an order to the army to cast away sharp blades and other weapons; then have someone take me to rally the native people to transport grain and fodder to you. If you kill this one person, the native chief, when they find out they'll panic even more."

When he finished speaking, the assembled officials deliberated, saying: "We've come this far, and the situation is critical. Moreover, we don't know the way through his territory. We're running out of grain. If we move onward, there'll be nothing for us or the animals to eat. We can only rely on him and see how things turn out. . . ."

In response to their decision, the emperor said, "You ministers do whatever is appropriate."

The assembled officials emerging from the court audience didn't think that heaven intended to have ruler and ministers scattered apart by the traitorous schemes of the Bhamo native chieftain. In any case they ordered his release and got someone to go with him as he summoned the native people to come peacefully. They also ordered men in the army to collect all the swords, knives, and such that they were carrying and to divest themselves of so much as an inch of iron. Then the native people began to come out one by one, and before long, grain and fodder were heaped in hillocks. All the men and horses in the whole camp got to eat their fill.

After eating for three days, who had reason to take precautions

---

*All the tribal chiefs in the far southwest had been at least nominally subordinate to the Mu ducal lineage since the beginning of the Ming dynasty, when Mu Ying (1345–92), the favorite adopted son of the Ming founding emperor, was granted special hereditary governing powers in the region. See n. 5.

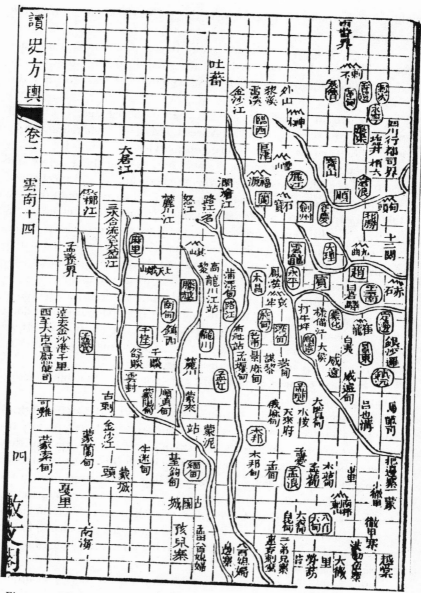

Figure 24. The border region between Yunnan Province, in China, and Myanmar (formerly Burma; Miandian in Chinese) as it was vaguely understood in the seventeenth century. Compare this to map 8.

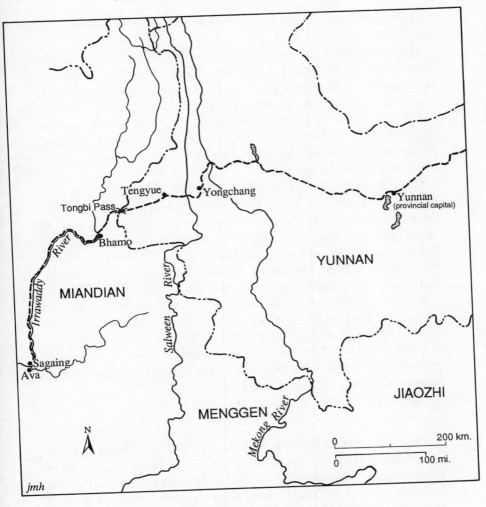

Map 8. The Terminal Route of the Yongli Court

against the natives' having a change of heart? But in the middle of the night of the fourth day, all that we could see were fires lit on the tops of the surrounding hills, and artillery fire sounded without end. Duke Mu led some men to protect the Imperial Carriage, and he ordered Commander Pan to tell his army not to do anything until the enemy came down. Then we could discern whether they were natives. If they were, we would certainly be able to tell, and then we could order some men to go down to the river and seize the boats. Further deliberations could wait until it was light.

When he finished speaking, Duke Mu joined the assembled civil and military officials in forming a protective guard around the quarters of the emperor, empress dowager, and empress. Right before dawn, someone came to report to the duke that all the natives brought by the chieftain had run away. Fortunately our men sensed their betrayal early. Otherwise, there might have been some danger of their seizing all the grain and fodder that we had requisitioned from them. Luckily it had been taken by our men.

When Duke Mu heard this, he memorialized the emperor, reporting that by dawn we had seized more than a hundred boats. He then requested that the Sage Carriage and members of the palace household board the boats. They were followed by the duke himself, along with the inner circle of senior civil and military officials. Only Commander Pan took his men and horses by the land route, and after this point Pan and his ruler did not see each other again.[8]

When Duke Mu and the other officials reached Myanmar, they expected that the king [Pindalè] would come to meet the Imperial Carriage. They never anticipated that he would stick the imperial party in a place of death.* By then, we could neither advance nor retreat; moreover, we didn't know their native language. So ruler and officials were confined there for three years.[†]

.   .   .

During those three years we endured many bitter troubles and anxieties. Those Myanmar scoundrels tried to lure Duke Mu, the inner group of senior civil and military officials, and other officials—altogether 106 men—[out of the Yongli camp] to go and "drink talisman water."[9] It was the 19th day, 7th month, 17th year of the Yongli reign [sic—August 21, 1663] when the Myanmar king [Pyè Min] sent an official to say: "The king of our country says that during the three years that the Emperor of the Heavenly Court has been residing here, he has seen no soldiers or cavalry of the Heavenly Court come to get the emperor, who for

---

*A rustic area called Sagaing, across the Irrawaddy River north of Ava.
†Omitted below is a long account of the gradual attrition of Li Dingguo's army in successive encounters with Qing forces, his abortive attempts to reestablish contact with the Yongli court, his near death from frustration, and his betrayal to the Qing by the eunuch in charge of his wife and son.

his part has shown no sign of moving. Could it be that you do not want to go? Even if you were to stay for ten years, in the end you still would have to leave. Now the king of my country says that tomorrow is an auspicious day. He wishes to invite you senior officials, along with Old Ancestral Master Mu, to drink talisman water. He wishes thereby to form a personal bond with you and come to one mind with you, the better to go out and pacify some territory. Then the emperor can be asked to return to China. If you intend to protect your emperor here in our country for a hundred years, that will not do."

When Duke Mu heard this, he burst into anger, saying: "This is not [an invitation] to drink talisman water. It's nothing but a traitorous scheme of you barbaric people to snare ruler and ministers all in one net. What's more, in the three years that we have lived in this region, your king has bound us here and not allowed our people to go to any distant point. [Even if we were free to go,] we are not familiar with your travel routes. Moreover, the status of your kingdom as a pacification office was originally bestowed by our China.[10] The ruler and ministers who have come here constitute the Heavenly Court of the superior realm. To accord with the principles of an inferior realm, your king should respond to our needs here. How is it that, on the contrary, he has confined ruler and ministers in this place? Also, we know very well that your country has long been rebellious at heart. That goes without saying. . . . You can go tell your king that the Emperor of the Heavenly Court is merely following heaven's will. Having come to the point of hopelessness, why should he have to take the insults of you natives besides? Although ruler and ministers are now in dire straits, we never thought that your king would treat us so discourteously. Bring on your million troops and thousand elephants! We, ruler and ministers, will simply follow heaven's command in going to our deaths. But afterward, others will surely come to settle accounts with you!"

When Duke Mu finished speaking, he and the assembled senior civil and military officials said with one voice, "We'll go early tomorrow morning. Tell your king to come out bright and early to meet us!" The native messenger assented and left.

·   ·   ·

The next day the Myanmar scoundrels surrounded the imperial compound with a hundred elephants and twenty thousand of their best troops. Shortly before noon the knaves themselves came to kill Duke

Mu and the others. In no time Duke Mu grabbed a wooden beam, and with it he beat to death several dozen natives before the horde of marauders surged forward and killed him, along with all the senior officials. Then they slew their way into the imperial compound and killed our young boys and old men—over fifteen in all[—who had moved there to protect the emperor's quarters]. Several thousand of those in the imperial party were killed; only eight people remained—the emperor, empress dowager, empress, crown prince, princess, two concubines, and this young eunuch. Also spared was a regional commander from Jiangxi, Jiang Shouren, who'd become ill and was no longer conscious. And there were three men who'd been left for dead but hadn't died. Pitifully, of ruler and servants—altogether several thousand people—only about a dozen remained alive.

In mid-afternoon we saw the Myanmar marauders regroup in one place, and we heard that their king had sent out an order to stop the killing. We also saw a large number of the Myanmar villains gather around their king. He was holding a document in one hand and pointing with the other toward the emperor,* but I don't know what the Myanmar king and his servitors were saying. Before long he left, leading away his foot soldiers and cavalry.

He then got four officials and three hundred soldiers to stand guard around the emperor, empress dowager, empress, crown prince, princess, imperial concubines, and women family members of the slain civil and military officials, all of whom were interned together on the upper floor of a building. After we'd been without food for three days, the scoundrels still wouldn't allow anyone to come downstairs. So this young eunuch, Yang Deze, having observed that the surrounding knaves had done nothing for three days and that the guards were gradually dwindling in number, submitted to the emperor that he might as well go out of the building to search for some food to sustain the imperial family.† After all, it wouldn't do for ruler and subjects to starve to death. The emperor replied, "Yes, you might as well go. But there's no need to look for anything just now except some cool water for us to drink."

It was the height of summer, and the weather was at its hottest.

---

*The document may have been a warning from the Qing that if the Yongli emperor was not turned over to them, a Qing army would attack Ava. See *SM*, pp. 175–76.

†From this point on, the author refers to himself as the little eunuch. Most instances are here rendered in the first person.

There were so many people in the building that the odor was becoming hard to take. So, having heard the emperor's instruction, I went downstairs and right away was tied up by the Myanmar scoundrels and taken to see their headman. When the headman saw me, he asked, "How old are you?" And I replied, "Twelve." Then the headman asked, "What did such a small boy as you with such big courage want to do in coming downstairs?" I replied: "So many of our people have been killed off, but you've neither killed my emperor and his followers nor done anything about us. Now it's been three days. What's more, the weather is terribly hot, the men and women are all in one place, and upstairs the stench is unbearable. So my master, the emperor of the Heavenly Court, directed that I come and ask you not to delay. If you intend to kill us, then do so. Otherwise, quickly send someone upstairs with some cool water to relieve the people."

When the headman heard my words, he said: "This has nothing to do with me or my men. The king of our country has sent down an order that you, ruler and followers, are to be deprived of food and not released until he issues another order. But because you say that you've been sent by your emperor, I won't kill you. Go on back."

When I heard him speak like that, I grew even more bold and said: "You say that your king has given you orders. But how could it be that he wants you to let my ruler and his followers slowly starve to death before going back and reporting to him? Now it's been three days and three nights. What sense is there in not allowing us to drink so much as one mouthful of water? I really must ask whether *you* need to eat every day or not?"

Thereupon the headman had four of the native soldiers detain me and not let me go while he went back to speak with his king. He was gone the whole morning and didn't return until noon. Then he said to me: "I repeated to my king everything that you said after coming downstairs. When he heard your words, he was pleased and commented on your being so young and yet so brave. Now we are to take your emperor and have him return to where he was living before without our keeping guard."

I then said, "How can you release us without even sending any rice?" The headman then laughed and said, "It's good enough that we're letting you go. But still you worry about your rice!" Then he had me untied and let me go back, after which I reported the words that he had brought back from his king.

When the emperor, empress dowager, empress, crown prince, princess, and concubines heard this, they hugged me and exclaimed, "Our son, today we've made things hard on you. You've really earned merit in rescuing the Imperial Carriage!" . . . [Shortly, we] were moved back into the imperial compound.

Unexpectedly a foreign monk came to see the emperor and said: "This king of ours is not a good man. Not long ago he had his own brother assassinated, and he seized the throne. Because he saw that the great affairs of the Heavenly Court could not be completed and that no one was in liaison with the court, he became of a mind to harm the Emperor. Why did he suddenly leave a few days ago without doing so? That was the Emperor's vast good fortune. Just when he was about to have the Emperor taken away, we saw that a document had arrived from the 'Heavenly Court.' We didn't know whether it was the Ming court or the Qing court. All we heard was that the court wanted the Emperor. When the king got the document, he gave a start, and because of its content, he went back [to Ava]. Was that not the Emperor's vast good fortune? . . . "

When the emperor heard what the foreign monk had to say, he thought the document surely was from the Prince of Jin. So he thanked some natives who'd [come with the monk and] brought firewood and rice, and the group took their leave.

When the Myanmar marauders' king heard that some natives had come with tribute, he ordered that they be taken away and hacked to death. And he also got over a thousand men to come and keep watch on the emperor, the palace household, and the others. So we again went hungry for two or three days. And after that, absolutely no natives came to our place.

Outside, from morning to night for over forty days, ghosts cried and spirits howled, and inside, mournful sounds never ceased. The desolation was hard to bear; nor did anyone come to sell anything. For our daily needs I could only go out at dusk and come back at dawn, searching through the night in various unsecured places for some wild vegetables or other edibles so ruler and servants, members of the palace household, and the group of women could make it through each day.

Suddenly one day the king of Myanmar again got someone to come and say, "The Emperor of China can no longer stay here. We suggest that you go somewhere else." . . . It was getting late in the evening, and it was the 9th month, when the weather got very cold. Nevertheless, [the Myanmar scoundrels] had the emperor, empress dowager, empress, crown prince, and princess mount into their old carriage. The rest of those in the palace household and all the titled women had to walk. We traveled until the middle of the night, when we reached the [Irrawaddy] river launch and boarded boats.

As the sky was about to turn light, I could see through the morning darkness several thousand men and horses on the opposite bank. I didn't know whether they were Qing troops or troops of the Ming court come to get us. I couldn't distinguish anything clearly. We could only go forward in the middle of [the Myanmar] army.

As it happened, the emperor's asthma flared, and the empress dowager and empress were full of anxiety. As dawn came, they had me go out the cabin door and take a look. I saw a chaotic profusion of men and horses but no pennants or insignia. I only heard people throughout the camp calling for Regional Commander Wang Hui and saw several large palanquins waiting on the shore. I also heard people say, "Let's wait a while longer, till it's light, before asking the empress dowager, emperor, and empress to start out." I submitted each thing I'd seen or heard to the imperial family.

When the empress dowager learned that the emperor was feeling somewhat more comfortable, she said to me: "These are Qing troops. It's Wang Hui who has come to meet us, but [if he were still loyal to the Ming] he would have greeted us promptly. Why would he delay boarding our boat? Go cautiously again and watch their movements. Regardless of your age, my son, you must do something in this emergency. Then you will be the most steadfast, loyal servant my Ming dynasty has had in three hundred years. It is important that you carefully and surely identify anyone out there who was one of our people before—all of whom you knew. You can sit at the doorway of the cabin and observe how the scoundrels are acting. Then come and report to me."

I received the empress dowager's directive and left. The emperor said to her: "The Mother Empress should be calm. Your son and servant thinks that if [the Manchu barbarians] have received the world that once was the Ming dynasty's, they naturally must treat people with decorum, and they surely will effect the rites appropriate to the emperor of our nation—the Son of Heaven. Even if the Qing troops get hold of us today, I wager that they will not dare be disrespectful. They have to report this information to [the barbarian Manchu leaders], so there is some time yet.* It would be reasonable if they would wait until your son's illness improves. So the Mother Empress need not be distressed."

Around mid-morning I saw over a hundred men—none carrying soldiers' blades—walk up to the prow of our boat. They looked up at me, and one of them said, "I am Wang Hui." I asked him, "Do you recognize me?" He said he didn't, and I retorted, "If you don't recognize me, then how can you say that you're Wang Hui?" Then the man spoke again: "Wang Hui will be here soon. I am a regional commander like him. I feared that the emperor would refuse to see someone he didn't know. So I hoped that you, Young Master, would say Wang Hui's name to him."

I asked who had sent them, and the men responded, "We've come to meet the emperor's carriage. As for who has sent us, we ask that the Young Master transmit our memorial requesting an audience with the emperor." I spoke again, saying, "It wouldn't be difficult for you to see my emperor if you had brought along any written identification." They asked what sort of written identification I wanted, and I said, "I'm still young and don't know. Why don't you go and think about it."

As I spoke, I saw Wang Hui coming. From far away he began chuckling and said, "In the three or four years since we last met, you've grown up, Young Master, seated so high. Our coming here with five thousand cavalrymen to meet the Ten Thousand Years [the emperor] was ordered by Li Thousand Years [Li Dingguo]."

I saw furtive glances darting among the men. Their manner was not as in earlier times, and what they said was not clear. I was suspicious but could only submit what they'd said to the emperor. When the emperor heard my words, he laughed jovially and said, "Go and tell them to come aboard. I'll ask them myself. You don't understand that this is a ploy by those bandits to delude me."

I followed this order and announced that Wang Hui could come aboard to see the Imperial Carriage. When Wang finished [the preliminary formalities of] a court audience, the emperor asked him for news of Li, the Prince of Jin, and also asked to see any confirming document. Wang Hui couldn't say a single sentence in reply. Then the emperor knew that he'd falsely claimed to have been sent by the Prince of Jin.

*Pejorative references to the Manchus, bracketed above, have been blanked out of surviving texts.

The emperor asked, "Wang Hui, have you been sent by Wu Sangui?" Wang dared not respond. Then the emperor said in a loud voice: "What wrong has Our Great Ming done to you that makes you determined to trap the whole Ming court in one net? I'd guess that you and the others won't receive any higher reward for this than a princedom. But if you kill this mother and son today, then you criminals will bring a curse upon yourselves and your ancestors for a thousand years. It would seem that I, though bereft, have not treated you ungenerously. Who could have imagined that you would not only scurrilously seek to preserve your own life but also betray your ruler!"

His denunciations went on to include Wu Sangui. The emperor's Dragon Visage showed great anger as he pointed his finger at Wang Hui, berating him severely: "You cowardly fellow, get off immediately. This is a place where loyal ministers and fine generals kneel. How do *you* have the cheek to kneel here? Haven't you gone yet?!"

Wang Hui, who was advanced in years and who was thoroughly shamed by this tongue-lashing from the emperor, lost his footing as he got off the boat, and he fell down on the riverbank. A bunch of people dashed to lift him up and ask what was wrong, but he was speechless.

Before long another man from the Qing camp boarded our boat to speak. . . . He came up, knelt, and submitted these words: "Your servant is the generalissimo of the vanguard of the forward battalion of the Qing army. I am named Ying'a, of the Plain White Banner.'' Recently I learned that the Carriage of the Sage Ruler of the Great Ming had arrived, so I have come to wish the Ten Thousand Years peace of mind."

The emperor said, "I am the Son of Heaven of a fallen nation. Why does the General accord me such great deference? You truly are a noble man who knows ritual propriety. I am an emperor of the Ming dynasty with no authority over you or your men. Yet you observe such grand ceremony. Thank you. What more do you have to say?"

The Qing general replied: "I have long heard that the Emperor is a ruler of sage virtue and radiant humanity. Indeed, the whole world knows this. Today's affairs are the results of heaven's command and at root have nothing to do with us as individuals. The Emperor, in his sageliness, comprehends [this], of course. Having requested that the Emperor come out of Myanmar, we naturally will write a memorial to inform our ruler that today we saw the Emperor's Dragon Visage,

which is as authentic as that of the Emperor of Zitong*—rarely seen
in the world. Previously someone who had seen the Emperor told our
ruler [of his extraordinary physiognomy], but our ruler did nòt believe
what he heard. Today the moment that this servant saw for himself,
he knew that after all, the Emperor's reputation had a foundation of
truth.

"When we set out with our troops, we were acting on an edict that
deputed us to invite the Emperor's Sage Carriage to accompany us to
the capital [so that you and our ruler can] enjoy reigning over the world
together. The edict also warned us that the Emperor's Dragon Body
absolutely was not to be agitated. Our ruler still wishes to see the
Emperor with his own eyes. Lest the Emperor disbelieve this, he gave
us an edict as we embarked, which has been brought here. We ask that
the Emperor's Dragon Eyes view it so he can judge with his sage
perspicacity whether our words are true or false."

Hearing the Qing officials' words, the emperor gave a big laugh and
said: "This shows the humane virtue of your emperor of the Qing
court. How could I be unaware of destiny? Heaven's command has
long since gone to the Qing dynasty. Alas, it was because the fortunes
of our Great Ming dynasty could not be prolonged that we have come
to the present day." But having said this, he cried hard as he went on:
"I have not taken leave of this world long since because my dear old
mother is advanced in age, and I could not just let things drop. Sir, if
you and the others could take care not to alarm my old mother in any
way, it would show your great virtue. Should you wish to make an
inspection and record our people's names, go and ask our young eunuch,
Yang Deze. I am ill and feeling poorly. I really cannot endure any
more."

. . . Then the emperor, ill as he was, traveled with the Qing units
for five months,[†] during which time the Qing officials were very respectful toward him. Each day they would come to pay court, and
when the emperor saw them coming, he would shed tears and say, "In
times past my family had [Ming] high ministers also do obeisance at
court. But today not one comes to see me." During those five months
on the road the emperor would not receive a single large vessel of food
or drink. All he did was write several poems each day and sob heavily,

---

*A Daoist deity whose main shrine was in Zitong, Sichuan Province. He was thought
to control men's fortunes in the civil service examinations and in gaining, as well as
advancing in, bureaucratic office.

[†]Other sources indicate that the trip took a more reasonable three months.

facing the lamp. Sometimes he kept the empress dowager company, and he would say to her through his tears, "Your son and servant is disloyal and unfilial—his criminality is so confirmed that he warrants execution. Why has he allowed his burden of guilt to cause the Mother Empress such distress!"

As the entourage was approaching the Yunnan [provincial seat], the emperor's asthma flared up badly; circumstances were perilous as well. But the emperor laughed heartily and said to himself, "How could I, a descendant of our venerable Heavenly Court, covet the wealth and honor of any other man?" Gradually the emperor's illness worsened, leaving him only one breath in a long interval.[12]

One day a man came and said, "Today a messenger has come from Beijing. He definitely wants me to ask the Emperor to go see him. He also has a directive that he wants to read aloud to you." The emperor said to the empress dowager, "Your son can no longer be filially obedient to his Mother. I think his time has come." When he finished speaking, sure enough, someone came for him. The emperor said nothing.

It was the 2nd day of the 4th month of the 18th year of the Yongli reign* when the emperor, the crown prince, and the young son of an imperial relative were executed together in the Yunnan [provincial seat]. The sky became murky and the earth dark. Before long there were thunderclaps and flashes of lightning, and hail filled the city. At the time the Qing troops and eight-banner cavalrymen wanted to rebel and forcibly preserve the Yongli emperor. Throughout and around the city, troops and commoners alike wailed for three days without ceasing. Then Wu Sangui himself felt some remorse, but he also feared that the Manchus would harm him to take revenge. So he sent word that the Manchu troops harbored seditious intentions and planned to avenge the Yongli emperor by rebelling. When the [Qing court's] edict came down, he proceeded to behead all the eight-banner troops. Sangui also had the empress dowager, the empress, and the remaining members of their immediate household, including the eunuchs, all sent to Beijing.

As it happened, the [Qing] Shunzhi emperor had died,[†] and four regents [Oboi, Soni, Suksaha, and Ebilun] were managing the gov-

---

*Eighteen is surely an error for sixteen, in which case the date would be May 19, 1662.

†On February 5, 1661.

ernment.[13] Not understanding greater principles, they put the empress
dowager in a palace home for the elderly and planned to marry off
the empress and the young princess. When she heard this, the empress
became very angry. After bowing four times to the empress dowager
and four times to the spirit of the Yongli emperor, she said: "Although
my husband, a grand and enlightened monarch, was unable to restore
the dynasty, he truly was like [the ancient sage rulers] Yao and Shun.
That he suffered from the terrible malice of those marauders was
heaven's will. I recall that when I was empress at [the Ming] court,
there never was the slightest lapse in respectful relations between
throne and ministers. That I am now being harassed like this by
such scoundrels is due to my shortcomings. I am a woman. How
can I fulfill my husband's great charge to sustain my life in order to
filially serve my mother-in-law? I think today that I should seek death
and have done with it."

As she was speaking, I saw a bunch of Manchu rogues coming into
our quarters. My lady rushed to get some sort of knife but in her haste
couldn't find one. So she smashed a porcelain bowl. Taking a piece of
it in her hand and using all her strength, she severed her throat. Immediately her breath was cut off and she died.

When the four regents heard about this, even they were taken aback.
So they sent down orders to the Ministry of Rites to hold a proper
funeral for an empress according to Ming court regulations.[14] At the
time no one in the capital or in any of the provinces knew of this. Not
a single former civil or military official of the Ming court was in attendance. There was only me, the young eunuch Yang Deze, who temporarily posed as the filial son and, wearing deep mourning, accompanied
the funeral procession the whole way. Afterward, the empress dowager
lived to the age of ninety-one before dying; the princess passed away
within two years after that. I accompanied both to their final resting
places.

From beginning to end, everything I knew or heard of while following
the court of a beleaguered state is still before my eyes. Item by item,
I have written those things out to tell the world and to do justice to
the ardent courage of the emperor, empress dowager, empress, crown
prince, princess, the Prince of Jin, Duke Mu, the civil and military
high officials, and the generals and soldiers of the army, who kept their
good names untarnished by dying for loyalty. Hearing of these things,
how can one not shed tears?

NOTES

DMB   L. C. Goodrich and Chaoying Fang, eds. *A Dictionary of Ming Biography (1368–1644)*. 2 vols. New York: Columbia University Press, 1976.

ECCP   Arthur W. Hummel, ed. *Eminent Chinese of the Ch'ing Period, 1644–1912*. 2 vols. Washington, D.C.: Library of Congress, 1943.

GE   Frederic Wakeman, Jr. *The Great Enterprise: The Manchu Reconstruction of Imperial Order in Seventeenth-Century China*. 2 vols. Berkeley: University of California Press, 1985.

SM   Lynn A. Struve. *The Southern Ming, 1644–1662*. New Haven: Yale University Press, 1984.

INTRODUCTION

1. This association is not discussed in an otherwise informative article by Charles E. Hammond, "An Excursion in Tiger Lore," *Asia Major*, 3rd ser., 4.1 (1991): 87–100. As a result, the author does not point out that a certain story of a "Righteous Tiger," told in 1661, could well be a politically ingratiating analogy for the Manchu-Qing dynasty—fearsome initially but bringing salvation after all (pp. 97–100). See also Mi Chu Wiens, "Anti-Manchu Thought during the Early Ch'ing, *Harvard Papers on China*, 22 (1969): 1–24.

2. The massive, crenellated stone structure that we think of today as the Great Wall was constructed in the mid to late Ming period as part of the dynasty's defense measures against the Mongols. Tactically it was intended to be used more in transmitting signals of approaching Mongol forces than in keeping them out. If Chinese armies were too weak or distracted to thwart such approaches, then the wall was of little effect in preventing

Mongol—or later, Manchu—incursions or invasions. See Arthur Waldron, *The Great Wall of China: From History to Myth* (Cambridge: Cambridge University Press, 1990), pp. 140–93.

3. See S. A. M. Adshead, "The Seventeenth Century General Crisis," *Asian Profile*, 1.2 (October 1973): 271–80; William S. Atwell, "Some Observations on the 'Seventeenth-Century Crisis' in China and Japan," *Journal of Asian Studies*, 45.2 (February 1986): 223–44; and Frederic E. Wakeman, Jr., "China and the Seventeenth-Century Crisis," *Late Imperial China*, 7.1 (June 1986): 1–26. On the widespread malaise attending the last decades of the Ming dynasty, see Ray Huang, *1587, a Year of No Significance: The Ming Dynasty in Decline* (New Haven: Yale University Press, 1981); or Albert Chan, *The Glory and Fall of the Ming Dynasty* (Norman: University of Oklahoma Press, 1982).

4. For narrative histories of this protracted struggle, see *GE* and *SM*.

5. The Manchus, a heavily Jurchen coalition of various tribes from the region of the Liao and Sungari river drainages, did not begin to call themselves *manju*, or *manzhou*, until 1635. See Pei Huang, "New Light on the Origins of the Manchus," *Harvard Journal of Asiatic Studies*, 50.1 (1990): 239–82. The famous Banners, first organized by Nurhaci (1559–1626) and expanded by his successors, consisted formally of Manchus, Mongols, and Chinese transfrontiersmen, but each of these categories was an ethnic amalgam, which could, for instance, include Korean elements. On this complicated subject, see Pamela Kyle Crossley, "The Qianlong Retrospect on the Chinese-Martial (*Hanjun*) Banners," *Late Imperial China*, 10.1 (June 1989): 63–107; and Crossley, *Orphan Warriors: Three Manchu Generations and the End of the Qing World* (Princeton: Princeton University Press, 1990), pp. 5, 14–15. Cohesion lay in a shared culture of horsemanship and archery for hunting and conquest. It was this culture, not any racial qualities, that most Chinese regarded as fearsomely alien.

6. For discussions of loyalism in the seventeenth-century context, see Lynn A. Struve, "Ambivalence and Action: Some Frustrated Scholars of the K'ang-hsi Period," in *From Ming to Ch'ing: Conquest, Region, and Continuity in Seventeenth-Century China*, ed. J. Spence and J. E. Wills, Jr. (New Haven: Yale University Press, 1979), pp. 326–28; and *GE*, chap. 15.

7. James B. Parsons, "The Culmination of a Chinese Peasant Rebellion: Chang Hsien-chung in Szechwan, 1644–46," *Journal of Asian Studies*, 16.3 (May 1957): 387–99.

8. See Peter Perdue, *Exhausting the Earth: State and Peasant in Hunan, 1500–1850* (Cambridge: Council on East Asian Studies of Harvard University, 1987), pp. 61–72. Also, see Chap. 10, introduction. On Wu Sangui, see Chap. 1, nn. 12, 15.

9. For studies of major figures of the conquest period, see, for instance, Frederic

Wakeman, Jr., "Romantics, Stoics, and Martyrs in Seventeenth-Century China," *Journal of Asian Studies*, 43.4 (August 1984): 631–66; Jerry Dennerline, *The Chia-ting Loyalists: Confucian Leadership and Social Change in Seventeenth-Century China* (New Haven: Yale University Press, 1981); and Kang-i Sun Chang, *The Late-Ming Poet Ch'en Tzu-lung: Crises of Love and Loyalism* (New Haven: Yale University Press, 1991). Regarding the "collective mentalities" that the Chinese voices in this volume might represent, see David Johnson, "Communication, Class, and Consciousness in Late Imperial China," in *Popular Culture in Late Imperial China*, ed. D. Johnson, A. J. Nathan, and E. S. Rawski (Berkeley: University of California Press, 1985), pp. 34–72.

10. See Pei-yi Wu, *The Confucian's Progress: Autobiographical Writings in Traditional China* (Princeton: Princeton University Press, 1990), esp. parts 2 and 4. In addition to the many exemplars treated by Wu, see Willard J. Peterson, *Bitter Gourd: Fang I-chih and the Impetus for Intellectual Change* (New Haven: Yale University Press, 1979).

CHAPTER 1. A SURVIVOR OF BEIJING

1. On traditional Chinese historians' predominant treatment of Li et al., see James B. Parsons, "Attitudes toward the Late Ming Rebellions," *Oriens Extremus*, 6 (1959): 177–91.

2. He was placed in the fourth of six categories of punishment: frontier garrison duty subject to monetary redemption.

3. This record was very little known until it was first published in the collection *Dingchou congbian* in 1936. A punctuated edition can be found in the *Mingmo Qingchu shiliao xuankan* series (Hangzhou: Zhejiang guji chubanshe, 1985), in the volume titled *Jiashen hezhen lue*.

4. See Jerry Dennerline, *The Chia-ting Loyalists: Confucian Leadership and Social Change in Seventeenth-Century China* (New Haven: Yale University Press, 1981), chaps. 9–10; or *GE*, I:656–61.

5. In the middle seventeenth century, China participated with much of the rest of the Northern Hemisphere in a "little ice age" of unusually cold temperatures and erratic weather. This certainly brought about more food shortages than usual and contributed to increases in disease, such as those mentioned below by Liu Shangyou. See William S. Atwell, "Some Observations on the 'Seventeenth-Century Crisis,'" *Journal of Asian Studies*, 45.2 (February 1986): 224–27; and Helen Dunstan, "The Late Ming Epidemics: A Preliminary Survey," *Ch'ing-shih wen-t'i*, 3.3 (November 1975): 1–59.

6. On Beijing and the imperial palace during the Ming and early Qing periods, see Nancy Shatzman Steinhardt, *Chinese Imperial City Planning* (Honolulu: University of Hawaii Press, 1990), pp. 169–78.

7. For a full narrative of the events reported below but in a wider context, see James B. Parsons, *Peasant Rebellions of the Late Ming Dynasty* (Tucson: University of Arizona Press, 1970), chap. 4.

8. For a different view, see Ray Huang, "Ni Yuan-lu: 'Realism' in a Neo-Confucian Scholar-Statesman," in *Self and Society in Ming Thought*, ed. W. T. de Bary (New York: Columbia University Press, 1970), pp. 415–49.

9. Paper money was used extensively in the first century of the Ming dynasty, but its use was officially discontinued in 1450. The government began printing it again in 1643 as a desperate measure to help save the dynasty's financial situation. See Li Chien-nung, "Price Control and Paper Currency in Ming," in *Chinese Social History: Translations of Selected Studies*, trans. and ed. E. Z. Sun and J. de Francis (New York: Octagon, 1966), pp. 293–94.

10. The tael (*liang*) was a standard weight of silver—about one ounce during the seventeenth century. Under the standard Chinese decimal system, a weight of silver called *qian* was one-tenth of a tael, and a *fen* was one-tenth of a qian, or one-hundredth of a tael. The character for *qian* can also refer to coins, usually made of copper alloy in this period. A "string" of one thousand coins was supposed to equal the value of one silver tael, though the exchange rate between copper and silver, the two basic metals of the Chinese monetary system, varied with time, region, and circumstance. For more on silver and the exchange system, see Chap. 2, nn. 14, 16; Chap. 4, n. 12; and p. 61*n*.

11. Here and below, the author uses the unspecific term *pao* for different sorts of firearms, probably ranging from full-sized cannon through middle-sized field guns to muskets. On the firearms used in China during this period, see Joseph Needham et al., *Science and Civilization in China*, vol. 5, part 7: *Military Technology; The Gunpowder Epic* (Cambridge: Cambridge University Press, 1986), pp. 365–414.

12. Besides *GE*, I:290–97, also see Angela Hsi, "Wu Sangui in 1644: A Reappraisal," *Journal of Asian Studies*, 34.2 (February 1975): 443–53.

13. Huang was much too far to the south, in the western part of South Zhili. The author has probably confused Huang with Liu Zeqing, who was summoned from far southern Hebei Province, but who turned southward, away from Beijing, instead of going to aid the city.

14. On the functions of court eunuchs in the Ming and Qing periods, see Taisuke Mitamura, *Chinese Eunuchs: The Structure of Intimate Politics*, trans. Charles A. Pomeroy (Rutland, Vt.: Tuttle, 1970), chap. 4. See also n. 22, below.

15. Ming sympathizers placed a great many false hopes on Wu Sangui. It was several months before Ming loyalists in the South became convinced that he had gone over to the Qing. In 1673, when Wu eventually did rebel against the Qing, the disillusionment was so thorough that few outside his

far southwestern satrapy supported his cause. See *GE*, II:1099–1127; and Kai-fu Tsao, "K'ang-hsi and the San-fan War," *Monumenta Serica*, 31 (1974–75): 108–30.

16. They committed suicide by hanging, the empress in her palace residence, the emperor in the large imperial park just north of the palace. The precise fate of the crown prince remains a mystery. Two different men who claimed to be the Chongzhen emperor's heir were captured later, one in the Beijing vicinity and one in Zhejiang, but both were eventually executed as impostors. See *GE*, I:528–35, 573–75, 581; and *SM*, pp. 35–36, 59.

17. Li may have staged this last-minute enthronement to reinforce claims to legitimacy that he might need to assert after being forced out of the capital.

18. See *ECCP*, I:215–19; or Erich Hauer, "Prinz Dorgon," *Ostasiatische Zeitschrift*, 13 (1926): 9–56.

19. He was captured at the age of twenty-two after impetuously leading a campaign against the Oirats into present-day Inner Mongolia in 1449, and he was returned to Beijing just over one year later. See *DMB*, I:290–91 (under Chu Ch'i-chen); and Frederick Mote, "The T'u-mu Incident of 1449," in *Chinese Ways in Warfare*, ed. F. Kierman, Jr., and J. K. Fairbank (Cambridge: Harvard University Press, 1974), pp. 243–72.

20. The head was shaved except for a patch of hair in the back, which was allowed to grow long and was braided into a queue. This coiffure was not unique to the Manchus. It had been common among various peoples of the Eurasian steppe region at least since the second century B.C. See Shiratori Kurakichi, "The Queue among the Peoples of North Asia," *Memoirs of the Research Department of the Toyo Bunko*, 4 (1929): 1–70. To the Chinese mind it was definitely a barbarian feature.

21. The various brigands referred to from this point on were independent groups, not parts of Li Zicheng's roving rebel army—though some of Li's men who were left stranded in southern Hebei and Shandong by the main army's quick retreat from Beijing probably turned to free-lance banditry. On security conditions in that region, see I Songgyu, "Shantung in the Shun-chih Reign: The Establishment of Local Control and the Gentry Response," trans. Joshua Fogel, *Ch'ing-shih wen-t'i*, 4.4 (December 1980): 1–34; 4.5 (June 1981): 1–31.

22. The two eunuchs are Wang Cheng'en, head of the Directorate of Ceremonial, who committed suicide with the Chongzhen emperor; and Wang Zhixin, head of the imperial secret service, who died under torture by the Chuang rebels. Eunuchs were probably more numerous, wealthy, and powerful during the Ming than under any other dynasty. In spite of their sexual incapacity, the more successful among them often kept wives and adopted sons to manage and inherit their wealth, including villas and manors outside the capital. See Chap. 15, introduction and nn. 1–3.

23. The home base, in central Shandong Province, of a colorful group of thieves in the popular novel *Shuihu zhuan* (variously translated into English as the *Water Margin, All Men Are Brothers,* and *Outlaws of the Marshes*). On the significance of themes in this work for people of the mid-seventeenth century in China, see Ellen Widmer, *The Margins of Utopia:* Shui-hu hou-chuan *and the Literature of Ming Loyalism* (Cambridge: Council on East Asian Studies of Harvard University, 1987). Apparently Liu's party was traversing the huge Wenan Swamp in central North Zhili (Hebei). See map 3.

24. That is, he had passed qualifying examinations and attained *shengyuan* status—he was eligible to take higher examinations for civil service degrees that might lead to an official career. By the seventeenth century, few shengyuan actually attended schools or became officials, but the status afforded many social and legal privileges. See Ichisada Miyazaki, *China's Examination Hell: The Civil Service Examinations in Imperial China,* trans. Conrad Schirokauer (Tokyo: John Weatherhill, 1976; New Haven: Yale University Press, 1981), chaps. 2, 3, 4. On the reasons why men from other parts of China found it advantageous to sit for the civil service examinations in Shuntian, rather than in their home prefectures, see Adam Y. C. Lui, *The Hanlin Academy: Training Ground for the Ambitious, 1644–1850* (Hamden, Conn.: Archon Books, 1981), pp. 129–30.

25. Their boat was probably suspended inside a pound-lock overnight. On the technology of locks along the Grand Canal, see Joseph Needham, *Science and Civilization in China,* vol. 4, part 3: *Civil Engineering and Nautics* (Cambridge: Cambridge University Press, 1971), pp. 344–63.

CHAPTER 2. THE MASSACRE OF YANGZHOU

1. For narrative accounts of this period, see *SM,* pp. 55–56; and *GE,* I:347–55, 399–404, 546–69.

2. Chinese biographies of Shi Kefa are legion, but published Western-language accounts of his life are few. See *ECCP,* II:651–52; and Wm. Henry Scott, trans., "The Official Biography of Shih K'o-fa (1602–1645)," *Annals of the Philippine Chinese History Association,* 7 (June 1977): 68–86.

3. See *ECCP,* I:215.

4. See Hellmut Wilhelm, "Ein Briefwechsel zwischen Durgan und Schï Kofa," *Sinica,* 8.5–6 (1933): 239–45.

5. The letters are included in most editions of Shi's collected writings. This translation is from the most recent edition, entitled *Shi Kefa ji,* ed. Luo Zhenchang (Shanghai: Shanghai guji chubanshe, 1984), which is based on the *Shi Daolin xiansheng yigao* (1697).

6. This bloodcurdling record of Manchu atrocities was a favorite among anti-Qing and anti-Japanese Chinese patriots from the beginning of the twen-

tieth century until the Communist revolution. The work has been published many times in slightly different versions. The translation below, which omits various passages for the sake of compactness, is based on the text of the *Yangzhou shiri ji* in the Guhuai shanfang edition of the *Jingtuo yishi* collectanea (Daoguang period, 1821–50). At a few points where that text is problematic, more felicitous characters or phrases have been adopted from the edition in the collectanea *Zhongguo neiluan waihuo lishi congshu* (Shanghai, 1947), vol. 3. The work has been fully translated into Western languages at least two previous times: P. Aucourt, "Journal d'un bourgeois de Yang-tcheou (1645)," *Bulletin de l'Ecole Française d'Extreme-Orient*, 7.3–4 (July–December 1907): 297–312; and Lucian Mao, "A Memoir of a Ten Days' Massacre in Yangchow," *T'ien Hsia Monthly*, 4.5 (May 1937): 515–37.

7. On the contemporary popularity of storybooks about female paragons, see Katherine Carlitz, "The Social Uses of Female Virtue in Late Ming Editions of *Lienü Zhuan*," *Late Imperial China*, 12.2 (December 1991): 117–48. The most influential late-Ming writer of admonitory guides for women did not favor dogmatic adherence to rules of conduct. He stressed that women should be resourceful in finding ways to preserve both virtue and practicality, especially in emergencies, as we find in the case of Wang Xiuchu's wife. See Joanna F. Handlin, "Lü K'un's New Audience: The Influence of Women's Literacy on Sixteenth-Century Thought," in *Women in Chinese Society*, ed. M. Wolf and R. Witke (Stanford: Stanford University Press, 1975), pp. 13–38. On widow chastity and widow suicide, see Chap. 6, esp. nn. 2, 14. Even fictional stories of this period placed an unusually strong emphasis on duty and on moral heroism. See Patrick Hanan, "The Fiction of Moral Duty: The Vernacular Story in the 1640s," in *Expressions of Self in Chinese Literature*, ed. R. Hegel and R. Hessney (New York: Columbia University Press, 1985), pp. 153–213.

8. His mother's surname was Yin. His father, Shi Congzhi, had died of illness in 1639. Because Shi's services were crucial at that time in resisting the incursions of roving rebel armies into the lower Yangzi region, the court allowed him to observe only two years' mourning for his father instead of the usual three.

9. Shi Dewei had the same surname as Shi Kefa, but they had no family relationship. Dewei arranged for the symbolic burial of some of Kefa's personal effects and the erection of a memorial shrine at a place called Plum Flower Ridge, north of the city of Yangzhou. Probably the most reliable account of Kefa's last days, the *Weiyang xunjie jilue* (Account of Martyrdom at Yangzhou), was written by Dewei later but was not published until 1812.

10. According to a study by one of Shi Kefa's chief biographers, this was Shi's

second wife, surnamed Yang, whom he married probably in 1638, not long after the death of his first wife. Shi did not take any concubines—unusual for a man of his status, especially considering that in the year of his death, Shi was still childless. See Zhu Wenzhang, "Shi Kefa furen xingshi kao" (Inquiry on the Surname of Madame Shi Kefa), 5th appendix to *Shi Kefa zhuan* (Biography of Shi Kefa) (Taipei: Commercial Press, 1974), pp. 112–17; for a partial rendering in English, see Chu Wen-djang, "Madame Shih K'e-fa," in *Studia Asiatica: Essays in Asian Studies in Felicitation of the Seventy-fifth Anniversary of Professor Ch'en Shou-yi*, ed. L. Thompson (San Francisco: Chinese Materials Center, 1975), pp. 91–97.

11. Because Kefa's only true brother, Kemo, had died prior to 1644, and Kefa usually referred to all agnates of his own generation as brothers, which expresses respect and affection, the identities of everyone addressed in this letter are not clear. It may be primarily directed to Kefa's second uncle, Benzhi, and the latter's sons (Kefa's second cousins), Kejian and Kecheng.

12. Shi wishes his wife to commit suicide, partly to reinforce his own martyrdom but also out of concern for her chastity should she fall into enemy hands. When this possibility arose before, Kefa repeatedly urged her to kill herself rather than be dishonored. Probably feeling an overriding need to care for her mother-in-law (who suffered from tuberculosis), she did not commit suicide at this time. Nevertheless, she seems not to have lived long after Kefa's mother died, which was perhaps in 1648.

13. On the organization of living space in traditional Chinese homes, principally among rooms, open courtyards, and verandas, see Ronald G. Knapp, *China's Vernacular Architecture: House Form and Culture* (Honolulu: University of Hawaii Press, 1989), esp. chap. 2.

14. On this medium of exchange in Ming-Qing China, see Lien-sheng Yang, *Money and Credit in China: A Short History*, Harvard-Yenching Monograph Series, vol. 13 (Cambridge: Harvard University Press, 1952); and Frank H. H. King, *Money and Monetary Policy in China, 1845–1895*, Harvard East Asian Series, no. 19 (Cambridge: Harvard University Press, 1965).

15. Such scenes had been familiar to ordinary Chinese people at least since the eighth century from murals on temple walls and from illustrated scrolls used by marketplace storytellers. By early Ming times, paintings of Buddhist hells were being mass-produced, probably using stencils, for sale in urban markets. See Stephen Teiser, " 'Having Once Died and Returned to Life': Representations of Hell in Medieval China," *Harvard Journal of Asiatic Studies*, 48.2 (December 1988): 445–46, 453.

16. The increased use of silver for small transactions had led, by late Ming times, to the common casting of ingots (*ding*) just five ounces in weight. In the Qing period ten-ounce ding were also in general use. See Yang, *Money*

and Credit in China, p. 46; and King, *Money and Monetary Policy in China*, p. 72.

17. The text gives the number 800,000. The figure is highly unlikely, for in the mid-seventeenth century the population of the city proper could hardly have exceeded 300,000. Only by including the whole of Yangzhou Prefecture could the figure have passed 800,000. See Zhang Defang, "Yangzhou shiri ji bianwu" (Discernment of Errors in the "Yangzhou shiri ji"), *Zhonghua wenshi luncong*, 5 (1964): 365–76.

CHAPTER 3. A MISSIONARY DESCRIBES THE MANCHUS

1. On Martini among his Jesuit colleagues, see George H. Dunne, *Generation of Giants: The Story of the Jesuits in China in the Last Decades of the Ming Dynasty* (London: Burns and Oates, 1962). For more on Martini's life and writings, see Giorgio Melis, ed., *Martino Martini: Geografo cartografo storico teologo* (Trent: Museo Tridentino di Scienze Naturali, 1983).

2. The title of the English translation is *Bellum Tartaricum, or the Conquest of the Great and Most Renowned Empire of China*. For critiques of the content of *De bello Tartarico*, see Piero Corradini, "Martino Martini as China's Historian: the *De bello Tartarico*," and Ma Yong, "Martino Martini's Activity in China and His Works on Chinese History and Geography," in Melis, ed., *Martino Martini*, pp. 185–94 and 248–62, respectively. For additional information, see D. E. Mungello, *Curious Land: Jesuit Accommodation and the Origins of Sinology* (Honolulu: University of Hawaii Press, 1989); Edwin J. Van Kley, "News from China: Seventeenth-Century European Notices of the Manchu Conquest," *Journal of Modern History*, 45.4 (December 1973): 561–82; and Donald F. Lach, *Asia in the Making of Europe*, vol. 2: *A Century of Wonder* (Chicago: University of Chicago Press, 1977), esp. book 3: "The Scholarly Disciplines." For another, more derogatory description of the Manchus by a Jesuit contemporary of Martini's, see Joseph S. Sebes, "A Description of the Tartars (Manchus) by the Jesuit Gabriel de Magalhaes in 1647 When He First Encountered Them at the Time of Their Conquest of China," *Manchu Studies Newsletter*, 4 (1980–81): 3–14.

3. Besides Manchus and Mongols, the Eight Banners included Chinese from Liaodong who had long held allegiance to the Manchus. See Liu Chia-chü, "The Creation of the Chinese Banners in the Early Ch'ing," trans. Pamela Crossley, *Chinese Studies in History*, 14.4 (Summer 1981): 47–75. Chinese soldiers who surrendered after the Qing crossed Shanhai Pass in May 1644 were organized separately and, as a rule, not made part of the eight-banner system. Initially the Plain White Banner was under the command of the young Shunzhi emperor's uncle, Prince Regent Dorgon, and the Plain

Yellow and Bordered Yellow banners were the emperor's. Plain White became the imperial banner only after Dorgon's death in November 1650.

4. At the time Alvarō Semedo (1585–1658) was the vice-provincial of the Jesuit China Mission. See *DMB*, II:1157–59.

5. Probably Shang Kexi (d. 1676), formerly a Ming commander in Liaodong and Shandong who defected to the Manchus in 1633. He was ennobled as a prince of the second degree, and after his conquest of Guangdong in 1650 he was given that province as a fief in recognition of his merit. See *ECCP*, II:635–36.

6. Sun Yuanhua, governor of Shandong, 1630–32. A Christian interested in the use of Western firearms, he was rewarded with arrest, trial, and execution for his efforts to prevent commanders from Liaodong, such as Shang Kexi, from defecting to the Manchus and returning to their home region. See *ECCP*, II:686.

CHAPTER 4. NANJING CHANGES HANDS

1. On the early history of the two Ming capitals, see F. W. Mote, "The Transformation of Nanking, 1350–1400," in *The City in Late Imperial China*, ed. G. W. Skinner (Stanford: Stanford University Press, 1977), pp. 101–53; and Edward L. Farmer, *Early Ming Government: The Evolution of Dual Capitals* (Cambridge: East Asian Research Center of Harvard University, 1976). For essays on Zhu Yuanzhang and Zhu Di, respectively, see *DMB*, I:381–92 and 355–65.

2. See Robert Crawford, "The Biography of Juan Ta-ch'eng," *Chinese Culture*, 6.2 (March 1965): 28–105.

3. For accounts of the Hongguang period, see *SM*, chap. 1; or *GE*, chap. 5.

4. This rare work, extant only in manuscript, is appended to the *Tongbian rilu* (Daily Record of the Disturbances in Tongcheng), by Jiang Chen, which is held by the National Central Library in Taipei. On the history of the Yao family, see Hilary J. Beattie, *Land and Lineage in China: A Study of T'ung-ch'eng County, Anhwei, in the Ming and Ch'ing Dynasties* (Cambridge: Cambridge University Press, 1979), pp. 37–41, 91–95.

5. See Hilary J. Beattie, "The Alternative to Resistance: The Case of T'ung-ch'eng, Anhwei," in *From Ming to Ch'ing: Conquest, Region, and Continuity in Seventeenth-Century China*, ed. J. Spence and J. E. Wills, Jr. (New Haven: Yale University Press, 1979), pp. 250–56.

6. Four more Dutch editions and seven translations into four other European languages appeared by the end of the century. On the enthusiasm in Europe for reports of this kind, see Edwin J. Van Kley, "News from China: Seventeenth-Century European Notices of the Manchu Conquest," *Journal of Modern History*, 45.4 (December 1973): 568–70. The excerpts below are

from an English translation of 1669 by John Ogilby. For short notices on Johann Nieuhof and his other writings, see Hartmut Walravens, *China illustrata: Das europäische Chinaverständnis im Spiegel des 16. bis 18. Jahrhunderts* (Weinheim: VCH Acta Humaniora, 1987), pp. 142-44.

7. See John E. Wills, Jr., *Pepper, Guns, and Parleys: The Dutch East India Company and China, 1662-1681* (Cambridge: Harvard University Press, 1974), chap. 1.

8. On two subsequent Dutch ambassadorial missions to the Chinese capital, in 1665-67 and 1685-87, see John E. Wills, Jr., *Embassies and Illusions: Dutch and Portuguese Envoys to K'ang-hsi, 1666-1687* (Cambridge: Harvard University Press, 1984), chaps. 2 and 5.

9. On the physical layout of Nanjing during the Ming period, see Nancy Shatzman Steinhardt, *Chinese Imperial City Planning* (Honolulu: University of Hawaii Press, 1990), pp. 163-66.

10. See Edward L. Farmer, *Early Ming Government: The Evolution of Dual Capitals*, Harvard East Asian Monographs, no. 66 (Cambridge: East Asian Research Center of Harvard University, 1976).

11. This was true in the early Ming period, but Beijing grew larger after the capital was transferred there in 1402-21 and probably remained the largest city in the world until about 1800, when its population was exceeded by that of London. See G. W. Skinner, "Introduction: Urban Development in Imperial China," and F. W. Mote, "The Transformation of Nanking, 1350-1400," in *The City in Late Imperial China*, ed. Skinner (Stanford: Stanford University Press, 1977), esp. pp. 29-30 and 151-53, respectively.

12. Lead, iron, and copper coins had been used for small payments since the Later Han dynasty (25-220). Although silver was rarely coined, it was routinely cast into small bars and ingots for use in larger transactions. Such ingots were not standard in fineness or weight, hence the prevalent use of scales. See Lien-sheng Yang, *Money and Credit in China* (Cambridge: Harvard University Press, 1952), chaps. 3 and 5; Frank H. H. King, *Money and Monetary Policy in China* (Cambridge: Harvard University Press, 1965), part 1, chap. 3; and Yeh-chien Wang, "Evolution of the Chinese Monetary System, 1644-1850," in *Modern Chinese Economic History*, ed. C. Hou and T. Yu (Taipei: Institute of Economics of the Academia Sinica, 1979), pp. 425-52. Silver was extremely important as a medium of international exchange in the seventeenth century. The degree to which the Chinese domestic economy was affected by sharp fluctuations in international bullion flow in the middle decades of the century remains a matter of debate. See William S. Atwell, "Notes on Silver, Foreign Trade, and the Late Ming Economy," *Ch'ing-shih wen-t'i*, 3.8 (1977): 1-33; Atwell, "International Bullion Flows and the Chinese Economy," *Past and Present*, 95 (May 1982): 68-90; and Brian Moloughney and Xia Weizhong, "Silver and the Fall of

the Ming: A Reassessment," *Papers on Far Eastern History*, 40 (September 1989): 51–78.

CHAPTER 5. CHANGSHU

1. For detailed studies of events in two other locales not far from Changshu, see Jerry Dennerline, *The Chia-ting Loyalists: Confucian Leadership and Social Change in Seventeenth-Century China* (New Haven: Yale University Press, 1981), chaps. 9–10; and Frederic Wakeman, Jr., "Localism and Loyalism during the Ch'ing Conquest of Kiangnan," in *Conflict and Control in Late Imperial China*, ed. Wakeman and C. Grant (Berkeley: University of California Press, 1975), pp. 43–85.

2. The works mentioned below, all anonymous or pseudonymous, survived only in manuscripts until they were published in the collectanea *Yuyang shuoyuan, jiabian* (Changshu, 1917).

3. Since the 1550s, when large-scale pirate raids began to trouble the South China coast, it had been considered important for cities and major military installations near the sea to have stout walls. On a region adjacent to Suzhou Prefecture, see Merrilyn Fitzpatrick, "Building Town Walls in Seven Districts of Northern Chekiang," *Papers on Far Eastern History: Ming and Early Qing*, no. 17 (1978): 15–51.

4. This chronicle refers to major figures by their formal names, whereas the old man's account and the story sequence use their sobriquets. To minimize confusion, formal names are used throughout this composite translation for Shi Min (sobriquet Ziqiu) and Hu Laigong (sobriquet Longguang); and the sobriquet Zizhang is used for Yan Shi. Shi Min obtained the highest civil service degree in 1637 and rose to the post of supervising secretary for the Ministry of War. Hu was born in Changshu County but left to seek his fortune in martial ventures up north. In 1643 he returned with stories of associating closely with famous Ming military leaders and pretentiously took up residence in Changshu city instead of his home village. In 1644, when the Hongguang court at Nanjing called for volunteers to aid in its defense, Hu put together a troop of mercenary marines and ingratiated himself with the commander in chief for river control to gain appointment as a regional commander. Yan attained the highest civil service degree in 1634 and served as a prefect and in the Bureau of Operations of the Ministry of War. He had close marriage relations with outstanding literati, but his agnatic family line emphasized the martial arts.

5. On the origins of this popular observance, see Stephen Teiser, *The Ghost Festival in Medieval China* (Princeton: Princeton University Press, 1988); chap. 3, n. 133, provides numerous citations of sources on the Ghost Festival in Qing times.

6. Many captives were sold or ransomed; others were kept as concubines or personal servants. See James L. Watson, "Transactions in People: The Chinese Market in Slaves, Servants, and Heirs," in *Asian and African Systems of Slavery*, ed. J. L. Watson (Oxford: Basil Blackwell, 1980), pp. 223–50. Slaveholding was an important part of the Manchu social economy in particular; see Pamela Kyle Crossley, *Orphan Warriors: Three Manchu Generations and the End of the Qing World* (Princeton: Princeton University Press, 1990, pp. 14–15. Many Han-Chinese residents of the Liao region whom the Manchus had enslaved before they entered Shanhai Pass fled their masters and returned to their family homes once the Manchus brought them into China proper. So the Manchus were trying to replenish their supplies of slaves, and through the 1650s there were continual efforts to halt the flight of slaves. See Ma Feng-ch'en, "Manchu-Chinese Social and Economic Conflicts in Early Ch'ing," in *Chinese Social History: Translations of Selected Studies*, trans. and ed. E. Z. Sun and J. de Francis (New York: Octagon, 1966), pp. 340–47. By no means were the lives of people who remained in bondage to the Manchus necessarily pitiful. They often shared in the power and wealth of their masters. See Jonathan Spence, *Ts'ao Yin and the K'ang-hsi Emperor: Bondservant and Master* (New Haven: Yale University Press, 1966), pp. 7–18. See also Chap. 6.

7. Changshu was frequently referred to as Yu or Yushan after a scenic stretch of hills located northwest of the county seat. Or it was called Haiyu—"the sea and Yu"—referring to the two most prominent geographical features of the county: the coastline and the Yu hills.

8. Certain Tong lineages in Liaodong had long been dedicated and successful servants of the Manchus, and some even claimed Manchu descent. The Tong surname appears frequently in records of the conquest and of the early Qing court. See Pamela Crossley, "The Tong in Two Worlds: Cultural Identities in Liaodong and Nurgan during the Thirteenth–Seventeenth Centuries," *Ch'ing-shih wen-t'i*, 4.9 (June 1983): 21–46.

9. On this belief in delayed supernatural retribution, common during the late Ming and early Qing periods, see Cynthia J. Brokaw, *The Ledgers of Merit and Demerit: Social Change and Moral Order in Late Imperial China* (Princeton: Princeton University Press, 1991), esp. chap. 1.

10. The Chinese regarded the liver as the center of people's most intimate feelings. Contemporaries reported that the Manchus often ate raw meat and were especially fond of fresh hot liver. See, for instance, Joseph S. Sebes, "A Description of the Tartars (Manchus) by the Jesuit Gabriel de Magalhaes in 1647 When He First Encountered Them at the Time of Their Conquest of China," *Manchu Studies Newsletter*, 4 (1980–81): 3–14. The Manchus were not, however, known to be cannibals. Such sensa-

tionalization of an item of vague knowledge is characteristic of the historical romance.

11. On representations of such scenes in Chinese paintings, see Lothar Ledderose, "A King of Hell," in *Suzuki Kei Sensei kanreki kinen Chūgoku kaiga shi ronshū* (Festschrift on the History of Chinese Painting for the Birthday of Suzuki Kei) (Tokyo: Suzuki Kei Sensei kanreki kinenkai, 1981), pp. 33–42. Popular conceptions of the netherworld as a bureaucratic realm of officials in courtlike chambers, and stories of people who returned to life and talked about their experiences in that realm, probably go back as far as the Former Han period (206 B.C.–A.D.8). See Robert F. Campany, "Return-from-Death Narratives in Early Medieval China," *Journal of Chinese Religions*, 18 (Fall 1990): 91–125.

CHAPTER 6. FROM ORPHAN TO PRINCESS

1. The strong emphasis in Chinese society on continuing ancestral sacrifices by generation after generation in the male line necessitated the adoption of boys, or even grown men, into households. According to the law, adoption of successors whose surnames differed from those of the adopting family was prohibited, but people often either were ignorant of this prohibition or ignored it. Cross-surname adoption was common during this period, particularly in this region. See Ann Waltner, *Getting an Heir: Adoption and the Construction of Kinship in Late Imperial China* (Honolulu: University of Hawaii Press, 1990), esp. chap. 2.

2. The difficult and ambiguous situation of widows and the powerlessness of any woman who lacked legitimate male support in Chinese society made suicide a frequent recourse even in normal times. See Susan Mann, "Widows in the Kinship, Class, and Community Structures of Qing Dynasty China," *Journal of Asian Studies*, 46.1 (February 1987): 37–56; Ann Waltner, "Widows and Remarriage in Ming and Early Qing China," *Historical Reflections*, 8.3 (Fall 1981): 129–46 (that issue has also been published as a monograph, *Women in China: Current Directions in Historical Scholarship*, ed. R. Guisso and S. Johannesen [Youngstown, N.Y.: Philo Press, 1981]); and Margery Wolf, "Women and Suicide in China," in *Women in Chinese Society*, ed. Wolf and R. Witke (Stanford: Stanford University Press, 1975), pp. 111–41; Chia-lin Pao Tao, "Chaste Widows and Institutions to Support Them in Late-Ch'ing China," *Asia Major*, 3rd ser., 4.1 (1991): 101–19. The heavy strictures on women and the lauding of "widow suicide" were not without critics in the late Ming and early Qing—including Manchu emperors. See Paul Ropp, "Signs of Change: Reflections on the Condition of Women in the Early and Mid Ch'ing," *Signs, Journal of Women in Culture and Society*, 2.1 (Autumn 1976): 5–23.

3. The edition used in this translation is in the *Yuyang shouyuan, jiabian*, 3rd fascicle (1917). It was collated from two different old manuscript copies and one previous printed edition (1878).

4. See Kang-i Sun Chang, *The Late-Ming Poet Ch'en Tzu-lung: Crises of Love and Loyalism* (New Haven: Yale University Press, 1991), chap. 2, esp. p. 11. Also of interest on this matter: Richard C. Hessney, "Beyond Beauty and Talent: The Moral and Chivalric Self in *The Fortunate Union*," in *Expressions of Self in Chinese Literature*, ed. R. Hegel and R. Hessney (New York: Columbia University Press, 1985), pp. 214–50. For another example of male elaboration on the life and writings of a historically unconfirmable late-Ming female figure, see Ellen Widmer, "Xiaoqing's Literary Legacy and the Place of the Woman Writer in Late Imperial China," *Late Imperial China*, 13.1 (June 1992): 111–55.

5. In the text he is usually referred to as Qian Sheng, "Student Qian," because he was preparing for the civil service examinations. His name, however, was Shenkun, and his sobriquet was Shijian.

6. Jiading County, southeast of Changshu, probably suffered the most under Li's heel. See Chap. 1, n. 4.

7. The Chinese character *hei* (black) was used to transliterate the first syllable of a number of common Manchu names. It was the governor of Jiangning, then based at Suzhou, Tu Guobao, who had taken charge of confiscating and transporting Li's household goods and personnel in late November or early December 1648.

8. See Howard S. Levy, *Chinese Footbinding: The History of a Curious Erotic Custom* (New York: Walton Rawls, 1966), esp. pp. 65–68. See also fig. 11 in this chapter.

9. For an explanation of the eroticism of the "lotus foot" in culturally comparative perspective, see William A. Rossi, *The Sex Life of the Foot and Shoe* (New York: Saturday Review Press and E. P. Dutton, 1976), chap. 5.

10. Probably *sain*, "good, auspicious," with the superlative suffix *lingu*. See Erich Hauer, *Handwörterbuch der Mandschusprache* (Weisbaden: Harrassowitz), vol. 1 (1952), pp. 44, 233; vol. 2 (1955), p. 759.

11. Ginseng, a medicinal root, had long been one of the most important trade commodities of the Manchurian region. See Van J. Symons, *Ch'ing Ginseng Management: Ch'ing Monopolies in Microcosm* (Tempe: Center for Asian Studies, Arizona State University, 1981).

12. Letter writing was an important medium of personal communication for educated women, given how sequestered they were compared to men. The quality of Liu's missives suggests that she participated in a surge of letter writing among women in the middle seventeenth century, which seems to have been instigated partly by the scattering of families and friends during

the Qing conquest. See Ellen Widmer, "The Epistolary World of Female Talent in Seventeenth-Century China," *Late Imperial China*, 10.2 (December 1989): 1-43. Dorothy Ko makes the point that intimacy between mother and daughter was often fostered by the education that the mother provided in the women's quarters of elite households; see "Pursuing Talent and Virtue: Education and Women's Culture in Seventeenth- and Eighteenth-Century China," *Late Imperial China*, 13.1 (June 1992): 12.

13. The brother here conflates the statuses and achievements of the Manchu princes Dorgon, Dodo, and Bolo. Certain late Qing recountings of this story assume uncritically that the prince was Bolo, a speculation that is mentioned in Chaoying Fang's biography of Bolo in *ECCP*, I:17. However, this identification is not tenable. For one thing, Bolo was not in the South during the year of Li Chengdong's revolt, which occasioned Liu's being brought to Nanjing. Moreover, by the time of his death in 1652, he had sired at least eight sons by four wives and one concubine, none of whom was either of the Ula tribe (see p. 106*n*) or surnamed Liu. A popular writer of Chinese historical fiction, Gao Yang, has portrayed the man in question as the second-degree Prince of Shuncheng, Lekdehun (*Liu Sanxiu* [Taipei, 1979]), but in historical fact, he was not stationed in the Jiangnan region in 1648-49. So the historical identity of our prince remains elusive. The one man whose circumstances correspond most closely to those described in *Guoxu zhigan* is Tantai (see *ECCP*, II:899), who was serving as Generalissimo Who Subdues the South in 1648-49; he was based in Nanjing while campaigning primarily in Jiangxi. Although Tantai was not of the imperial lineage, and although his highest rank was duke, not prince, his power and prestige at the time of Liu's captivity was very high, not least because he was a confidant of, and troubleshooter for, the man who actually ruled the Qing dynasty until 1650, Prince Regent Dorgon (see Chap. 1, n. 18). After Tantai returned to Beijing, he gained even greater power as head of the Ministry of Personnel. He was, however, more than ten years older than Liu's prince.

14. Liu's two elder brothers had also been at odds over her betrothal to Huang Lianggong. Since women were supposed to be loyal and obedient to their brothers and their husbands alike, tensions among these crucial male figures often brought on, or exacerbated, suicidal behavior in Chinese women. See Andrew C. K. Hsieh and Jonathan Spence, "Suicide and the Family in Premodern Chinese Society," in *Normal and Abnormal Behavior in Chinese Culture*, ed. A. Kleinman and T. Lin (Boston: Reidel, 1981), esp. p. 31.

15. This, like many terms and phrases in this account, is a classical reference, here to the *Zuo Commentary* to the *Spring and Autumn Annals* (*Chunqiu*). See James Legge, trans., *The Chinese Classics*, vol. 5: *The* Ch'un Ts'ew *with the* Tso Chuen (rpt., Taipei: Jinxue shuju, 1969), p. 850.

16. Ibid., pp. 92–93, 296–97.

17. The editor of the *Yuyang shuoyuan* edition here follows an earlier text by including the character for "junior uncle." None of the uncles of the Shunzhi emperor could have been the prince in question, however.

18. By this time the empress dowager was probably Xiaozhuang, the true mother of Fulin, the Shunzhi emperor. She was elevated to the position of empress dowager after the death of her aunt, Xiaoduan (who had been the principal consort of Fulin's father, Khungtaiji), in May 1649. See *ECCP*, I:255, 300–301, 304. For a remarkably natural color portrait of this influential woman, see Wan Yi et al., comps., *Daily Life in the Forbidden City: The Qing Dynasty, 1644–1912*, trans. Rosemary Scott and Erica Shipley (New York: Viking Penguin, 1988), p. 26.

19. This occurred at a time when the Qing court had been struggling to find ways to ameliorate increasing conflicts between the Manchu and Han-Chinese populaces. In October 1648, probably not long after the union of the prince and Liu, the court formally announced that marriages between Manchus and Han-Chinese, including officials, were not only permissible but desirable for overcoming divisions between the two peoples. The idea that intermarriage between Manchus and Chinese was prohibited during the Qing period is more common than accurate. It seems to have arisen from regulations that affected only men in the imperial clan (the Aisin-Gioro) and bannermen stationed in the capital, who were limited to taking and giving wives within the Eight Banners (which were 75 percent Liaodong Chinese in the mid-seventeenth century).

20. See Adam Y. C. Lui, "The Imperial College (*Kuo-tzu-chien*) in the Early Ch'ing (1644–1795)," *Papers on Far Eastern History*, 10 (September 1974), esp. pp. 162–63.

CHAPTER 7. REQUESTING AID FROM JAPAN

1. See *ECCP*, I:180–81; and Richard C. Rudolph, "The Real Tomb of the Ming Regent, Prince of Lu," *Monumenta Serica*, 29 (1970–71): 484–95.

2. See *SM*, pp. 76–77, 92–97.

3. Ibid., pp. 117–20.

4. Ronald P. Toby, *State and Diplomacy in Early Modern Japan: Asia in the Development of the Tokugawa Bakufu* (Princeton: Princeton University Press, 1984), pp. 112–40.

5. Yi-t'ung Wang, *Official Relations between China and Japan, 1368–1549*, Harvard-Yenching Institute Studies, no. 9 (Cambridge: Harvard University Press, 1953).

6. See Kwan-wai So, *Japanese Piracy in Ming China during the Sixteenth Century*

(East Lansing: Michigan State University Press, 1975); and Charles O. Hucker, "Hu Tsung-hsien's Campaign against Hsü Hai, 1556," in *Chinese Ways in Warfare*, ed. F. Kierman, Jr., and J. K. Fairbank (Cambridge: Harvard University Press, 1974), pp. 273–307.

7. For an account of Hideyoshi's ill-fated campaign in Korea, see James Murdoch, *A History of Japan*, vol. 2 (New York: Ungar, 1964), pp. 302–59. On the Ming fiscal sacrifice, see Ray Huang, *Taxation and Governmental Finance in Sixteenth-Century Ming China* (Cambridge: Cambridge University Press, 1974), p. 302.

8. See Charles R. Boxer, *Fidalgos in the Far East, 1550–1770*, 2nd rev. ed. (London: Oxford University Press, 1968).

9. See George Sansom, *A History of Japan, 1615–1867* (Stanford: Stanford University Press, 1963).

10. See Charles R. Boxer, *The Christian Century in Japan, 1549–1650* (Berkeley: University of California Press, 1967); and George Elison, *Deus Destroyed: The Image of Christianity in Early Modern Japan* (Cambridge: Harvard University Press, 1973).

11. See Iwao Seiichi, "Japanese Foreign Trade in the Sixteenth and Seventeenth Centuries," *Acta Asiatica* (Tokyo), 30 (1976): 1–18; and Renchuan Lin, "Fukien's Private Sea-Trade in the Sixteenth and Seventeenth Centuries," trans. Barend ter Haar, in *Development and Decline of Fukien Province in the Seventeenth and Eighteenth Centuries*, ed. E. B. Vermeer (Leiden: E. J. Brill, 1990), pp. 181–83.

12. Confucian scholars were also welcome, however, and the turbulence in China during this time did cause some to take refuge in Japan. The most famous, whose teachings had long-lasting effects on Japanese Neo-Confucian philosophy, was Zhu Zhiyu (sobriquet Shunshui, hence Shu Shunsui in Japanese). See *ECCP*, I:179–80; and Julia Ching, "Chu Shunshui, 1600–82—a Chinese Confucian Scholar in Tokugawa Japan," *Monumenta Serica*, 30.2 (Summer 1975): 177–91.

13. Little is known about the author, Zhang Linbo, except that he was a stipendiary student from Shanghai who served the court of Regent Lu as a drafter in the secretariat—that is, as a handler of documents. His account is found in a collection titled *Nanyou lu* (Records of Hardship Travels) within a larger manuscript collection, the *Mingji yeshi zachao* (National Library of Beijing). An altered version can be found in an abridgement of the *Nanyou lu*, a manuscript titled *Fuhai ji* (Record of Floating at Sea) (rpt. with *Suozhi lu* in *Zhongguo xueshu mingzhu*, no. 7, ed. Li Zongtong [Taipei: Shijie shuju, 1971]; also published in printed form in *Taiwan wenxian congkan*, no. 309 [Taipei: Economic Research Office of the Bank of Taiwan, 1962]). However, according to other historical records, the heads of this

mission were surnamed Ren and Yu, not Zhang. So the identity of the original author of the *Fengshi Riben jilue* remains uncertain.

14. The author goes on to refer to Ruan by his personal name. Ruan Jin began adult life as a small-scale pirate but soon was taken under the wing of the Ming naval commander Zhang Mingzhen (Chang Ming-chen; see *ECCP*, I:46–47). Ruan served the regime of Regent Lu in its offshore phase loyally and energetically, thereby rising to the rank of marquis.

15. The Tripitaka (called the Dazang or Sanzang in China) was a supposedly complete collection of all the Buddhist scriptures. It included sermons, rules governing Buddhist practice, treatises, and miscellaneous works, some originally written in Chinese and the rest translated into Chinese. For a brief introduction to the three "baskets" (*pitaka*) of the Pali scriptures, see Henry C. Warren, *Buddhism in Translations* (Cambridge: Harvard University Press, 1953), pp. xi–xiv. For a more extensive introduction, see Hirakawa Akira, "Buddhist Literature: Survey of Texts," trans. Paul Groner, in *The Encyclopedia of Religion*, ed. M. Eliade, vol. 2 (New York: Macmillan, 1987), pp. 509–29.

16. There was only one empress dowager surnamed Li during the Ming dynasty, the assertive mother of the Wanli emperor, best known by her honorific title Zisheng (1546–1614). Her posthumous honorific was not Xianmu, as given in the text. See *DMB*, I:856–59.

17. The Dragon King is a god of waters—usually rain and rivers, but in this case the sea. Before embarking on a voyage such as this, Chinese sailors probably obtained paper decrees and shiny plaques from temples along the seacoast in which the Dragon King was worshiped. More commonly worshiped by Chinese seamen since the Song period has been a goddess, variously known as the Dragon Girl (*longnü*), the Empress of Heaven (*tianhou*), or Grandma (*mazu*), who is revered for her ability to tame the sea and bring order to the coast. See James L. Watson, "Standardizing the Gods: The Promotion of T'ien Hou ('Empress of Heaven') along the South China Coast, 960–1960," in *Popular Culture in Late Imperial China*, ed. D. Johnson, A. J. Nathan, and E. S. Rawski (Berkeley: University of California Press, 1985), pp. 292–324; and Bodo Wiethoff, "Der staatliche Matsu Kult," *Zeitschrift der Deutschen Morgenländischen Gesellschaft*, 116.2 (1966): 311–57. It is known that on certain festive occasions all the creatures in the sea, the whales in particular, were believed to gather and pay court to her, causing very high winds and waves. See Liu Changpo, *Taiwan soushen ji* (Spirits in Taiwan—A Record of Investigations) (Taipei: Liming wenhua, 1981), p. 166. Apparently a similar belief is at work in this narrative, with the sailors using decrees and plaques to dismiss the fish and whales from a watery court assembly and thereby calm the sea.

18. According to the Japanese translators with whom the author-envoy spoke, Zhanwei had left his monastery in Nagasaki to promote his teachings to Japanese people in a small, remote place who had never known a Chinese cleric before. He had gained a following, and some of his writings had come to the attention of the shogun in Edo. The shogunal authorities, suspecting him of having connections with the strictly proscribed Christian proselytizers from the "western seas," severely punished his followers and spared Zhanwei's life only because of a regulation against killing Chinese monks. He was deported and warned that if he tried to come back, everyone on the same boat would be killed with him. Zhanwei had hoped that the gift of the Tripitaka would earn him readmission to Japan and to his former monastery.

19. That is, the bakufu commissioner in Nagasaki. Between 1633 and the 1680s, usually two commissioners served concurrently; one was on duty in Nagasaki, and the other was resident in Edo, where he served as a foreign-affairs adviser to the shogun. In 1649 the Nagasaki commissioner was Yamazaki Gonpachirō, and the Edo commissioner was Baba Saburozaemon. See Sasama Yoshihiko, *Edo bakufu yakushoku shūsei* (Collected [Materials on] Edo Bakufu Officeholding) (Tokyo: Yūzankaku, 1974), pp. 272–73.

20. At least one decree from Regent Lu was forwarded to the shogun in Edo. It simply announced that the Tripitaka was to be given to Zhanwei's former monastery in Nagasaki to promote good relations between China and Japan. See Hayashi Shunshō and Hayashi Nobuatsu, comps., *Ka'i hentai* (Changing Situation of the Chinese and the Barbarians), vol. 1 (Tokyo: Tōyō Bunko, 1958–59), p. 44.

CHAPTER 8.   A RIGHTEOUS MINISTER'S LAST CRUSADE

1. See *ECCP*, I:345–47; and *SM*, pp. 89–92.
2. See Charles O. Hucker, "The Tung-lin Movement of the Late Ming Period," in *Chinese Thought and Institutions*, ed. J. K. Fairbank (Chicago: University of Chicago Press, 1957), pp. 132–62; Heinrich Busch, "The Tung-lin Academy and Its Political and Philosophical Significance," *Monumenta Serica*, 14 (1949–55): 1–163; William S. Atwell, "From Education to Politics: The Fu She," in *The Unfolding of Neo-Confucianism*, ed. W. T. de Bary (New York: Columbia University Press, 1975), pp. 333–65; and Jerry Dennerline, *The Chia-ting Loyalists: Confucian Leadership and Social Change in Seventeenth-Century China* (New Haven: Yale University Press, 1981), chaps. 1–2.
   See *ECCP*, I:196–98 (under the prince's actual name, Zhu Yujian [Chu Yü-chien]); and *SM*, pp. 77, 80–81.

4. On Zheng Zhilong and the rise of the Zheng regime, see Chap. 12. For a brief biographical sketch of Zheng Hongkui (Cheng Hung-k'uei), see *ECCP*, I:112–13.

5. The memorials excerpted below are preserved in the *Huang Zhangpu ji* (Collected Works of Huang from Zhangpu; sometimes cited by the inside title, *Ming Zhangpu Huang Zhongduan Gong quanji*), ed. Chen Shouqi (1830), *juan* 5–6.

6. On the founding emperor of the Ming, Zhu Yuanzhang (Chu Yuan-chang, 1328–98), see *DMB*, I:381–92; Edward L. Dreyer, *Early Ming Government: A Political History, 1355–1435* (Stanford: Stanford University Press, 1982), chap. 2; and F. W. Mote, *The Poet Kao Ch'i, 1336–1374* (Princeton: Princeton University Press, 1962), chap. 1, esp. pp. 30–36.

7. On the Guangwu emperor, Liu Xiu (Liu Hsiu, 4 B.C.–A.D. 57), see *The Cambridge History of China*, vol. 1: *The Ch'in and Han Empires, 221 B.C.–A.D. 220*, ed. D. Twitchett and M. Loewe (Cambridge: Cambridge University Press, 1986), pp. 245–56.

8. On Deng Yu (Teng Yü, A.D. 1–58), see Herbert A. Giles, *A Chinese Biographical Dictionary*, vol. 2 (Taipei: Literature House, 1962), p. 724.

9. A reference to Han Xin (Han Hsin, also known as Han Wang Hsin, d. 196 B.C.), one of the chief supporters of Liu Bang (Liu Pang, 247–195 B.C.) in his struggle to found the Han dynasty. See Giles, *Chinese Biographical Dictionary*, II:246–49; and the *Cambridge History of China*, I:117–18.

10. Deng Zhi (Teng Chih) was a prominent minister, diplomat, and general of the Shu-Han state of the Three Kingdoms period. In a successful mission from Shu-Han (in the Sichuan Basin) to the state of Wu (in the lower Yangzi region) in 223, he persuaded the Wu ruler, Sun Quan (Sun Ch'üan), to abandon his alliance with the state of Wei and, instead, ally with Shu-Han against Wei. In 228 he assisted the Shu-Han leader Zhuge Liang (Chu-ko Liang) in a bold campaign northward against Wei, which held the traditional capital of China, Chang'an. See Ssu-ma Kuang, *The Chronicle of the Three Kingdoms (220–265): Chapters 69–78 from the* Tzu Chih T'ung Chien, trans. Achilles Fang, vol. 1, Harvard-Yenching Studies, no. 6 (Cambridge: Harvard University Press, 1965), pp. 144–45, 162–64, 250–52.

11. The great general Ma Yuan (14 B.C.–A.D. 49) aided Liu Xiu (see n. 7) in reestablishing the Han dynasty by defeating forces loyal to the Xin dynasty's ruler, Wang Mang. Later he fought against the Qiang people in the far northwest and quelled a rebellion of the Yue people in the Red River delta (present-day northern Vietnam). In spite of his advanced age, Ma continued to lead far-flung campaigns against the Xiongnu in the north and against aboriginal tribes in the south. He died during the latter effort. See *DMB*, II:572–73; and *Cambridge History of China*, I:271–72, 275–76, 426, 454.

12. These are further references to the campaigns of Liu Xiu—specifically, to famous victories in areas of present-day Henan and southwestern Shanxi.

13. Allusions to Emperor Yuan (r. 318–23) of the Eastern Jin and Emperor Zhaolie (r. 221–23) of the Shu-Han state of the Three Kingdoms period, respectively. Both men refounded dynasties that had collapsed, but both also had relatively short, ineffectual reigns. The governments that they established were never able to restore the political unity and security of their respective predecessors, the Western Jin and the Later Han dynasties.

14. Cen was a local official under the regime of Wang Mang, but he whole-heartedly joined Liu Xiu's movement to reestablish the Han dynasty.

15. Probably a reference to a commander named Peng Le of the Northern Wei (360–534) who, when in battle against Yuwen Tai, the future founder of the Northern Qi dynasty (500–77), became impaled in the abdomen such that his intestines spilled out. Unable to stuff them all back in, he cut off the excess and went on fighting. He made such an impression on Yuwen Tai that the latter gave him a high position when the Northern Qi was established.

16. Reference to a passage in the *Analects*, VII.10.3; see James Legge, trans., *The Chinese Classics*, vol. 1 (rpt., Taipei: Jinxue shuju, 1969), p. 198.

17. An allusion to the "Western Inscription" by the famous Neo-Confucian thinker Zhang Zai (1021–77), which in turn refers to the falsely accused Shensheng in the *Liji* (Book of Rites). See Wing-tsit Chan, trans. and comp., *A Source Book in Chinese Philosophy* (Princeton: Princeton University Press, 1963), p. 498.

18. An allusion to the words of the border guard at Zhangwu in the "Zeyang" chapter of the *Zhuangzi*. See Burton Watson, trans., *The Complete Works of Chuang Tzu* (New York: Columbia University Press, 1968), p. 286. On Shen Nong, the Founder of Agriculture alluded to here, see n. 19.

19. Legendary sage-rulers of Chinese antiquity. See Derk Bodde, "Myths of Ancient China," in *Mythologies of the Ancient World*, ed. S. N. Kramer (New York: Doubleday, 1961), pp. 367–405, reprinted in *Essays on Chinese Civilization by Derk Bodde*, ed. C. Le Blanc and D. Borei (Princeton: Princeton University Press, 1981), pp. 45–84.

20. An allusion to a story about Emperor Dezong (r. 780–804) of the Tang dynasty. At that time of exigency, titles like earl and marquis were liberally conferred on higher-ranking military officers.

21. Literally, "with the chin of a frog and the arms of a mantis"—referring to the self-satisfaction of such reptiles and insects in their small worlds. See the "Heaven and Earth" and "Autumn Floods" chapters of the *Zhuangzi*, in Watson, trans., *Complete Works*, pp. 133, 186.

22. See Zhuang Qichou, *Zhangpu Huang xiansheng nianpu* (Biographical Chronicle of Huang from Zhangpu), in *Huang Zhangpu wenxuan*, vol. 3, *Taiwan*

wenxian congkan series, no. 137 (Taipei: Economic Research Office of the Bank of Taiwan, 1962), pp. 466–67.

CHAPTER 9.   A QING VICEROY PLEADS FOR MERCY

1. See *ECCP*, I:358–60; Chen-main Wang, "The Life and Career of Hung Ch'eng-ch'ou (1593–1665): Public Service in a Time of Dynastic Change" (Ph.D. diss., University of Arizona, 1984); and *GE*, I:211–16 and II:728–40, 1025–35.
2. See James B. Parsons, *Peasant Rebellions of the Late Ming Dynasty* (Tucson: University of Arizona Press, 1970), chaps. 2–3.
3. See *DMB*, II:1538–42.
4. Apparently Hong did not agree to assume any official position in the Qing government until after the fall of Beijing to rebels in 1644. See Wang, "Life and Career of Hung Ch'eng-ch'ou," p. 105.
5. From the *Ming-Qing shiliao* (Ming-Qing Historical Materials), comp. Institute of History and Philology of the Academia Sinica, *jia* series (Shanghai, 1930–36), II:181; VI:577, 584, 598; and *bing* series, II:111. A photocopy of an original of the first document can be found in *Ming-Qing dang'an* (Ming-Qing Archival Documents), ed. Zhang Weiren, vol. 5 (Taipei: Institute of History and Philology of the Academia Sinica, 1986), pp. B2389–90. These particular memorials were of the type called *jietie*. On this type of document and others in the early Qing period, see Silas H. L. Wu, *Communication and Imperial Control in China: Evolution of the Palace Memorial System, 1693–1735* (Cambridge: East Asian Research Center of Harvard University, 1970), chap. 4.
6. This response is appended to a slightly different text of the above memorial, entitled "Hong Chengchou bingmu ben" (Document on Hong Chengchou's Eye Disease), in *Biji xiaoshuo daguan*, 12th ser., vol. 12 (Taipei: Xinxing shuju, 1976), pp. 5602–4. I thank Chen-main Wang for calling my attention to this.

CHAPTER 10.   A MERCHANT SURVIVES SLAUGHTER

1. See James B. Parsons, *The Peasant Rebellions of the Late Ming Dynasty* (Tucson: University of Arizona Press, 1970), pp. 149–56.
2. For a brief biography of Zuo (Tso Liang-yü), see *ECCP*, II:761–62. For an explanation of the whole complicated situation, see *SM*, pp. 70–73.
3. See p. 29*n*; and Harriet T. Zürndorfer, *Change and Continuity in Chinese Local History: The Development of Hui-chou Prefecture, 800–1800* (Leiden: E. J. Brill, 1989), chap. 3.
4. Printed in the *Xiangtan xianzhi* (Gazetteer of Xiangtan County), comp.

Zhang Yun'ao (1818), fascicle 14, *juan* 31, from an earlier, Kangxi-period collection that commemorated those who died in the Xiangtan massacre of 1649.

5. See Helen Dunstan, "The Late Ming Epidemics: A Preliminary Survey," *Ch'ing-shih wen-t'i*, 3.3 (November 1975): 5.

6. See N. H. Van Straten, *Concepts of Health, Disease and Vitality in Traditional Chinese Society: A Psychological Interpretation* (Wiesbaden: Franz Steiner Verlag, 1983), pp. 50–55; and Carol Benedict, "Bubonic Plague in Nineteenth-Century China," *Modern China*, 14.2 (1988), esp. pp. 137–45.

7. Ma began his career as a bandit but surrendered to the Ming general Zuo Liangyu in 1637 and entered Zuo's command. When Zuo's army disintegrated in 1645, Ma joined the command of the Southern Ming viceroy for Huguang, He Tengjiao, but he never submitted to very close control.

8. Prince-of-the-Blood of Zheng, Jirgalang (1599–1655)—a nephew of the founder of the Manchu nation, Nurhaci. He was one of the most vigorous Manchu leaders since the 1630s. See *ECCP*, I:397–98.

9. Kong Youde (d. 1652), Shang Kexi (d. 1676), and Geng Zhongming (d. 1649), who campaigned in Huguang and Jiangxi the previous year. For brief biographies, see *ECCP*, I:416–17, 435–36, and II:635–36. On the circumstances under which these men joined the Qing, see *GE*, I:196–210.

10. As in previous selections, "Great" is rendered "Qing" in such references to armed forces.

11. This was a false rumor. He Tengjiao, the Ming viceroy of Huguang appointed by the Yongli court, went to Xiangtan to try to improve the bad relations that had developed between Ma Jinzhong and the Ming (Yongli) governor of Huguang, Du Yinxi. There he, too, was caught off guard by the sudden arrival of the Qing contingent. He was captured and subsequently executed in Changsha, whereas Ma escaped westward to Baoqing. The death of He, a widely respected leader who was skilled at effecting cooperation among disparate elements, was one of the most crucial misfortunes in the history of the Ming resistance. See *SM*, pp. 136–40.

12. On Chinese herbal medicine, see Paul U. Unschuld, *Medicine in China: A History of Pharmaceutics* (Berkeley: University of California Press, 1986).

13. The cult of the Wuxian, or Wutong—the Five Manifestation Gods—had its origins in the Tang period, apparently through the application of the Buddhist term for the Five Supernatural Powers to mountain demons. The cult went through several transformations, reaching its peak of popularity in the late Yuan and early Ming periods. The powers attributed to the five, singly or collectively, varied a great deal but seem to have consistently included the power to cause illness. From this story it seems that the power to give disease implied the power to take it away as well, which the god(s) might do if propitiated. See Richard Von Glahn, "The Enchantment of

Wealth: The God Wutong in the Social History of Jiangnan," *Harvard Journal of Asiatic Studies*, 51.2 (1991): 651–714; and Ursula-Angelika Cedzich, "Wu-t'ung: Zur bewegten Geschichte eines Kultes," *Religion und Philosophie in Ostasien: Festschrift für Hans Steininger zum 65. Geburtstag*, ed. G. Naundorf et al. (Würzburg: Könighausen und Neumann, 1985), pp. 33–60.

CHAPTER 11.   AN ARTIST'S FILIAL TREK

1. See *ECCP*, I:489–90 and II:679, on Li and Sun, respectively. For more on Li Dingguo, see Chap. 15.
2. See *SM*, pp. 144–54.
3. Titled "A Ten-Thousand Li Search for [My] Parents," this twelve-leaf album is held in the Sackler Collection of the Metropolitan Museum of Art in New York (see fig. 17). An eight-foot handscroll by Huang, of scenery from Yunnan and Guizhou, is also extant, apparently in a private collection.
4. The translation below is excerpted from the account of his trip westward, the *Huang xiaozi xunqin jicheng* (Travelogue of the Filial Son Huang in Search of His Parents). It has been published several times, along with his account of the trip back, the *Dianhuan riji* (Daily Record of a Return from Yunnan). The particular text on which this translation is based can be found in the compendium of collectanea *Congshu jicheng chubian*, vol. 124 (Shanghai: Commercial Press, 1935–45).
5. James Hargett, "Travel Record Literature," in *The Indiana Companion to Traditional Chinese Literature*, comp. and ed. W. Nienhauser (Bloomington: Indiana University Press, 1986), pp. 936–39.
6. See Li Chi, *The Travel Diaries of Hsü Hsia-k'o* (Hong Kong: Chinese University of Hong Kong, 1974). Xu was from Jiangyin, just to the northwest of Changshu, the home county of Huang's lineage.
7. See James Cahill, *The Compelling Image: Nature and Style in Seventeenth-Century Chinese Painting* (Cambridge: Harvard University Press, 1982), p. 27.
8. See Kenneth Ganza, "The Artist as Traveler: The Origin and Development of Travel as a Theme in Chinese Landscape Painting of the Fourteenth to Seventeenth Centuries" (Ph.D. diss., Indiana University, 1989).
9. One common method of indicating dates was to use a sixty-combination (sexagenary) cycle of ten "stem" characters (in this case, *xin*) and twelve "branch" characters (in this case, *mao*). See Joseph Needham with Wang Ling, *Science and Civilization in China*, vol. 3: *Mathematics and the Sciences of the Heavens and the Earth* (Cambridge: Cambridge University Press, 1959), pp. 396–98.

10. The Liao people are now more commonly known as the Yi. On the Yi and Miao peoples, see F. M. Savina, *Histoire des Miao* (Hong Kong: Société des Missions-Etrangères, 1924), chap. 2; Herold J. Wiens, *China's March toward the Tropics* (Hamden, Conn.: Shoe String Press, 1954), pp. 70–93; Wolfram Eberhard, *China's Minorities: Yesterday and Today* (Belmont, Calif.: Wadsworth, 1982), chap. 6.

11. The population of Yunnan and Guizhou had grown vigorously from the thirteenth through the sixteenth centuries, and it increased again dramatically in the eighteenth. But the devastation of the Ming-Qing transition, from the revolt of Sha Dingzhou in 1646 to the defeat of the Rebellion of the Three Feudatories in 1681, was sufficient to prevent any population growth at all in the seventeenth century. See James Lee, "Food Supply and Population Growth in Southwest China, 1250–1850," *Journal of Asian Studies*, 41.4 (August 1982): 711–46.

12. Guanyin is the Chinese name for the bodhisattva Avalokitesvara. Closely associated with the principle of compassion, Guanyin was considered a potent savior in times of life-threatening dangers. See John H. Chamberlayne, "The Development of Kuan Yin, Chinese Goddess of Mercy," *Numen*, 9 (1962): 45–52. Fuxi is a legendary Chinese culture hero who devised the linear complexes of the *Yi*, or *Yijing* (Book of Changes). See Hellmut Wilhelm, *Eight Lectures on the I Ching*, trans. Cary F. Baynes, Bollingen Series, no. 62 (Princeton: Princeton University Press, 1960), p. 10. For a general introduction to the *Yi*, see Wilhelm, *Heaven, Earth, and Man in the Book of Changes* (Seattle: University of Washington Press, 1977). These items were especially appropriate for a learned man who had withdrawn from the world of public affairs. For discussions of how subscribing to Confucian values (like filiality and reverence for one's ancestors), belief in miscellaneous gods, and devotion to Buddhist teachings fit into the spiritual lives of Chinese people, see C. K. Yang, *Religion in Chinese Society* (Berkeley: University of California Press, 1961); and Robert P. Weller, *Unities and Diversities in Chinese Religion* (Seattle: University of Washington Press, 1987).

13. See *SM*, p. 147.

CHAPTER 12.   FATHER AND SON CHOOSE OPPOSITE SIDES

1. On the meaning and image of Zheng Chenggong in China and Japan since the seventeenth century, see Ralph C. Croizier, *Koxinga and Chinese Nationalism: History, Myth, and the Hero*, Harvard East Asian Monographs, no. 67 (Cambridge: East Asian Research Center of Harvard University, 1977).

2. See *DMB*, I:871–84; and Iwao Seiichi, "Li Tan, Chief of the Chinese

Residents at Hirado, Japan, in the Last Days of the Ming Dynasty," *Memoirs of the Research Department of the Toyo Bunko*, 17 (1958): 27–83. The Chinese government banned direct trade with Japan in 1547, but illicit and indirect trade (the latter mostly through Taiwan and the Ryukyu Islands) had continued and even burgeoned. See Chap. 7.

3. For insights on continuities in the conditions for piracy in this region, see Dian H. Murray, *Pirates of the South China Coast, 1790–1810* (Stanford: Stanford University Press, 1987).

4. See Harry J. Lamley, "Lineage and Surname Feuds in Southern Fukien and Eastern Kwangtung under the Ch'ing," in *Orthodoxy in Late Imperial China*, ed. K. C. Liu (Berkeley: University of California Press, 1990), pp. 255–78.

5. See *ECCP*, I:110–11; Charles R. Boxer, "The Rise and Fall of Nicholas Iquan," *T'ien Hsia Monthly*, 11.5 (April–May 1939): 401–39; and Leonard Blussé, "Minnan-jen or Cosmopolitan? The Rise of Cheng Chih-lung Alias Nicolas Iquan," in *Development and Decline of Fukien Province in the Seventeenth and Eighteenth Centuries*, ed. E. B. Vermeer (Leiden: E. J. Brill, 1990), pp. 245–64.

6. Chenggong remained loyal to him by following the Longwu-promulgated calendar until the 8th lunar month of 1648, when he learned of the Yongli emperor's enthronement in Guangdong. Although he never acknowledged the legitimacy of Regent Lu's regime (see Chap. 7), he did offer safe haven to the Prince of Lu after that regime was finally defeated on Zhoushan Island in 1656.

7. See Chang Pin-tsun, "Maritime Trade and Local Economy in Late Ming Fukien," in *Development and Decline of Fukien Province*, pp. 67–69. In that same volume, consult Cheng K'o-ch'eng, "Cheng Ch'eng-kung's Maritime Expansion and Early Ch'ing Coastal Prohibition," trans. Burchard Mansvelt Beck, pp. 217–44. See also Yamawaki Teijirō, "The Great Trading Merchants, Cocksinja and His Son," *Acta Asiatica* (Tokyo), 30 (1976): 106–16.

8. When a photocopy of that remnant manuscript was published by the Institute of History and Philology in 1931, with a detailed explanatory preface by Zhu Xizu, the title *Yanping Wang huguan Yang Ying congzheng shilu* (Veritable Record of Following Campaigns, by the Prince of Yanping's Fiscal Officer, Yang Ying) was used. Later researchers concluded that the more probable title was *Xian Wang shilu* (Veritable Record of the Former Prince), and it was published under that title in 1981 in a printed, punctuated edition thoroughly edited, annotated, and collated by Chen Bisheng (Fujian renmin chubanshe). The translation below is based on the 1981 edition. I consulted the 1931 edition at points and interpolated some material from Qing memorials published in the *Ming-Qing shiliao* (Ming-Qing

Historical Materials), comp. Institute of History and Philology of the Academia Sinica, *ding* series (Shanghai, 1950).

9. An allusion to the *Zuo Commentary* to the *Spring and Autumn Annals* (*Chunqiu*). See James Legge, trans., *The Chinese Classics*, vol. 5: *The* Ch'un Ts'ew *with the* Tso Chuen (rpt., Taipei: Jinxue shuju, 1969), p. 17.

10. This move into Chaozhou Prefecture was occasioned by a famine in Fujian, but it also gave Chenggong a chance to establish local strongmen who were reliably loyal to him and thereby stabilize his sources of supply from that area. Activities such as this show that the Zheng organization was virtually an amphibious state system.

11. The chief culprit on the Qing side was Regional Commander Ma Degong. Ma, as a regional commander under the Ming, had ingratiated himself with the Qing by turning over the Hongguang emperor after the latter's flight from Nanjing. His zealousness in several actions in Fujian shows how eager men in his surrendered position were to prove themselves with their new masters. But Ma was temporarily cashiered later when the Qing wanted to placate Zheng Chenggong. See *ECCP*, I:559.

12. Various members of the Zheng organization were in touch with the Japanese authorities before and after this point. Some supplies eventually came, but no soldiers were ever sent. See Chap. 7. See also *SM*, pp. 117–20. I know of no corroboration in primary sources of Chenggong's claim to be expecting soldiers from Kampuchea.

13. Probably the former Prince Regent Dorgon, as indicated in the summary of this edict in the Veritable Record of the Shunzhi reign, the *Da Qing Shizu Zhang Huangdi shilu*, 75/8b, vol. 2 (rpt., Taipei: Huawen shuju, 1964), p. 886. After Dorgon's death in December 1650, resentment against his high-handed methods was openly expressed in Qing leadership circles, and it became convenient to blame policy failings before 1650 on him.

14. The version of this edict in the *Xian Wang shilu* has been supplemented using the copy published in the *Ming-Qing shiliao, ding* series, I:87. Although the *Xian Wang shilu* places this edict in the second lunar month, the *Ming-Qing shiliao* copy is dated 5th month, 10th day (June 24, 1654).

15. This edict is not in Yang Ying's text, though it is quoted from (with one character altered homophonously) in Chenggong's last letter to his father. It has been translated from the copy in the *Ming-Qing shiliao, ding* series, II:101.

16. These are allusions to famous cases in Chinese history in which brothers chose different allegiances during periods of political disunity. The first case is that of Zhuge Jin (Chu-ko Chin; 173–241) who, after the fall of the Later Han, became an important minister under Sun Quan, king of the state of Wu, while his younger brother, the more famous Zhuge Liang (Chu-ko Liang; 181–234) became a general of legendary powers under the king of

the Shu-Han state, Liu Bei, during the Three Kingdoms period. See Herbert A. Giles, *A Chinese Biographical Dictionary*, vol. 1 (Taipei: Literature House, 1962), pp. 181–82. Both brothers steadfastly held to the principle that the relation between sovereign and subject is more important than that between brothers. See Achilles Fang, trans., *The Chronicle of the Three Kingdoms (220–265)*, vol. 1 (Cambridge: Harvard University Press, 1965), p. 51. For the popular form of this story, see Lo Kuang-chung, *Three Kingdoms: China's Epic Drama*, trans. and ed. M. Roberts (New York: Pantheon, 1976), esp. pp. 159–60. The second case is even more applicable to the situation of the Zheng brothers: During the Spring and Autumn period (722–481 B.C.), King Ping of the state of Chu unwisely became convinced that the crown prince was plotting against him, and he determined to eliminate able officials who respected the prince. The king held the prince's tutor, Wu She, hostage, saying that he would be killed unless both of Wu's sons, Shang and Yuan (sobriquet Zixu), came to court. Shang, "a man of goodness," went, and he was executed along with the father. Yuan, on the other hand, "a man of fierce determination, willing to bear disgrace and capable of accomplishing great things," saw what was in store for all of them and fled from Chu into the state of Wu. There he actively promoted attacks on Chu to avenge the deaths of his father and brother. See Burton Watson, trans., "The Biography of Wu Tzu-hsü," in *Records of the Historian: Chapters from the* Shih Chi *of Ssu-ma Ch'ien* (New York: Columbia University Press, 1958), pp. 16–29.

CHAPTER 13.   DUTCH AND CHINESE VIEWS OF A BATTLE

1. A revolt of the Chinese populace (as distinct from the natives of the island) against the Dutch in 1652, although it seems to have had nothing to do with Zheng Chenggong's movement, fixed in the Dutch colonists' minds a direct relation between restiveness among the Chinese and Zheng agents among them. See Johannes Huber, "Chinese Settlers against the Dutch East India Company: The Rebellion Led by Kuo Huai-i on Taiwan in 1652," in *Development and Decline of Fukien Province in the Seventeenth and Eighteenth Centuries*, ed. E. B. Vermeer (Leiden: E. J. Brill, 1990), pp. 265–96.

2. On the former, see John E. Wills, Jr., *Pepper, Guns, and Parleys: The Dutch East India Company and China, 1662–1681*, esp. chap. 3. On the latter, see Young-tsu Wong, "Security and Warfare on the China Coast: The Taiwan Question in the Seventeenth Century," *Monumenta Serica*, 35 (1981–83): 111–96. For a study of Coyet's account, see C. R. Boxer, "The Siege of Fort Zeelandia and the Capture of Formosa from the Dutch, 1661–1662,"

Transactions and Proceedings of the Japan Society of London, 24 (1926–27): 16–47.

3. The work was published under the initials C.E.S., presumed to stand for the sobriquet Coyet et socii. An English translation from the Dutch constitutes part 3 of William Campbell's *Formosa under the Dutch, Described from Contemporary Records* (London: Kegan Paul, Trench, and Trubner, 1903). The excerpts here are from Campbell's translation, pp. 322–23 and 412–57. It was published again in English—with additions by Pierre Martin Lambach and A. Blussé van Oud-Alblas [Leonard Blussé] and edited by Inez de Beauclair—under the title *Neglected Formosa*, by the Chinese Materials Center (San Francisco) in 1975 (Occasional Series, no. 21). A German translation appeared in 1677, and a Japanese translation in 1930.

4. On Yang Ying and his chronicle, see Chap. 12, introduction and n. 8. On comparing Dutch and Chinese accounts from this period, see also Leonard Blussé, "The VOC as Sorcerer's Apprentice: Stereotypes and Social Engineering on the China Coast," in *Leyden Studies in Sinology*, ed. W. L. Idema (Leiden: E. J. Brill, 1981), pp. 87–105.

5. A well-known passage in the *Analects* (XVII.2) states: "[People] are born similar but diverge in their practices."

6. Coyet suggests the force of Zheng Chenggong's movement by comparing him with Prince William of Orange (1533–84), who took up leadership of a widespread revolt in the 1570s against the rule of the Spanish Hapsburg king, Philip II. This eventually led to the formation of the United Provinces of the Free Netherlands. See Pieter Geyl, *The Revolt of the Netherlands, 1555–1609*, 2nd ed. (London: Ernest Benn, 1966), chaps. 2–4. On the relation between that Eighty Years' War and the ascendancy of Dutch sea power, see Charles R. Boxer, *The Dutch Seaborne Empire, 1600–1800* (London: Hutchinson, 1965), chap. 1.

7. To recover Leiden from Spanish control, in 1574 the Dutch resistance broke the dikes and flooded the city. See Geyl, *Revolt of the Netherlands*, pp. 136–38.

8. Zheng Chenggong began recognizing the Yongli, rather than the Longwu, calendar in 1648. See Chap. 12, n. 6.

9. Beginning in 1655, Zheng planned, and approached in stages, a major campaign in the Jiangnan region, which climaxed in the summer of 1659 with a siege of Nanjing. Qing counterattacks caused this effort to collapse rapidly. See *SM*, pp. 182–89.

10. For an introduction to Chinese beliefs about auspicious and inauspicious forces in the topography (*fengshui*), see Andrew L. March, "An Appreciation of Chinese Geomancy," *Journal of Asian Studies*, 27.2 (February 1968): 253–67; and Stephan D. Feuchtwang, *An Anthropological Analysis of Chinese Geomancy*, Connaissance de l'Asie, vol. 1 (Vientiane, Laos: Vithagna, 1974).

11. Although Zheng's military organization had many idiosyncratic features, he basically adopted the standard Ming five-part division, with center, front, rear, left, and right guards. In Zheng's case, each army had land, naval, and amphibious forces. There was no separate nomenclature in Chinese for land-based and waterborne military men or units.

12. Even before the Dutch departed, Zheng changed the name of Sakam to Dongdu Mingjing, the "Ming Eastern Capital," and established a prefecture around it named Chengtian (Comply with Heaven), signifying continued loyalty to the Ming. The area is present-day Tainan.

13. In maritime East Asia winds blow predominantly from the south from about the beginning of May and predominantly from the north starting in November. Zheng knew that after the first week of May, it would be very difficult for any Dutch ship to carry the alarm from Tai Bay to Batavia. See Masatoshi M. Yoshino, "Winter and Summer Monsoons and the Navigation in East Asia in Historical Age," *Geojournal* (Wiesbaden), 3.2 (1979): 161–69.

14. The two extant eyewitness accounts of this momentous day, Frederik Coyet's and Yang Ying's, give different dates. Coyet's is, furthermore, a nonexistent April 31. This discrepancy has been the subject of some specialized studies (see *SM*, p. 254, n. 83). Generally, April 30 is favored as the accurate date of the Zheng landing.

15. Chinese seamen were struck by the fast-hull form of the European clippers, which tapered downward, unlike Chinese boats and ships with wide hulls, which usually tapered upward. For illustrations of the sorts of troop and transport ships used in the Fuzhou-Xiamen maritime region, see Valentin A. Sokoloff, *Ships of China* (San Bruno, Calif.: V. A. Sokoloff, 1982), pp. 25, 31, 35.

16. This is an overstatement of what occurred in 1624 after considerable hostilities. See John E. Wills, Jr., "Maritime China from Wang Chih to Shih Lang: Themes in Peripheral History," in *From Ming to Ch'ing*, ed. J. Spence and J. Wills (New Haven: Yale University Press, 1979), p. 216. It is doubtful that the Ming central government formally authorized this move, though provincial authorities may have.

17. These natives, who were eventually forced off the best agricultural land by the Han-Chinese, later became known as the hill-area people. The Minnanese-speaking Chinese settlers and members of Zheng's organization were the ancestors of inhabitants who were later called the Taiwanese. See Wen-hsiung Hsu, "From Aboriginal Island to Chinese Frontier: The Development of Taiwan before 1683," and I-shou Wang, "Cultural Contact and the Migration of Taiwan's Aborigines: A Historical Perspective," in *China's Island Frontier: Studies in the Historical Geography of Taiwan*, ed. R. G. Knapp (Honolulu: University of Hawaii Press, 1980), pp. 3–28 and

31–54, respectively. In the early 1650s the Dutch estimated that there were fifteen thousand to twenty thousand Chinese settlers in the southeastern part of Formosa and a total population, mostly aboriginal natives, of a hundred thousand. See Huber, "Chinese Settlers against the Dutch East India Company," p. 274.

18. For other comments on the historical consequences of this Dutch loss, see Boxer, "Siege of Fort Zeelandia," pp. 43–44.

CHAPTER 14. AN EMPRESS APPEALS TO THE POPE

1. See *SM*, chap. 5.
2. On Shang, see Chap. 3, n. 5; on Geng, see Chap. 10, n. 9.
3. The letters are preserved in the Vatican archives. The translation has been done by comparing a photograph of the original document—published in Nigel Cameron, *Barbarians and Mandarins* (Tokyo: John Weatherhill, 1970), p. 223—with a transcription taken by Mizukuri Genpachi, published by Mizukuri, with Tanaka Yoshinari, in "Min no Ō Taikō yori Rōma hōō ni okurishi yubun" (Imperial Document from the Ming Empress Dowager to the Roman Pope), *Shigaku zasshi*, 3.37 (1892), and printed again in Ishihara Michihiro, "Minmatsu Shinsho seien Rōma shimatsu" (Narrative Account of a Request for Assistance from Rome at the End of the Ming and Beginning of the Qing), *Rekishigaku kenkyū*, 79 (1942): 209–10.
4. For more details, see Robert Chabrie, *Michel Boym jesuite polonais et la fin des Ming en Chine (1646–1662)* (Paris: Pierre Bossuet, 1933), corrected and supplemented by Paul Pelliot in "Michel Boym," *T'oung Pao*, 2nd ser., 31.1–2 (1935): 95–151. See also George H. Dunne, *Generation of Giants* (London: Burns and Oates, 1962), chap. 20; and Fritz Jäger, "Die letzen Tage des Kü Schï-sï," *Sinica*, 8.5–6 (1933): 197–207.

CHAPTER 15. A BOY EUNUCH SEES THE BITTER END

1. See Robert B. Crawford, "Eunuch Power in the Ming Dynasty, *T'oung Pao*, 49.3 (1961): 115–48; and Shih-Shan Henry Tsai, "The Demand and Supply of Ming Eunuchs," *Journal of Asian History*, 25.2 (1991): 121–46.
2. For a general history, see Taisuke Mitamura, *Chinese Eunuchs: The Structure of Intimate Politics* (Rutland, Vt.: Charles Tuttle, 1970). For a study that draws on religious psychology, see Orlando Patterson, *Slavery and Social Death: A Comparative Study* (Cambridge: Harvard University Press, 1982), pp. 314–26.
3. See *The Cambridge History of China*, vol. 7: *The Ming Dynasty, 1368–1644*, part 1, ed. F. W. Mote and D. Twitchett (London: Cambridge University Press, 1988), pp. 595–614; and Ulrich Mammitsch, "Wei Chung-hsien

(1568–1628): A Reappraisal of the Eunuch and the Factional Strife at the Late Ming Court" (Ph.D. diss., University of Michigan, 1968).

4. At least three manuscripts of this account are extant. A somewhat spruced-up printed version can be found in the collectanea *Yujian zhai congshu*, comp. Luo Zhenyu (Shanyu, 1910), part 1, fascicle 3. Even spruced up, the prose is redundant and awkward, mixing stiff, formal phrases with low-brow words.

5. On Li, see Chap. 11, n. 1; and *SM*, chap. 7. On the hereditary noble line in which Mu Tianbo was the last duke and the special place of this lineage in Yunnan and in Ming history, see Mu Ying, in *DMB*, II:1079–83; and Peter R. Lighte, "The Mongols and Mu Ying in Yunnan—at the Empire's Edge" (Ph.D. diss., Princeton University, 1981).

6. This probably refers to the time in 1654 when Li was campaigning on behalf of the Yongli regime in Guangdong and Guangxi provinces, and the Yongli court, isolated in a small locale in southwestern Guizhou Province, was endangered by the designs of Li's erstwhile fellow rebel leader Sun Kewang. The Yongli emperor surreptitiously offered Li the status of first-degree prince if he could free the court from Sun's clutches. Li subsequently did accomplish this. See *SM*, p. 153.

7. That is, Emperor Xuanzong (r. 712–56), whose court was forced to flee southwestward from the capital, Chang'an, during the rebellion led by An Lushan. His son, the future Emperor Suzong (r. 756–62), remained northwest of the capital, where he successfully rallied support for a restoration. See *The Cambridge History of China*, vol. 3: *Sui and T'ang China, 589–906*, part 1, ed. D. Twitchett (London: Cambridge University Press, 1979), pp. 453–61.

8. Pan's contingent of nine hundred soldiers was later slaughtered when it approached the Myanmar capital, Ava, ahead of the imperial party, which had been delayed on the river route. For a larger picture of Chinese activities in the extreme southwestern border region during this time, see *SM*, pp. 171–73. Regarding historical developments internal to the lower Irrawaddy region in the sixteenth and seventeenth centuries, see Victor B. Lieberman, "Provincial Reforms in Toung-ngu Burma," *Bulletin of the School of Oriental and African Studies*, 43.3 (1980): 548–69. For the natives' perspective on the intrusions of the fugitive Ming court and various Chinese renegade armies, see U [Maung] Htin Aung, *A History of Burma* (New York: Columbia University Press, 1967), pp. 149–50.

9. Here the author apparently applies a term for a Chinese Daoist practice aimed at effecting good health to a superficially similar practice in Indianized states, which was aimed at bringing supernatural sanction to oaths of loyalty. For a reference to the ceremonial drinking of "water of allegiance" at the Burmese court, see J. George Scott and J. P. Hardiman, *Gazetteer*

of Upper Burma and the Shan States, part 1, vol. 2 (Rangoon: Superintendent of Government Printing, 1900), pp. 100–101.

10. The small tribal state of Miandian (from which developed present-day Myanmar) was incorporated into the Ming suzerain sphere as a "pacification office" (*xuanweisi*) during the late fourteenth and early fifteenth centuries. But by the latter part of the sixteenth century Miandian had grown powerful enough to make incursions across the Yunnan border and had engaged in hostilities with Ming forces. Relations between the Ming court and Miandian were strained through the turn of the seventeenth century, and there was no contact between them at all after the second decade of the century. On the waxing and waning of the Han-Chinese presence in the far southwestern border region and on frontier policy and tribal administration during the Ming period, see C. P. Fitzgerald, *The Southern Expansion of the Chinese People* (New York: Praeger, 1972), chaps. 3–4; and Herold J. Wiens, *China's March toward the Tropics* (Hamden, Conn.: Shoe String Press, 1954), chaps. 4, 6–7.

11. This probably was the Generalissimo Who Pacifies the West, Aisingga, a Manchu duke of an illustrious military lineage. He was of the Plain Yellow, not the Plain White, Banner.

12. Here the printed text becomes elliptical, and after a few lines, half a page is excised. Other printed editions and most manuscript copies omit this section. One rare manuscript copy, held in the National Library of Beijing, preserves the missing part. My translation follows that manuscript for most of the following six paragraphs. The bearing of this passage on the unsolved mysteries surrounding the execution of the Yongli emperor is discussed in Lynn A. Struve, "The Bitter End: Notes on the Demise of the Yongli Emperor," *Ming Studies*, 21 (Spring 1986): 62–76.

13. See Robert B. Oxman, *Ruling from Horseback: Manchu Politics in the Oboi Regency, 1661–1669* (Chicago: University of Chicago Press, 1975).

14. Although this funeral was not conducted in a completely standard way, some idea of what might have transpired can be derived from James L. Watson, "The Structure of Chinese Funerary Rites: Elementary Forms, Ritual Sequence, and the Primacy of Performance," and Evelyn S. Rawski, "The Imperial Way of Death: Ming and Ch'ing Emperors and Death Ritual," in *Death Ritual in Late Imperial and Modern China*, ed. Watson and Rawski (Berkeley: University of California Press, 1988), pp. 3–19 and 228–53, respectively.

ILLUSTRATION CREDITS

Figure 1. From the *Morokoshi meishō zue*, comp. Okada Gyokuzan (Osaka, Preface 1805), vol. 4.

Figure 2. From the *Morokoshi meishō zue*, vol. 6.

Figure 3. From an inscription on Shi's memorial shrine in Yangzhou as reproduced in Zhu Wenzhang, *Shi Kefa zhuan*, rev. ed. (Taipei: Taiwan Commercial Press, 1974).

Figure 4. From the *Luchen congshu* edition (1903) of the *Yangzhou shiri ji*.

Figure 5. Courtesy of the Lilly Library, Indiana University at Bloomington.

Figure 6. *Ma Chang Attacking the Enemy's Camp*, by Giuseppe Castiglione, is in the collection of the National Palace Museum, Taiwan, Republic of China.

Figure 7. From Johann Nieuhof, *L'ambassade de la compagnie orientale des Provinces Unies ver l'empereur de la Chine*...(Leiden, 1665). Courtesy of the Lilly Library, Indiana University at Bloomington. The original watercolor drawings from this Dutch legation have been published in Leonard Blussé and R. Falkenberg, *Johan Nieuhofs beelden van een Chinareis, 1655–1657* (Middelburg, Neth.: Stichting VOC Publicaties, 1987).

Figure 8. From Nieuhof, *L'ambassade de la compagnie orientale des Provinces Unies ver l'empereur de la Chine.* . . . Courtesy of the Lilly Library, Indiana University at Bloomington.

Figures 9 and 10. From Deng Fu, comp., *Changshu xianzhi* (1539). Courtesy of the Library of Congress.

Figure 11. From Alicia E. N. Bewicke Little, *Intimate China* (London: Hutchinson, 1899).

Figure 12. From the *Morokoshi meishō zue*, vol. 1.

Figure 13. From Qin Yueceng, comp., *Chongxiu Nanhai Putuoshan zhi* (1832).

Figure 14. Courtesy of the Honorable Tamisuke Watanuki.

Figure 15. From the *Zhongyang yanjiuyuan ershi niandu zong baogao* (General

Bulletin of the Academia Sinica, 1931). Courtesy of the Fu Ssu-nien Library, Institute of History and Philology of the Academia Sinica, Taipei.

Figure 16. From the famous seventeenth-century pharmacopoeia of Li Shizhen, *Bencao gangmu* (republication of 1885).

Figure 17. From the Metropolitan Museum of Art (The Sackler Fund, 1970.2.1). All rights reserved.

Figure 18. From the glass slide collection of the late S. Y. Teng, textual source not known.

Figures 19 and 20. From Olfert Dapper, ed., *Gedenkwaerdig bedryf der Nederlandsche Oost-Indische Maertschappye, op de Kuste en in het Keizerrijk van Taising of Sina* (Amsterdam, 1670). Courtesy of the Lilly Library, Indiana University at Bloomington.

Figures 21 and 22. From C.E.S., *'t Verwaerloosde Formosa* (Amsterdam, 1675). Courtesy of the Lilly Library, Indiana University at Bloomington.

Figure 23. From the *Morokoshi meishō zue*, vol. 6.

Figure 24. From Gu Zuyu (1631–72), *Dushi fangyu jiyao* (Xue family edition, 1879), "Yutu yaolan" sec., chap. 2. Courtesy of the Harvard-Yenching Library, Harvard University.

Map 7. The inset map was adapted from a sketch in Charles R. Boxer, "The Siege of Fort Zeelandia and the Capture of Formosa from the Dutch, 1661–1662," *Transactions and Proceedings of the Japan Society of London,* 24 (1926–27): plate I (facing p. 20). A seventeenth-century Dutch map of Tai Bay and its environs, held in the Algemeen Rijks-Archief, The Hague, Netherlands, is reproduced in Johannes Huber, "Chinese Settlers against the Dutch East India Company: The Rebellion Led by Kuo Huai-i on Taiwan in 1652," in *Development and Decline of Fukien Province in the Seventeenth and Eighteenth Centuries,* ed. E. B. Vermeer (Leiden: E. J. Brill, 1990), p. 267.

INDEX